Teaching Writing from a Writer's Point of View

Teaching Writing from a Writer's Point of View

Edited by

Terry Hermsen
The Ohio State University, Marion

Robert Fox
The Ohio Arts Council

National Council of Teachers of English
1111 W. Kenyon Road, Urbana, Illinois 61801-1096

Staff Editor: Kurt Austin

Interior Design: Doug Burnett

Cover Design: Evelyn C. Shapiro

Cover Photographs © Elizabeth Crews

NCTE Stock Number: 55170-3050

The programs described in this book are made possible with the support of the National Endowment for the Arts.

Library of Congress Cataloging-in-Publication Data

Teaching writing from a writer's point of view/edited by Terry Hermsen and
    Robert Fox.
        p.   cm.
    Based on a summer writing seminar cosponsored by Wright State
University and Ohio Arts Council.
    Includes bibliographical references.
    ISBN 0-8141-5517-0
    1. English language—Composition and exercises—Congresses.
2. Creative writing—Study and teaching—Congresses. I. Hermsen,
Terry, 1950- . II. Fox, Robert, 1943- .
PE1404.T3994 1998
808'.042—dc21   98-29894
                                                                          CIP

Contents

Preface

Thus, helplessly, there on the bridge
While gazing down upon those birds—
How strange to be above the birds!—

    . . . the spelling mind
Imposes with its grammar book
Unreal relations . . .

O swallows, swallows, poems are not
The point. Finding again the world,
That is the point.

Howard Nemerov, "The Blue Swallows"

The purpose of this book is to demonstrate various ways in which writing can help us, as teachers (whatever our training) or students (whatever our age), to find again the world. Writing that pulls in upon itself, that speaks only to "the spelling mind," as Nemerov puts it, or only to a select group of connoisseurs, eventually withers. To thrive, and to find its true voice in us, writing must lead us to gaze over the swallows, from the bridge that links our common life, and supply us with new ways of visualizing our interaction with each other.

On one level, *Teaching Writing from a Writer's Point of View* details ways that writers in Ohio have been working with teachers and their students to uncover new methods of using writing in the classroom. There are, thus, plenty of lesson ideas that might be taken back and applied "on Monday morning," as they say. The essays in Section I, from writers in the Ohio Arts Council's Artists in Education program, in particular provide practical ideas for preschool through high school, along with sample student writings. But you will also find ways of revamping curricula or constructing new writing assignments in Scott Russell Sanders's thoughts on the personal essay in Section IV, for instance; in the essays by Ohio teachers in Section III; or even in the samplings of students poems and stories in Section II. Each section complements and presents a dialogue with the other sections.

In addition, the book offers more than interesting lesson plans. It gives testimony to the value of collaborations between teachers and writers who love to teach, and presents models. It also intends to shake the foundations of writing on a much deeper level. In essence it is asking us, in the words of Ron Carlson, "to turn the desk," to put away the yellowed lesson plan, the approach we always got by with, the formula or the proven scheme, and begin listening again to the scratch of pen across paper or of fingers across keys—to writing discovering where it needs to go.

Such has been the experience of Mary Noble, an Ohio teacher who has opened up her teaching so that poems, stories, and essays (both personal and formal) interact with each other as complementary tools rather than isolated units. Or of Debra Conner, a poet from Parkersburg, West Virginia, who when working with preschoolers in a Head Start center found that all her old "tricks of the trade" were inappropriate. All she could do was return to "the thing I do best—write" in order to guide herself toward meeting the children on their own level.

Here you will find also MaryAnn Titus, a third-grade teacher who discovered that her students *could* understand—actually, the better word is *love*—the poems of Blake, Coleridge, David Waggoner, and that in amazing ways they could then apply what they learned in poetry to grapple with perimeters in math, or the natural processes in the woods behind their school, or concepts as complex as paradox and ambiguity and point of view. And more, they learned that writing helped make them less of just a class and more of a learning community. In that room, one student wrote:

> All the stuff inside my head
> won't come to a stop.
> It seems like I lost the key
> and now all the good ideas
> are plunging out the back
> too fast for me to know
> so I'm writing
> whatever I can catch in my net . . .

> Andy Foley

Like Howard Nemerov, like third grader Andy Foley, or like any committed writer, we've all lost the key. But maybe we've found it too. All we can do is gather what we can in our net—as those good ideas we thought we had go racing by us, faster than we can keep up. The same goes for this book. From our experience of writing, from teaching it, struggling with it and glorying in it, from the grit of the classroom to the height of the bridge, here's our catch.

Terry Hermsen

Acknowledgments

This book has been created through the Arts in Education Program at the Ohio Arts Council, a state agency supported by tax dollars.

We are indebted to OAC Executive Director Dr. Wayne P. Lawson, whose leadership continues to be relentlessly innovative; Deputy Director Sue Neumann, for her wise, reliable, and pragmatic counsel; Barbara Robinson, Chair, whose leadership on the state and national levels continues to be an incentive to the staff; Vonnie Sanford, who supported the launching of this book as director of the Arts in Education Program; AIE Director Mary Campbell-Zopf, for her support for the book and enthusiasm for the teaching of writing; the AIE Program staff: Joanne Eubanks, Christy Farnbaugh, and Anita Collinger; and the rest of the OAC staff, supportive beyond expectations.

Our programs would not be possible without support from the Arts in Education and Literature Programs of the National Endowment for the Arts, a federal agency in Washington, D.C. Specifically, we would like to acknowledge Doug Herbert, Director of the AIE Program, and the former Literature Program staff whose Summer Seminars grants made *Change Course!* possible: Director Gigi Bradford, Assistant Director Mike Shay, and Program Specialist Thea Temple.

At Wright State University, thanks go to James Thomas, Rich Bullock, and Nancy Mack for a successful and enduring partnership; C. J. Baker, whose command of logistics and intuition was indispensable; and to Henry Limouze, Chair, English Department; Perry Moore, Dean of Liberal Arts; Bill Rickert, Assistant Dean of Liberal Arts; Lily Howard, Assistant Provost; and Ralph Alexander of the WSU bookstore for their interest and support.

Thanks as well to the many artists, teachers, and students in Ohio and throughout the country whose hard work, generosity, and commitment continue to teach us all.

—The Editors

Introduction
The Experience of Writing: A Summer Institute

Robert Fox

In the mid-1970s, as I drove from my Meigs County farm to a month-long poetry residency I conducted in the Scioto County schools, I noticed every isolated country school. It saddened me to think of all the students who did not work with artists, who would not have the opportunity to engage in a process that could jog their imaginations, enable them to see the world and themselves differently, and discover that they had a skill or ability lurking within them which was never expressed. And I wondered what would happen to the students I worked with after I left.

I knew they were in good hands with teachers like Jaq Sylvia and Carmen Westerfield at Wheelersburg High School, who went beyond their curricula to nurture their students. I worked with other good teachers elsewhere. I knew there were more, waiting in the rye to catch kids at the edge of cliffs, just as Daniel Keyes and Lou and Eleanor Ehrenkranz had been there for me at Thomas Jefferson High School.

How did we find such teachers? What did we do with them when we did?

Art truly does save lives: working with artists challenges and positively changes student attitudes, but it seemed to me then, as I drove through rural southeast Ohio, that more change could not take place unless we altered how teachers were taught and what they did in their classrooms. As an undergraduate in the 1960s, I proceeded toward secondary certification, and after several courses dropped it. My introduction to the education establishment—stultifying bureaucracy rather than enthusiasm for learning—disillusioned me. The kind of change I envisioned seemed off in the distant future.

The impression I had while driving through Meigs, about the necessity of changing methodologies and teacher attitudes, was supported not long afterward during a residency I did for the Springfield City Schools, when I was asked to conduct a district-wide teacher workshop. What a wonderful opportunity, I thought, to meet the teachers of the fifth graders who were bussed to my central location. I looked forward to the possibility of extending the impact of my residency, holding the kind of discussions we normally would have held had I been in their buildings.

I flattered myself thinking that the teachers were coming of their own volition, after school, to learn more about what I was doing with their students. Little did I know that I was conducting a regularly scheduled inservice, an activity they were required to attend. Lynne V. Cheney, former Chair of the National Endowment for the Humanities, once remarked that teachers used the term as a verb: "to be inserviced" sounded like having something unpleasant done to you against your will.

I arrived early, unpacked my books and manuscripts, awaiting my allies, my potential friends. I greeted them with enthusiasm as they trickled in; they regarded me warily, and despite my invitation to move up to the front, they clustered as close to the rear as possible. Their voices had an edge of both fatigue and complaint. I wasn't certain, but I sensed that they did not choose to be there.

My introducer misread my bio and left. As soon as I started my presentation, a variation of one I'd done to several receptive groups, one teacher after another folded her arms and closed her eyes. I read funny poems. No one laughed. I decided against presenting a writing exercise and instead talked about my work in the classroom and read some unusual student writing I was getting. An abrupt snore startled me.

I had worked with enthusiastic groups of teachers who wrote mischievous responses to my exercises, who tried Kenneth Koch's ideas in their classrooms with encouraging success, and so I was disconcerted. When I asked if there were questions, one teacher shot her hand up. She wanted to know how to recognize a good student poem. This was one I had fielded before.

Several teachers had told me they could talk about the mechanics of rhyme and meter but didn't know how to recognize what made a poem successful. I emphasized vision, imagination, and a sensibility that sees meaning in what might otherwise be pedestrian or go unnoticed. I spoke about unusual comparisons, the music of assonance or internal rhyme. A student poem should be praised even for just one outstanding image or line. "Yes," she said. "But how do you *assess* it?" I thought for a moment and replied, "You say it's good and tell them to write more." Her face darkened and she looked at the floor. It was obvious I wasn't going to provide her with what she needed—a formula, perhaps.

Several years after I joined the staff of the Ohio Arts Council, the writers who visited schools through the Arts in Education Program wanted to gather and discuss their residencies. AIE Coordinator Vonnie Sanford agreed to a meeting. Among other concerns, the writers wanted to know about the aftermath of residencies: Did teachers follow up on the exercises and resource lists left by the writers? Did they buy their own copies of *The Whole Word Catalogue*, or Kenneth Koch's books, or any of the numerous individual collections introduced in their classrooms, books by contemporary poets and writers as diverse as Michael Harper, Phillip Lopate, Rita Dove, Louise Glück, Sybil James? Usually not, return visits indicated.

A memorable moment came when Joel Lipman recalled having Robert Frost as a poet in residence in his Chicago prep school. "He didn't teach," Joel said. "He didn't lecture about poetry or go around to the classes reading his poems. He was just *there*. His door was open and you could go talk to him. He was a *presence*." Joel attributes having become a poet to Frost's residency in his school.

I was reminded of an early aim of the National Endowment for the Arts' Poets in the Schools Program, that the artists' successes would inspire schools to create permanent positions, hiring poets with their own funds. While this may seem naive now, Leonard Randolph, then director of the NEA Literature Program, was able to successfully lobby members of Congress to increase NEA appropriations using samplers of student poetry from their districts.

In Ohio at least, despite the success of the residency program, it was unlikely that schools would create permanent positions for poets. (However, a visual artist was hired away from our roster by a private school in Lucas County.) We asked ourselves what we could do, as writers, as a state arts agency, to have more lasting impact on the way reading and writing were taught and to give writers more credibility.

Hale Chatfield, who taught teachers before, suggested a creative writing summer institute. Teachers needed graduate credit and advanced degrees to receive raises and promotions. And, we were sure, a number of teachers would need no other motivation than the chance of renewal, of a professional development opportunity unlike anything else available to them. If we found an attractive campus, such as Ohio University in the hills of southeast Ohio, they could regard it as a sort of vacation.

The writers supported the idea and Vonnie and I were enthusiastic. The OAC was about to embark on a summer institute for teachers in media arts. If that venture was successful, then institutes could also be created in writing as well as other arts disciplines.

Why was media first? The reasons were compelling: (1) schools had invested heavily in video cameras and editing equipment, 35 mm still cameras and darkrooms, and had not invested in teacher training—in many schools the equipment remained behind locked doors; (2) we live in a media-saturated culture manipulating how we think, feel, live, and it's crucial to learn to respond critically; and, (3) the media offer exciting possibilities for the creation of art.

Award-winning Ohio filmmakers Julia Reichert and Jim Kline helped establish the Summer Media Institute "Develop Yourself" at Wright State University where they taught. It moved two years later to Ohio University in Athens. The Institute, a six-day workshop, offered still photography, video documentary, audio documentary, computer animation, and more recently, computer imaging. Workshop leaders have included such nationally known artists as Jane Aaron, Skip Blumberg, and National Public Radio's Elizabeth Perez-Luna. The media institute has attracted a steady following of teachers and administrators, and each year the waiting list equals the number of participants.

A few years later, when the arts council received one of the largest arts-in-education grants in the country from the NEA, the time for the creative writing institute had arrived. An increasing number of residency requests referred to a change from traditional English curricula to language arts or whole language methodologies. Applicants spoke of the writing process. They proposed that practicing creative writers could help participants understand this new approach, recently mandated by the state department of education.

I learned that the writing process approach in this country was formalized at the University of California-Berkeley's National Writing Project, a program now offered by most states. Ohio's version, the Ohio Writing Project (OWP), was located in the Composition and Rhetoric Program at Miami University, Oxford, Ohio, and was a major force in converting Ohio schools and districts to the writing process approach.

The writing process was exactly what the name said, a flexible, organic way of teaching writing that takes students through the same steps that professional writers use: brainstorming, drafting, and revising. I wondered if the five-paragraph theme, thesis, and topic sentences were things of the past. I learned that many writing process exercises, or "prompts" mirrored those used by poets in schools for the past three decades. Were process advocates copying the pedagogy that evolved in Poets in the Schools programs? I found it odd that the OWP encouraged participants to write poetry, fiction, and creative nonfiction, and to publish, and that none of the teachers were publishing creative writers. It was also odd that the writing process advocated the techniques used by creative writers, but that most of the texts were written by teachers and theorists, not writers. I had never heard of McCrory, Murray, Atwell, and Calkins. I could not find any communication between the two parallel schools of pedagogy.

Only in this country, I thought, could an all-encompassing discipline like writing become an academic specialty segregated from those who write as a profession! In the sciences, for example, physicists, astronomers, and biologists have begun to converse beyond their specialties about such common interests as ontology and cosmology. Writers who teach and writing theorists should learn from their example.

I approached the Ohio Writing Project with the idea of sponsoring creative writers in their program, but they were not interested in collaborating. I mentioned this to James Thomas one day. James had recently come to Wright State University in Dayton from the University of Utah, where he had founded *Quarterly West* magazine, the Writers at Work conference, and co-edited the first of several anthologies of "sudden" or short short fiction. James suggested we talk with Rich Bullock and Nancy Mack, his colleagues in the English Department, who had recently started the Wright State Institute on Writing and Its Teaching, held on the campus of Antioch University in Yellow Springs.

Their Institute was a two-week program for teachers K–12. The first week was "Writing and Its Teaching," taught by Nancy Mack with the help of innovative teachers from the local public schools. The course taught how to create writers workshops in the classroom, introduced current research on how writers write and read, and held lesson-planning workshops adapted to all grade levels. The second week, "Responding to Writing: From Grading to Portfolios," was taught by Rich Bullock. This course was an intensive study of assessment, emphasizing the use of peer evaluation and how portfolios could encourage risk taking and more meaningful learning while still providing accountability in grading. Both courses armed teachers with mini-lessons, flexible curricula, and strategies for dealing with school politics.

The Institute was held for the first time in the summer of 1990, and in 1991, James and I, with the help of several Wright State graduate assistants, coordinated a third week entitled "Creative Writing and the Classroom," which later became "The Experience of Writing."

Like the media institute, the creative writing institute offered specialization in a particular genre: fiction, poetry, or nonfiction. As with artist residencies in the schools, in addition to "core group" specialization, "peripheral group" exposure to the other two genres was important.

James and I spent many months tinkering with the schedule and the details. He wanted to define the curricula; I was for leaving it open, up to the workshop leaders.

Our faculty consisted of fiction writers Ron Carlson and Pamela Painter, the versatile Eve Shelnutt, poet and nonfiction writer Christopher Merrill, nonfiction writer Mark Shelton, and poet Terry Hermsen, all writers committed to teaching. Terry reminded me recently of our faculty meeting that first Sunday morning. We gathered on the pleasant screened-in porch of the Morgan House Bed and Breakfast, where most of us were staying. The faculty wanted to know what James and I had in mind for them to do. We presented the schedule and said, "The rest is up to you." Ron Carlson responded immediately, "Okay. Now this is how we do it. . . ."

Later the first day, at the Antioch Union, I knew we were off to a good start when I overheard teachers at the wine, cheese, and hors d'oeuvres near the registration desk. "This is the first time I have been treated professionally at a professional conference," became a refrain.

Our first session attracted thirty participants, about half of what we anticipated, but not a bad response given that we had less than a year to plan and publicize the program. The next year, registration almost doubled.

The first few days were difficult. Many teachers had not written in a long time, some not at all. Now they had to write daily, and begin if not complete a ten- to twenty-page project in order to receive graduate credit. "When are we supposed to write?" some participants asked, hoping to be excused from peripheral groups and the readings. "Why do we have open blocks of time on the schedule?" others wanted to know. "The open spaces are writing time," we said. Some resented having to attend the evening readings, wanted their day to end at 5:00 p.m. By the third day, however, the teachers were staying up late sharing their writing on the stairways of the dorms. Everyone wrote. The workshop leaders gave their time selflessly. Meals and meetings of the staff were cut short when workshop leaders needed to meet with participants. Apart from the scheduled group dinners, workshop leaders often strolled uptown with members of their core group for lunch. The end of the week came too soon. On Friday, workshop leaders met their core groups for the last time, and then we squeezed into a room barely large enough for a group reading. There was no shortage of volunteers to start. Some were emboldened by their predecessors. A couple of very shy people had their work read by others. Every new piece was a surprise—the strength and range of their voices was astonishing. Few rushed off after the reading, wondering where the time had gone. Goodbyes were long, departures slow.

James and I knew that something magical had happened during the previous week. The teachers truly had become writers, but what exactly did that mean? We learned more when we received their written evaluations, which contained some of the following statements:

> I *experienced* what I ask of my students
>
> —Pam Woods, Worthington Christian High School

> If I could pick the most important thing I learned at the Institute it would be that you have to be a good writer in order to teach good writing
>
> —Sandi Anderson, South High School, Springfield

> It was a revelation to me to hear Eve [Shelnutt] say that a writer can have faith in herself, and let her story tell her where it wants to go rather than the reverse—that's quite a concept for a control freak like me to grasp. And I loved Pam's [Painter] suggestion that a well-kept house is a sign of a misspent life. You will be happy to hear that during the past two weeks my house has gone uncleaned
>
> —Mary Jo White, Mills Lawn School, Yellow Springs

In Section III, you'll learn in more detail what past participants of the week came away with.

We've made many small changes over the years, many of those in response to comments on our evaluations. The basic components have not changed and can be used as a model for similar programs of varying lengths. The Experience of Writing lasts six full days. It could be spread out over two weeks but such an extension would sacrifice intensity unless additional genres were added, and it would cost more. The components are as follows:

(1) core group meetings every morning

(2) peripheral group meetings on two afternoons so that participants would experience all three genres—fiction, poetry, and nonfiction (Monday and Tuesday in our schedule); sometimes these are team taught

(3) readings by all the workshop leaders—we've changed the schedule from an hour to half hour per reader, doubling them up and including the staff of publishing writers as well

(4) a panel discussion by the workshop leaders involving the whole group, focusing on motivating students, developing teaching strategies, and discussing their lives as writers

(5) "repeat offenders" panel (self-named)—veteran participants discuss successes and failures of the previous year

(6) individual conferences with workshop leaders about projects

(7) participant readings to core groups on the last day, with a few selected for the whole group reading

(8) a panel on publishing—to acquaint participants with how one gets published and introduce teachers to the world of literary publishing by hearing from magazine editors and book publishers from around the state

(9) meals together—we start with an opening banquet on Sunday, on campus, then go off campus to different restaurants on Tuesday and Thursday nights. Yes, it's more time to "bond," but the playtime as a group is important in a week of intense productivity

Our work with teachers reached a new level when we were able to take what was now a four-week program and create *Change Course!* A major grant from the Literature Program of the National Endowment for the Arts (one of two given nationally) enabled our planning team of James Thomas and myself, Nancy Mack, Rich Bullock, and Cynthia (C. J.) Baker, to work with twelve competitively selected secondary teachers for a full year. Some of the accomplishment of *Change Course!* is related in Rich Bullock's book, *Why Workshop? Changing Course in 7–12 English.*

During the year that I dropped out of the secondary education sequence as an undergraduate, I participated as a visiting poet in the High School Reading Program of the Academy of American Poets. It was an eye-opener, teaching me the power of art in education. I was impressed with how quickly students understood that poetry could give voice to their confusion, heal, and be fun as well. Since then I've had an unplanned career as an educator, in partnership with teachers and schools. The programs I've witnessed and participated in over four decades began with readings by poets; became longer term writers' visits, (residencies) where students (and some teachers) wrote; and led to The Experience of Writing, some of whose participants you'll meet later in this book.

Change in the schools has been happening much more rapidly than I imagined it would twenty years ago. We may never see a resident writer in every school or district, but when I drive by schools in unfamiliar geographies, instead of regretting the lack of a resident artist, I wonder instead what innovative ways teachers are using to incorporate the arts into their curricula. New research on the brain and how we learn affirms the importance of the arts in learning. Meigs County, unreceptive to residencies while I lived there, now has a local arts council which regularly sponsors school residencies. Teachers have been discovering a natural partnership with artists: venture capital grants from the state Department of Education have resulted in many new residencies around Ohio. Schools, with their own funding, hire artists from our roster and follow our residency guidelines.

Throughout the country one can find poetry readings in coffee shops, taverns, parks, and community centers. Young people and old search for language that elevates rather than diminishes the individual, which creates a community rather than divides us. We desperately need a higher level of discourse, an honest dialectic to confront and heal our differences and to construct a civil life in the twenty-first century.

❙ Wild Cards: Essays by Ohio Writers in the Schools

❙n the early days of poetry in the schools, Lewis MacAdams called the poets and other visiting artists "the wild cards in the school deck." Because a writer is often visiting a classroom for a brief time, two to four weeks usually, he or she comes in "cold," ready to try several ideas which may spark an interest some students never knew they had; and because the lesson usually grows out of the writer's own work and concerns, intriguing possibilities emerge for combining life experience with the students' learning.

Poetry in the Schools (later renamed Writers in the Schools as playwrights and prose writers participated) has always been something of a "living experiment," as Anne Sexton dubbed it when she collaborated with high school English teacher Bob Clawson in 1967. The essays included in this section are ample evidence that the experiment begun by MacAdams, Sexton, and so many others is alive and vital. They represent writers taking on the kind of challenges art—and education itself—has always thrived on, offering us renewed inspiration for what can happen when we come at the teaching of writing afresh. In poet Debra Conner's journal, "Doing Our Own Possibility," for instance, we see the unfolding insights of a writer working with very young children (three- and four-year-olds at a Head Start Center in eastern Ohio). Here she is doubly, as MacAdams puts it, "from the outside." As a person not trained in early childhood theory, and as someone without young children of her own, it is fascinating to follow her journey as she discovers that preschoolers already speak a form of fantastical poetry. She recognizes herself as a child, and our view of early childhood is enriched.

Similarly, watch as Michael London, a playwright from Dayton, walks into a high school in west-central Ohio to uncover the theatrical skills in 11th and 12th graders—indeed, to help them discover the sources of drama in what they sometimes think of as a boring landscape.

Admittedly, there is an educational theory at work in his approach, but it is one born out of Michael's own concerns as a playwright, his "obsessions," if you will, with the everyday talk and stories passed down over generations. (Notice this, too, as you read his own play, "Blood in the Valley," included here as a model for the kind of writing he is asking students to do.)

Perhaps as much as any piece here, Oberlin poet Lynn Powell's essay shows a writer working close to her own life . . . in this case, at her daughter's elementary school "Just across the Street." Here is an award-winning poet who is also a parent trying to find ways to bring her own art to the teachers of kindergartners through second graders. Hers is the story of an educational collaboration between teachers grounded in theory and the daily work of the school and a poet with a vision of how poetry can awaken a young life.

Most often, when a life grows, our view of the world and the words we have for it create a new interchange. So it is when Nick Muska brings translytics—a loose and experimental version of translation—into the classroom. Words, both foreign and familiar, take on a more elusive and electric quality. And in Terry Hermsen's essay on poetry night hikes, we hope you will see students rethinking their assumptions—and their language—about the night, another of the familiar unfamiliars.

The classroom also is such a familiar place that we often take it for granted. Not so for poet David Hassler, approaching his first visit to a fifth-grade room near his hometown. His essay serves as a reminder to keep our sense of possibility awake when we engage the ready minds of students, even when they're ready to re-invent the universe.

Lewis MacAdams said that "the school . . . the neighborhood . . . the city and the town, in fact the whole human construct is made of words at its roots." Now, even further into the electronic age, not so much has changed. We are still in need of visions, as he puts it. But that's what writing is for.

Doing Our Own Possibility: Journal of a Residency at Columbiana County Head Start Centers

Debra Conner

> *Debra: What did your mother teach you?*
> *Child: To do my own possibility.*

Introduction

The following journal entries are drawn from a journal I kept during a five-week residency in Columbiana County, Ohio, which took place in the spring of 1995. As part of the Ohio Arts Council's artist-in-residence program, I lived and worked as a writer in four different Head Start classrooms located throughout the county: Lisbon, two Salem sites, the Salvation Army, and United. My actual residence was an office in the Lisbon center, which the staff had transformed into an office/bedroom, complete with computer, rented bed, and dresser. This arrangement provided me with the comforts of home—which was three hours away in Parkersburg, West Virginia—and most important of all, solitude and time to write. In some ways, the decision to write an account of this residency was born of desperation. How could I do a successful creative writing residency with Head Start children, ages three to five, with five-minute attention spans who weren't old enough to write or read? None of my usual classroom activities would work. I was starting at ground zero, operating on my instincts and the awareness that these children's imaginations offered plenty of material.

Thus, I turned to the thing I do best—write. I simply asked questions, listened, and observed. At the end of the day, I collected what they had given me and marveled at it. It was the perfect marriage of talents.

In addition to working with preschoolers, this residency included work with parents, who met with me to work on a special book of family stories and reminiscences called a Mapbook. (See pages 6–8 for the assignment.) During the residency's final week, writer Lynne Hugo collected material from teachers to form the last section of the seventy-plus page account. Its title, "Doing Our Own Possibility" comes from one child's answer to my question "What did your mother teach you?"

4-3-95—Monday—Lisbon #2 (Week 1)

On the road again. I've chosen to make the trip to Lisbon early this morning, rather than drive up on Sunday night, so I leave Parkersburg by 6:30 a.m. Now that we've changed to Daylight Savings time, it's dark as I head north, but I welcome the chance to see the sunrise and to look for spring's subtle alterations.

The morning light is as pink as that from any sunset and frost adds a touch of silver. Hawks show up here and there above the highway. For the first time, I see a pair, side by side on a limb, easily visible in the still-bare trees. The willows are the only trees with green leaves, but the Bradford pears and the crab apples offer explosions of color. Spring, unlike other seasons, arrives in such distinct stages.

My room at the Lisbon Head Start Center, although officially the storage room, is nevertheless carpeted and clean and as nice as any hotel. I settle in quickly and head upstairs to work with the children in Vickie Warnick's Lisbon 1 class. These students didn't see me during my planning week, so many are shy and hesitant.

One of the more outgoing ones is Brent, who talks to me about his cat, Wiley Burp Sheriff Tonka. Wiley, he explains, is black and white and something of an orphan, since his mom and one brother ran away and one brother died. Wiley, however, has wasted no time grieving. He spends his days hunting mice, foxes, and deer.

After a few minutes watching another child, Rancy, shape and pat "root beer meat" and talking to him about his pigs, Ozzie and Janice, I settle in for a long conversation with Amanda, who is putting together puzzles. Amanda tells me that she has taken a bicycle trip past my house and has seen me there, cleaning. I'm more skeptical about the cleaning part than about the distance she'd have to travel—three hours by car—to Parkersburg, but she's adamant. She even mentions that her mother packed a drink for her in case she got hot along the way. "What's your roll call?" Amanda asks me after a while, which must be her way of asking my name.

I ask Amanda a question: what would you do if you could do something you've never done? She tells me she'd dance "because my belly wants me to dance in a dress with bunnies on it." She contends that she can go outside and call bunnies and they will come to her.

As clean-up time is announced, Amanda's final bit of information has to do with Elvis. Elvis, it seems, has been listening to her and no longer wants her to sing "You Ain't Nothing but a Hound Dog."

I admit that I see something of myself in Amanda, and remember the times my mother had to come to school to talk with Mrs. Vore, my kindergarten teacher, because I lied a lot of the time. Both my mother and Mrs. Vore worried about my penchant for making up things. But I lied simply because lies were usually more interesting than the truth, not because I wanted to hurt anyone. Now, as a writer, I get to lie all the time. I love the distinction made by writer John Cheever: "I lie in order to tell a more significant truth."

After a dance/movement routine to the "Jungle, Rumble Boogie," it's on to "circle time," an important part of the day where the children learn about the calendar, the weather, and then listen to a story or have a group discussion. Today's story, about a baby duck, teaches me something I didn't know. Baby ducks can't swim until their mother rubs them with oil from her feathers. Motherless ducks must wait until they are old enough to develop the glands that produce the oil that will make them "waterproof."

Circle time leads to a discussion about spring, and I compile a poem, based on their ideas.

How Do We Know It's Spring?
Lisbon #1 class—a.m.

Bright sun and warm.
Millions of flowers are in my woods.
Because we can think again.
I saw a million butterflies come out of one cocoon.
Flies really fly.
Ice melts and I sweat and I want a drink.
When the sun goes down, it's Friday.
Bees fly—but be nice to them.
Moles come out and eat radishes
And rattlesnakes fly.

After finishing with the students, I have just enough time to set up the room and the art supplies for my first Mapbook session with parents. Since my plan is to have them work tonight on a map of their own lives, I set up an easel and create a version of my own life map, pinpointing and finding symbols for memories and events. As is always the case, I'm surprised by what surfaces:

my mother's warning that there were tigers in the field next to our house. Her way of insuring that my brother and I didn't venture in there;

a man—part of a crew of carpenters building houses in my neighborhood—who caused me months of terror after he told me he was going to cut off my ears.

The parents who come for the Mapbook session (all mothers) work for an hour or so on their own life maps. One of them, Wanda, remembers having a turkey who plucked at the orange flowers on a jacket she had. Mitzi remembers playing Mary in a Christmas play and being scared to death.

At the conclusion of the Mapbook session, the children come downstairs to work with their mothers to draw symbols for themselves and their family members and to find a way to identify themselves as a *tribe*. One of my favorite ideas comes from a girl who symbolizes her older, makeup-obsessed sister by a pair of bright pink lips.

The Family Mapbook

The family mapbook is a reinterpretation of the traditional family scrapbook. Instead of being a collection of photographs and mementos, your mapbook will map the terrain of your family's life. It will include the past, the present, and the future. It will pinpoint landmarks in the form of past experiences (for example: describe your and your child's favorite Christmas gift) and it will uncover landmarks within your imagination (for example: explain what kind of animals you and your child would be if you were animals). Along with the writing, the mapbook might contain photographs and artwork, created by you and your child. Your child will also contribute ideas, which you can record, if your child is too young to write. Other members of the family—grandparents, brothers and sisters, aunts and uncles—are welcome to contribute.

As your writing coach, I will supply you with examples of poetry and prose on subjects such as family, childhood, and identity. These can serve as models for your own writing and can increase your appreciation for literature.

Here are some ideas for your mapbook:

The Map

**Draw a map of your life. Locate and explain the significant peaks and valleys, the rivers, the forests, buildings, bridges, and other important landmarks. Write about some of the more significant experiences. Ask your child to do the same.

**Imagine you live in a prehistoric time. You have been asked to decorate the cave walls with symbols of great significance to your tribe (family). What would you include? What is the name of your tribe?

Self-Portraits

**Find (or draw) a picture of an animal and an object that represents you. Write an explanation of why you chose this animal and object as your self-portrait.

**If you were a room in your house, which one would you be? Draw or photograph the room and explain why it is like you.

**Make a collage, containing words and pictures cut from newspapers and magazines, that explains who you are.

Memories

**Describe your earliest memory.

**Compare memories with your child of things such as:
     a favorite pair of shoes
     a favorite toy and/or game
     a time when you were sad, frightened, angry, disappointed
     an enjoyable trip or vacation

**Write a funny family story

**Write about an eccentric relative

**Write an account of something you did when you were close to your child's age

**Write down ten or more cherished memories

Likes and Dislikes

**Compare some of the following with your child
     favorite foods
     favorite season
     favorite book, movie, song
     heroes and heroines
     dreams

**Take a photo of a cherished object. Write about why this object is important to you.

**Make up a Top 10 list for yourself and one for your child

Journals

**Each day, for a period of one week, record at least one noteworthy thing that happened to you and your child. Ask your child to contribute one or two things from his/her day.

Gifts

**Using pictures, drawings and description, create a gallery of people and things you'd like to bestow on your child. What "gifts" would you give your child to carry through life? Write about why these are important to you.

Letters

**Write a letter to your child. Write one to be opened next year, five years from now, ten years from now.

Stories

**Write a story in which you, your child and other members of your family appear as characters.

**Write a story from your child's point of view.

4-4-95—Tuesday—Salem #2 and Salvation Army

I arrive late at the Salem site, thanks to a series of wrong turns. Over lunch, I talk with the kids and discover that the boys at my table are eager to play with toy guns after school. When one little boy announces that he has "lots of guns and swords and Ninja stuff" his friend asks if he can come over and play. "No," says the first little boy, "my house is too messy." The other boy recommends that his mother clean it up so people can come over. The boy with the guns tells me that he also has real koala bears at his house. At the Salvation Army site, I'm able to work with small groups of students who seem unusually talkative and attentive. Together, we create a number of poems.

What Makes Me Cry?
Salvation Army class

When Mommy and Daddy leave
I cry when I get spanked and when I got stabbed
People cry when you hit them
When my sister stuck her tongue out, I cried
You cry if tigers eat you
and alligators make you cry
When I hit my tooth I cried
When I cried at the dentist, someone put a hand over my mouth
    and we never went back there again
I cried in a monster movie and when a man tried to put fire
    in a hole where a girl was
Mom cried when the landlord said we couldn't go camping and I
    gave her a kiss

Things That Are Cold

Wind
If you never read or play with something, it gets cold
When the heater is broken
The basement floor is dirty and cold
Mashed potatoes that you never eat

When I brush my teeth I get cold
Elephants have to stay outside and they get cold because they don't
    have a home
Bags that are empty

Back at the afternoon class at Salem #2, the students produce these poems:

Things That Are Spring
Salem #2—p.m. class

We put hair ribbons in our hair or eat them
We see the sun and cars driving the road
We see red and yellow flowers and green grass
We cut down trees and they fall
We see snow and rain and a castle
Kites fly with nobody holding on
We play tug-of-war and guns
Money flew on the trees when the wind blew it
We see koala bears and snakes in the pond
The school bus drives on the road
We see clothespins on the ground
We eat marshmallows and drink pop and play on the swings
I draw your face on the road

What Are Feet For?

For stepping and tapping and stomping and walking.
For running and kicking.
To walk on the sky.
To kick other shoes.
Feet can eat snow and swim.
Feet can hit rain.

4-5-95—Wednesday—Lisbon #2

The day gets under way with a fire safety program, where the kids learn "Stop, Drop, and Roll." Their student teacher reads them a book with characters from Sesame Street called *I Want to Be a Fireman.* Afterward, a couple of the boys announce that they'd like to be firemen, but Vince, the boy next to me, confides that he wants to be a cowboy.

As part of their lesson in fire safety, the children are asked to draw a picture of their houses and to plan their evacuation route, which the teacher writes on the back. Jerry has an elaborate and inventive plan involving breaking holes in the ceiling, sliding down the roof, and climbing a tree with his family. It's so detailed and far-fetched that the teacher can't get it written down, and she urges him to make a real plan. Indignantly, he dismisses her, saying, "I'll just dream about it." Jerry tells me that if his house were burning, he'd take a white Harley out of the basement and ride it up a tree. He confesses that he doesn't have a Harley, but one day he plans to have three—one white, one yellow, and one green. In the afternoon class, two of the girls, Jessie and Donna, tell me about their "screening" which, I assume, is a test they've recently been given. Jessie says she doesn't think she did very well because she didn't know where her hips were. When I ask them what day the screening took place, Jessie says: "On the day it was oily," meaning two days ago when the center had a gas leak and the kids were sent home early.

While the children are playing, I walk around, asking them questions about things grown-ups do. Here are their ideas:

Cook

Hang up clothes

Eat seeds in apples

Take pictures

Play with real tigers

Drive cars backwards, then straight

Ride motorcycles

Work and sleep and drink beer

Don't cry

Timmy tells me that after age nine you're grown up. Jessica thinks it's after age seven, and Erin believes grown-up life begins at age ten.

I press on with my questions, even after Timmy asks me to play with the plastic animals. Finally, he says, "How come you use up all those words? I don't want to talk. I'm tired." I get the message.

At the evening's first Mapbook session, nine parents show up, including my first father. I'm intrigued by the different approaches the parents take to the book. Some meticulously record dates and events, using great care in drawing or cutting out pictures to serve as images. Others are more spontaneous. There's a clear sense that everyone's enjoying the chance to look back at their life experiences. Many images are stories in miniature—a woman whose chaotic home life left her on her own as a young teen; another whose daughter almost died of diabetes at age 2. One woman tells a story about taking a car on a test drive and "forgetting" to return it. I regret that we don't have more time for sharing. The hour passes too quickly, leaving most parents still in the beginning stages of their life map. I'm aware that I have enough ideas to carry out a six-month Mapbook project, and I urge the parents to work on their books at home in order to finish their life map. In addition, I suggest that they do these activities throughout the week:

- create a map of their child's life

- enlist grandparents and other relatives to do a map in the book

- write letters to their child—one for now, one for a year from now, one for five years from now, and one for ten years from now

4-6-95—Thursday—Salem #1 and Salvation Army

The students at Salem are watching the video "Thumbelina," in which Thumbelina, a fairy princess, falls in love with a fairy prince named Cornelius. While they eat lunch, I ask them how they know when someone's in love. Here are their answers:

How Do You Know You're In Love?
Salem #1—a.m. class

Because you get hugged by a prince
Because you have a ring
They ride together
Because the princess is beautiful
Because the prince gets into your heart and the prince
    thinks of you all the time
Because "you was just right."

Megan tells me that she won't get a boyfriend until she's sixteen, but she used to be in love with her classmate, Billy. They even went trick-or-treating together. "We kissed on the lips and everything," she says.

The students at the Salvation Army site give me answers to the question I asked yesterday about grown-ups:

What Do Grown-Ups Do That Kids Don't?
Salem #1—a.m. class

They cook and smoke cigarettes
They don't play with toys but they play outside
If you're tired, they do clean up for you
Make people cry
Take care of babies and sing them to sleep
They don't go to school
When grown-ups don't answer the phone, I pick it up and pretend
    to be my mom.
They can shoot bows into monsters.

Because it's a windy day, I also ask them what happens when the wind blows.

4-10-95—Monday—Salem #1 & #2 (Week 2)

It's storming—a genuine thunder and lightning storm—as I leave home at 6:20 a.m., the second storm of the morning. From 2:00 to 3:00 a.m. I was awake with my dog, who's afraid of storms and doesn't calm down until we've had three or four for the season and he realizes everything's OK. Sometimes, we can fool him into settling down a little by turning on the TV. He thinks the storm comes from it, and he stops being afraid. I'm struck by the absurdity of trying to sleep with the clamor of a storm, the dog pacing and panting, and the TV playing the weather reports on the Weather Channel.

Thunderstorms always remind me of my mother, who cowers in closets and under furniture during them, and I wonder how I escaped inheriting her fear, since I witnessed it from earliest childhood. Once, I jokingly told a friend of mine, a psychologist, that I thought the next major breakthrough in her field—comparable in importance to Freud's theories—would be that NOTHING in our character or personality is inherited from our parents. She told me that there are studies being done now that show I might be right.

When I arrive at the Lisbon center, things are unsettled. The gas leak—the one that forced the classrooms upstairs to close last week—reappeared on Friday. The furnace has been off since Friday, and there are no classes today. The building is cool downstairs, since it's only 35 degrees outside. The staff is concerned about my comfort, and even though I brought an extra blanket, I wonder if I'll be warm enough. I also worry that tonight's Mapbook session will have to be canceled—a big disappointment. My intuition tells me to wait until afternoon before making a decision on anything.

Because there's no school here at Lisbon, I change my schedule and set off for Salem, where I have a chat with the students in Salem #2 about a magic flower. What would you do, I ask them, if you had a magic flower?

> Tara—open it up and find a pretty girl inside
>
> Sierra—make bears that eat pink food
>
> Jacob–turn flowers into gold
>
> William—growl
>
> Ashley—plant it so the bumble bees could go inside and eat honey
>
> Audrey—I would pick it and then call the cops. They would put handcuffs on it because they're wrong.
>
> Brandy—I would give it to my Mommy and she'd give it to my

daddy and to my sister. And then it would go to my little brother, Jonathon, who is one year old and he would eat it. My mom says three kids are all she needs. That's it.

At the Salvation Army site, I talk with the kids over lunch about the Easter Bunny, who dominates their conversations. I collect their ideas, with the intention of using them as material to write a poem of my own, which I work on later.

While We Sleep in Salem, Ohio
Debra Conner

The day is deep in rain
and no one's seen a rabbit talking
no clue to who's been good
or to explain how crumbs
make your hair curly.
Bunnies come at night
then leave, knowing secrets
about people and their dogs
and their curling irons.
They store them in the North
where they dwell in silence,
eating the hair off the ground.

4-12-95—Wednesday—Lisbon

This residency is allowing me to do so many things I'd never be able to do in a typical school setting. One thing I've done is to give my magnetic poetry kit to members of the staff here and urge them to create poems for their office doorways. The kit, which contains words printed on flexible magnetic material, can be used to assemble poems. At first, the staff is reluctant. "Oh, I can't write poems" or "I was never good at poetry in school" are typical responses. But before long, I see them linger in front of their doors, kit in hand, making poems. Here are some of the products:

Staff Poems

A friend is like
the sweet rain
you leave behind

Worship life
the repulsive
    womany
    mother

love is
true dream
shadow
for those
who cry

live through spring
and take a picture
of a gorgeous butt

roses
essential to winter

```
        play
              fast
        with
    the light
          soar lazy
    smear languid
          diamonds
    over the sky
```

Another advantage to being truly *in residence* and living at the Lisbon center is that others see me writing. Unlike in a school setting, where I arrive and leave with the teachers, the staff at Lisbon sees me working at my desk throughout the day, during times when I'm not with children or parents. I'm always surprised how few people understand that writers sit at their desks and work—much like anyone else with an office job. The difference is that writers keep on working after the rest of the world goes home for the day and before they arrive in the morning. I love the distinction the poet Marvin Bell makes:

> Poetry is a way of life, not a career. A career means you solicit the powerful and the famous. A way of life means you live where you are with the people around you. A career means you become an authority. A way of life means you stay a student, even if you teach for a living. A career means your life increasingly comes from your art. A way of life means your art continues to arise from your life.

The best residencies supply me with material for my writing. A give and take.

In the afternoon, I join the children for lunch and talk with them while they eat. When I comment on how eagerly they eat their raw vegetables, they tell me that celery and carrots are good for you. "How do you know if a food is good for you?" I ask. One child says that it helps you to climb trees. Another child offers a more unusual answer: "You smell better."

The discussion turns to bats as some of the children open the book *In the Tall, Tall Grass,* to look at the pictures inside, one of which shows bats. Brittany tells me that she's seen bats flying in the car like butterflies. Trevor saw a bat hanging upside down on his door. Amanda launches into a more fanciful discussion of bats, telling me that she has a bat inside her house that cleans up her room. "He gives me straws from the cupboard and puts them in my drink. He gives me company and kisses me," she says.

The number of parents who show up for tonight's Mapbook session is something of a disappointment, especially since I had extras at the Monday night session. How to explain? Maybe it's because spring vacation began today in the schools.

The small turnout has its advantages, however: it allows me time to continue working on my life map. I'm pleased to find that Terry Hermsen, who's been visiting today from the Ohio Arts Council, wants to work on a map of his life. The longer I work on this project, the more I'm convinced that it's not the milestones in our lives that matter, but the smaller, more ordinary moments. For example: it's probably not interesting to report that you took a trip to the Grand Canyon. But it is more interesting to note that you stole a piece of petrified wood and have felt guilty about it all your life. Some examples of striking material from tonight's session: Terry shows his drawing of huge, smoky pine trees, trees he had to crawl through as a child to get to his garage. One of the parents talks of jumping down from the hayloft into a pile of hay and watching the cows feed around her. I remember seeing—and I swear this is true—a winged horse fly across the sky behind our house. Some years ago, I learned that Pegasus, the winged horse, was the Greeks' symbol for poetry. That's what I want these Mapbooks to capture.

Tonight, we also have extra time to talk about items on our list of LIKES and DISLIKES. Amy loves scary movies and hates nylon jogging suits. I love the sense of power I get from using the garage door opener. My dislikes? Going barefoot, the feel of Styrofoam, and talking on the phone. Again, it's the personal, individual items that stand out.

4-24-95—Monday—Lisbon (Week 3)

The drive to Lisbon has become a routine now, with familiar landmarks along the way. I've even formed the habit of stopping at the same McDonald's drive-thru for a cup of hot tea to drink on the way. This need for routine and familiarity is part of our nature, I guess, and gives us a sense of safety. Nearly every retiree in my family has spoken of the need to get up in the morning, get dressed, and get moving.

I've also been told that our need for routine lies behind the success of chain motels and restaurants, beginning with Howard Johnson's orange roofs and McDonald's golden arches. Travelers, seeking the familiar, tend to stop at places they recognize—hence, the success of chains and the demise of the small independents.

Like the rest of us, the Head Start students have routines and daily "plans" (of their own choosing) to follow. All this prepares them for regular school and gives them a sense of safety. Again and again, I'm impressed by how much these children learn. My mother was a typical 1950s era stay-at-home mother, but she never could have offered me all that these children receive in the classroom. Being here has opened my eyes, shown me what a good program, with a good staff, can accomplish.

In Lisbon, after the children move to playtime, I continue talking with them in small groups or one-on-one. Jessica says she puts a bone in her dog's "machine." When Matthew tries to correct her, she's indignant. "It's NOT a dog bowl," she snaps. "It's a dog *machine.*" I love a woman who won't back down.

Matthew and Mitchell, the twins, are building a house with blocks. "What would your house be like?" I ask them. "It wouldn't have anything to eat inside and we'd have to get Swiss steak at the Sparkle," they tell me, emphasizing that Swiss steak is their favorite food. Like true artists, they insist that the only furniture they'd need would be a paint easel.

The children seem interested in watching me write, even though they're not—of course—writing themselves. I'm reminded of how important it is for them to see an adult writing, and remember something I read in an issue of *Teachers and Writers* magazine. The author points out that in order to learn anything we must imitate others who are more skilled or competent. With writing, "in order to become writers, young children must have plenty of opportunities to observe and imitate people writing, including teachers, older children, and *ideally parents*" (italics mine).

Tyler tells me that he's going to get tubes put in his ears and that he's been to the hospital to get blood taken out. "What do they do with the blood they take out?" I ask him and the three other children at the table. They offer these answers: (1) they put it back in when they give you a shot; (2) they put it in a bag; (3) they put it in a "tube-a-luck" (?).

Since we're on the subject of health, I ask the class what kids have to do to stay healthy. Most of their answers are what I'd expect—eat apples and carrots, play outside, go to the doctor—but several have more unusual ideas:

Some Kids' Ways to Stay Healthy
Lisbon #1—p.m. class

Eat cheeseburgers and fries and eggs
Eat candy and ice cream and cinnamon rolls
Catch flies and moths
Play with a hawk and a frog
Eat potato pies
Play with lions and tigers
Climb trees to reach the sun, moon and stars

The evening's Mapbook session with parents attracts a large group, including one family, the Orsborns, who come with mother, grandmother, and thirteen-year-old daughter, Danielle. Danielle is working on her own Mapbook and is doing a beautiful job. At thirteen, she doesn't have much of a sense of her past, and has chosen instead to create pages that have to do with her current identity—what she likes, what's special to her. Her father began the project but hasn't attended any of the recent sessions, making me wonder if it's difficult for some men to examine their lives. When I urged him to look for small, seemingly insignificant memories, he claimed he didn't remember anything prior to age sixteen. The same disappearing act happened with another of the fathers who, on the first night, summarized his life with one page of symbols: a log cabin, a deer, and (I think) a rifle.

I talk to the parents about how much I love family stories and stories about eccentric relatives, and I have used a number of them as the basis for poems. One poem came from a story about my aunt who, as a young woman during World War II, thought she needed a set of fox furs in order to attract a man. The trouble was, she couldn't afford a set, so she and a friend shared the cost and wore them on alternate Saturdays. Another poem came from a story, told to me by my grandmother, of the death of her nine-year-old brother, who was stomped to death by striking coal miners when they mistook him for a scab. I also read them a short humorous essay about a family vacation. For tonight, and in the week to come, I suggest they collect family stories for their Mapbook. Stories, I remind them, don't necessarily have to be long or elaborate. For instance, it would only take me a couple of sentences to record that my nephew, at age five or so, once washed his hair with Neet hair remover, thinking it was shampoo.

4-25-95—Tuesday—United

The day gets off to a bumpy start. I can't even manage to write my usual morning journal entry—so many things keep crowding in. When I meet with Cindy, the parent activities coordinator for Head Start, to make plans for my final week, she's interrupted again and again, and I feel like I'm only adding to her burdens. So much work goes into a residency and the staff here has been wonderful, doing everything from making meals and providing babysitting for the Mapbook sessions to furnishing my room. It's not fair that I get the credit when things go well. The final bumble of the morning occurs when I lock myself out of my room, leaving my purse inside with the key.

Happily, things go more smoothly when I arrive at United in Hanoverton. I park myself at a table with a girl named Victoria, who is eating lunch. When I tell her she has the same name as a queen, Queen

Victoria, she says she's never heard of Queen Victoria and she doesn't want to be a queen, she wants to be a teacher who teaches about mittens. "Could you be a queen?" I ask her. "No," she answers, "because I live in a trailer." She says that she has a fancy dress but she doesn't have a princess hat. "All I have is a baseball cap," she tells me.

Some of the other children chime in with their ideas about queens. Jessie knows all about them, telling me that they sleep, wear necklaces and earrings, and have sprinkles on their tennis shoes. They also, in her mind, can climb trees on summer days.

Drake has his own ideas. Queens, he says, wear purple tennis shoes and write. They also like God and other queens. They sniff flowers. Jessie's ideas are wrong, Drake claims. "Queens don't climb trees because they always have on their good clothes."

4-26-95—Wednesday—Lisbon

If there's one quality needed for a successful residency, it's persistence. So often, when things reach a lull, I need to remind myself to hang on and ride it out. Today was just such a day.

One of the problems I've faced in working with such young children has been their inability to make metaphors and similes—key ingredients for poetry. When I urge them to compare one thing to something else, it rarely works. Saying, for example, "A butterfly looks like a _____" or "Cats' whiskers feel like _____" usually yields nothing except blank looks. But in today's afternoon class, a breakthrough occurred. Working with a few students at a time, and looking at an oversized picture book of animals, I found the right prompt.

Instead of relying on them to make the simile, I made it for them, using their ideas. For example, when they recognized the picture of the lion, I asked them, "What else do you know that's this color/shape/feel?" When I pointed to the lion's tail, somebody said, "A pine cone." When I asked what other thing was the same color as the lion, someone said, "A treasure chest with gold." The key? Being more specific in my question.

Polar Bear
Lisbon #4—afternoon

Polar bear, white snow bear,
you listen to dragons and eagles
and reindeer playing in the grass.
You live in dark blue caves
like when you go to sleep.
Your fur is deer fur, your legs
like goats' or a soft

belly, frozen.
You're white as paper,
with red and black eyes like a train.
You scratch with your claws
until people are bones.

Lion
Lisbon #4—afternoon

Lion, tiger of teeth,
blood tiger, whose tail
is like a pine cone.
Green circle eyes, a tongue
and white teeth, fur
like gold in a treasure box.
You make the vultures come.

5-1-95—Monday—Lisbon (Week 4)

Interstate 70 bisects Ohio in more than one way, I discover. South of the interstate, spring's in full flower, with blooming dogwood and azaleas, leafy trees. But to the north, most everything's bare. There's a line in a Lisel Mueller poem that describes the changes she sees in the landscape as she drives south in the spring: "Spring unrolls like a proper novel." I think of Penelope in *The Odyssey* unraveling her weaving to fool the suitors. Nature does the same thing to me as I travel back and forth from home. She offers me spring, then takes it away. The children in Corra's class, Lisbon #3, warm my heart when I arrive to find them in their places, looking at books. Admittedly, books don't have everyone's full attention, a few of the children are holding theirs in the air, covers spread, like airplanes. But the fact that they're spending time *with* books, getting to know them, impresses me. In almost every Head Start class, the children ask me to read to them. I find this encouraging and hope a love of the printed/written word has taken root.

One of the little girls in Lisbon #3, Thomasanne, announces proudly that her mom has recently given her two books. I ask their names, but find she's only familiar with the story. "One's about a girl who eats an apple that's dangerous," she says. "She was covered with ice, but then her eyes got opened." The other is about "a thing that grows tall." I only need one guess: *Snow White* and *Jack and the Beanstalk*.

Most of the adults I've worked with remember a favorite childhood book, something they wanted read aloud over and over. My favorite was *Daniel the Cocker Spaniel*. I wonder if it's still around. Daniel, who wins a blue ribbon in a dog show, provided the inspiration for a neighborhood dog show I held in my parents' garage. The much anticipated event ended abruptly, however, when two of the canine competitors got into a fight, literally making the fur fly.

In the Lisbon 1 afternoon class, I read the children a book about barnyard animals called *The Big Red Barn* and ask them to help me make a poem by pretending to be one of the animals. This is what they concoct.

Night Time at the Barn
Lisbon #1—p.m. class

When we go to sleep,
we get shadows on ourselves.
We go outside
and catch lightning bugs.
We need covers
so we don't turn to ice.
We need flashlights.
Cows jump over the moon
and the moon's shadow
is in the water.
The scarecrow stands and dances.

Today brings an additional treat. Another poet, Lynne Hugo, arrives to participate in the final week of the residency. Lynne will work with teachers, staff, and the children of parents in the Mapbook group to collect additional stories and anecdotes for this project. Her presence energizes me, giving me new ideas and a fresh perspective.

Lynne shares a haunting family story of her own at tonight's Mapbook session, one based on an experience of an elderly aunt. The mothers who have come for tonight's session warm to her immediately, and they feel at ease sharing their books with her. I'm impressed by the amount of work all of them have done, and while I wish we'd had larger numbers of parents to participate, the ones who have come have worked diligently.

For this week's activity, I suggest they do a REMEMBER ME page in their book, recording things they hope their child or children will remember about them. These could be events (Remember the time we . . .) or characteristics (I hope you will remember that I was . . .) What do they hope they'll be remembered for?

5-2-95—Tuesday—United

Lynne and I spend much of the morning tending to the details of her visit and the final days of the residency. One Thursday evening, we'll be giving a public reading and talk at the vocational school; therefore, much time lately has gone into publicizing it and making the necessary arrangements. We also set appointments with the Head Start teachers, who will supply Lynne with their own family stories and with stories about the children. Neither of us wants to impose on the teachers by arriving at an inconvenient time.

At United today, I don't succeed in getting many creative responses to my questions about their bedtime routines, but the question "What has your mother taught you?" works better.

Things Mommy Taught Me
United—p.m. class

To say *please* and *thank you*
Not to do drugs
To feed the baby sister
    she's going to have in 60 days
To brush my teeth and play football
To fix my toys when they're broken
To have prayers
To jump the creek
To weed
Not to play with the dog
    because he has lice and fleas
To style my hair with a curling iron
To say "Twinkle, twinkle, little star"
To "do my own possibility"

Afterword

At the close of this unique and very successful residency, Debra Conner and Lynne Hugo hosted a celebration in which parents read their work, Mapbooks were displayed, and listeners were treated to a reading of the preschoolers' poems.

Everyone agreed the gains—for parents, students, and the Head Start Program itself—were incalculable. The following year, both writers returned for an additional five weeks each, working in Columbiana County.

Playwriting: A Teaching Approach Using the Stories of Our Lives

Michael McGee London

> Scene 1
>
> Setting: A classroom in Miami East High School near Troy, Ohio
>
> Cast: 30 Senior Drama Students
> Fredia Summers—Drama Teacher
> Michael London—Playwright
>
> Time: A meeting in the fall of 1993
>
> *Fredia:*   *(speaks with excitement and anticipation)* This is Mr. London. He's our Artist-in-Residence this year. You all know that he is a playwright. I've told you all about him. Mr. London, we're really excited to have you here. So, I won't keep talking. I'll just turn it over to you. Welcome!
>
> *(The students react with a combination of blank stares, polite half-smiles, and faces filled with nervous uncertainty.)*
>
> *Michael:*   *(speaks quietly to himself)* I hope this works.

That's where we began. In this essay I want to describe an approach to teaching playwriting that has worked for me and has worked for others. If you are interested in teaching playwriting, it might work for you.

> *Michael:*   *(He looks at their questioning eyes.)* What is a play?
>
> *Student 1:*   It's in the theater.
>
> *Michael:*   That's where it takes place, but what is it?
>
> *Student 2:*   You mean like it's a story or something?

So I told the group like a story or something. I told them a story about the day my grandmother and grandfather got married.

Michael: My grandmother's name was Amelia, and when she got married, at the age of fifteen, she was a very beautiful woman. There were lots of young men in the county who wanted to marry her, but her husband-to-be was my grandfather, Louie. This disappointed some of the young men in the county and angered one in particular.

They planned to have a small wedding with just the immediate family. A small wedding with just the immediate family was, of course, one attended by well over a hundred people. After the wedding, they were to go, by carriage, through the mountains to a quiet honeymoon spot in another county.

My grandmother's brother, Uncle Pete, had been out drinking a few nights before the wedding. He heard from some drunken mountain men about a man's plan to ambush the wedding carriage at a very narrow pass in the mountains. At that ambush, the plans were to kill Louie and kidnap Amelia. Uncle Pete had heard this man's name before, the man who wanted to kidnap Amelia.

Without ever telling Amelia or Louie, Uncle Pete gathered up some of their brothers and cousins and they went into the mountains to the site where they knew the ambush would take place. There they waited, hidden in the forest. It wasn't long before they saw a group of four men riding through the mountain pass. They watched as the men dismounted and hid in the trees. Uncle Pete and all the brothers and cousins could see what was happening. Now it was their turn. Having tracked and hunted many animals, they quietly surrounded them and surprised the would-be kidnappers and killers with an ambush of their own.

Uncle Pete was a big man. He and the brothers overcame the small band of ambushers very quickly. Although I was not there, I have been told that none of these men were as handsome after the fight as they had been before.

Uncle Pete, who had a mean streak inside of him, stood over the man who wanted to kidnap and marry Amelia. He had his foot on the man's throat. Uncle Pete pulled out a gun and aimed it at the man's forehead. He said in a very quiet and offhand way, "We really don't have a lot of time here today, so you must make a decision. You see, I have been waiting a long time in the mountains for you. I am getting hungry and my Michealina has dinner on the table waiting for me, so you must make a decision. I can kill you now or I can let you go and you will never again come anywhere near this county." He pressed hard on the man's neck with his large heavy boot. "It makes no difference to me. So hurry up and make a decision. I'm hungry." Uncle Pete pulled the hammer back on the gun. When the man heard the click of the hammer, his eyes widened with fear and he quickly agreed to leave the county and never come back.

Uncle Pete leaned down close to the man's face, grabbed him by the shirt, and raised him up so the man could feel and smell Uncle Pete's breath on his face. Uncle Pete breathed heavy on the man's face as he spoke. "If you forget and you come back I will have to kill you. It will be easy as eating my dinner. So don't forget!" And with that Uncle Pete dropped the man on the ground, kicked him, and told him to get up and get out.

Uncle Pete, Uncle Mike, Uncle Jimmy, and the rest kept all of the horses and stood quietly as the four men went limping as quickly as they could through the mountain forest. They watched as the men disappeared. Then they sat quietly, high in the forest, and looked down upon the narrow pass where the carriage would come. Finally it came. The black carriage bounced through the forest in the dappled sunlight. In it were the newlyweds who never knew of the danger on their wedding day.

After I told this story, the students and I discussed what it was that they thought was interesting, exciting, or uninteresting about the story. The students had a great time talking about the parts of the story that were funny, exciting, silly, suspenseful, etc. This was an exercise in listening.

I did not explain the overall plan of our playwriting residency to the students at this point. I wanted them to focus on gathering stories. I walked the students through some exercises in pairs and groups. They practiced interviewing techniques by interviewing each other, asking about stories in their own lives. About half of the class had only a general instruction for this process. The other half had some special instructions.

The special instructions might help make any stories that were being told by another student more interesting. First, they were to ask how people felt about the story. How did they feel when it was happening? Secondly, they were to prompt the storyteller for as much detail as they could possibly get.

I knew that these key elements of gathering stories, these essential elements of interviewing, were things I could not teach the students. But I did know that each of them was capable of learning this lesson. Discovering the emotional impact of these memories is to discover the heart of the story. Recalling the colors, seasons, shapes, names, ages, faces, and all is to paint a picture in the minds of the listeners that will frame the story in our memories. I knew that if the students could experience hearing the difference between the bland and the rich they might learn more about how to gather stories.

At the end of this interviewing exercise, a variety of students from both groups volunteered to retell the stories that they collected.

Michael:	Who wants to tell us a story? *(The students look around at each other, at the ceiling, at the floor, anywhere except at the Playwright. Then, after moments of quiet, one student raises her hand.)*
Student # 3:	I'll tell you one. I interviewed Janie. She told me a story about when she and her brother got into a fight when she was younger and they made a mess in the kitchen and her mother punished both of them.
Michael:	OK. That's good. What else did she tell you?
Student # 3:	That's it. That's all she told me.
Michael:	How old was she?
Student # 3:	I don't know.
Michael:	What did she say when you asked her if this was a funny story or a sad story?
Student # 3:	Nothing. I didn't know I was supposed to ask her that.
Michael:	*(Looks around the room and sees the quizzical looks of the faces of many of the students. They know he's up to something but they're not sure what.)* Let's try a story from someone in the second group of interviewers. *(A hand quickly goes into the air.)* Go ahead.
Student # 4:	*(She looks at one of the students and asks permission with her raised eyebrows.)* Is it OK?
Student # 5:	Yeah. It's cool.
Student # 4:	Terry told me a story about when he moved here. He was about ten years old and his parents told

him and his sister that they were moving to Ohio.
At first he got real mad at his parents but that kept
getting him grounded. So then he just pretended
like it wasn't going to happen. But then he'd find
out that he couldn't go with the Boy Scouts on the
summer campout, or his sister would talk about
the move constantly, or someone at school would
give him their address so Terry could write them
when he left. So, when pretending didn't work he
tried to bribe his parents not to go. He would like
sit in the kitchen while his mother was cooking and
promise to do all kinds of chores and never do
anything wrong. He asked his dad if he got straight
A's at school could they stay. But they wouldn't
agree, so none of that worked. Then he got really
mad. He didn't talk to anybody at home. He never
cleaned his room. He quit doing his homework. He
left stuff laying around the house. He was rude to
his parents and mean to his sister. And then he
burned down the dog house. He told his parents
that it was an accident but it wasn't. His father was
so mad. He didn't hit Terry, but Terry knew that he
wanted to. He went to his room and like started
throwing things against the wall. Finally his dad
came in and sat down. He didn't say anything at
first. He just watched Terry throwing stuff. Terry
stopped and sat on his bed. "You're trying to act
like you don't care about anything," is what his dad
said. Terry said, "I don't." Then his dad comes over
to Terry and they just like sat there forever. They
didn't talk or anything. Finally after an hour or so
of just sitting there, his dad said, "Are you going to
be OK?" and Terry says, "Yeah." And the thing that
was really strange was that he really was OK. He
wasn't happy but he didn't like get mad anymore or
any of that other stuff. He moved to Ohio. And
now that he's here, Terry and his dad still have
these times when they sit and don't talk. *(The
Playwright starts the applause and everyone else follows
along.)*

Michael: How did you get this story out of Terry?

Student # 4: I just kept asking him questions. Like, I says,
              "What's the hardest thing you ever had to do? You
              know the really hardest!" and then he starts telling
              me that it was when his family moved to Ohio. So,
              like I says, "Why?" and then he sort of tells me a

little more. So then I ask him how did you feel about that, like you told us. An' it was real cool. Like his face changes and everything, an' I know I was like gonna find something out. He didn't want to really talk about it and yet he did. So I told him that I wouldn't tell anyone what he told me. You know. Like I'm doin' now. *(Everyone laughs.)* Anyhow, so he like tells me all this really deep stuff and it was so cool, 'cause it was like when my grandpa died. I felt the same way. Anyhow, after we were done I ask him if I could tell his story 'cause it was really cool. Everybody felt like that when they were a kid. And he finally said OK, mostly 'cause I really bugged him a lot.

It became obvious to the group as a whole that the most interesting stories, the most fascinating stories, the most fun stories, were those that told something about how people felt and those that gave as much detailed information as possible.

This exercise was a simple one but a great learning experience for the students. They were able to identify for themselves which stories were interesting to listen to and which ones were not.

It was at this point that I gave the students the overview for the process that we were going to use in creating a play. Each of the students would first gather stories from their elders. It might be elders in their families or elders who were neighbors of friends. They would gather these stories using videotapes or cassette tapes. We spent time reviewing many guidelines on how to use equipment effectively in an interview.

I then explained that we would examine and explore these interviews, to determine which had the most potential for becoming a play. We would study the structure of a play, how to put a play together, how to write dialogue effectively, and how to write about dramatic action. From there we would choose stories, write them as plays, and, hopefully, present them back to our community, especially those elders whom they interviewed.

That is what we did. The students went out on their own with guidelines for interviewing. Some worked alone and some worked with a partner, and they began to interview their elders. As they gathered the stories, I asked them to focus on their elders' memories of childhood or teenage years.

We came together to discuss the gathering process. Many students were quite surprised to learn about their parents' and grandparents' lives. One girl said that she finally started to become closer to a grandmother that she always disliked. It was easier now that she understood her life. Another student quietly explained that it was important to his mother that he wanted to know about her life. It was especially valuable to both of them because his mother was dying of cancer.

Some students were frustrated because they couldn't seem to get some relatives to talk. Some got only parts of a story.

> *Michael:*   What were you thinking about after your father refused to talk anymore about this obviously important event in his life?
>
> *Student #6:*   I kept thinking, did he really do it? And if he did, why did he do it? I got a whole bunch of newspaper clippings and found out that he really did take Grandpa's plane up for a ride when he skipped school that day. But I can't get anyone to tell me why he did it.
>
> *Michael:*   Can you take a guess?
>
> *Student #6:*   Yeah, but it would feel weird to write about it and get it wrong.
>
> *Michael:*   What if you changed the names and just used this as a base for a small play? Would that feel wrong?
>
> *Student #6:*   I guess that would work. Yeah, that could be cool.
>
> *Michael:*   We can all do that. We don't have to write these stories exactly as they happened. We can use them as a base. We can change things and magnify others. We can dramatize them.

After the students had a sufficient period of time to collect stories and had begun to transcribe them, we came together in a workshop to share and evaluate the stories.

> *Michael:*   Well, what did you think of this last story? *(He looks around. It is clear that no one wants to answer.)* So, everyone liked it. Is that it?
>
> *Female student:*   No, I didn't like it. I mean, it's not that I didn't like it, it just wasn't very interesting.
>
> *Michael:*   Why wasn't it interesting?
>
> *Male student:*   Because it was boring, nobody did anything. It was boring. *(He turns and looks at the class.)* I'm sorry, I didn't mean to offend anybody but it really was boring.

We went through many stories that day and the students did a very good job of identifying which of them were interesting and which of them weren't and which of them had real dramatic potential. The potential to be a play. I also made available a short script of my own, "Blood in the Valley," which came from a story about a boy who lived down the valley from my father. *(A copy of the script follows this essay.)*

In order to help the students understand how to take a story and create a play from it, I asked them to choose a story from the ones we had just heard that they were really excited about. The one they chose came from the grandfather of an exchange student who was part of our class. It was the story of a young boy living in Germany during World War II. His favorite place to play was defiled when he and his boyhood chums discovered Polish prisoners of war being murdered on their soccer field.

I took the story and, with the students watching, proceeded to outline a series of scenes based upon the story. I first showed them how to draft an overall outline. Next, with the students alternately observing and then assisting, I wrote one of the scenes with a critical turning point of the story.

This process of having the students go through a common writing experience was very important. They had the opportunity to observe an experienced writer attack the script and they had the opportunity to be part of the process with prompting by myself. I believe it helped to give them a point of departure for turning their stories into plays.

Male student: Cool man! So that's how you do it. I can do that!

The students then had an assignment. They could work in groups or they could work alone. They should find one story or one part of a story that they found had the most dramatic potential. It could be a story that they collected themselves or one that was collected by someone else. (Most students chose to work in groups and most chose stories that were collected by someone else.)

They were then to outline a script. Their drama could be character-driven or plot-driven. (All of the students were clear that when we used the word *drama* we meant not only those stories that were serious but those that were funny and mysterious and all the rest.) Students were asked to draft the first scene, the last scene, and the scene which would be the critical turning point in their play.

After the students began producing a lot of work, we met together and they read their scripts. It wasn't long before they became critics and advisors to each other.

They learned about feedback by modeling the approach that their teacher and I used as we publicly evaluated what we heard and what we saw. Our approach was very supportive. We always identified the strengths and the weaknesses. The students identified which plays worked and which didn't, as well as *why* plays worked and why they didn't. Then it came time for them to complete their first drafts.

After they completed their drafts, I met privately with each playwright or group of playwrights and went through a detailed advising session on the editing of their piece. For some it meant minor adjustments, for others it meant major rewrites, but most students were now very excited about completing their work.

(Session #5)

Michael:	How do you want the audience to react to this? Are we sad or do you want us to laugh?
Student #1:	*(Looks at his partner.)* Well, I guess we're not sure?
Michael:	It shows. If you're not sure, then the audience will be confused right along with you.
Student #2:	*(Looks at his partner with frustration.)* I told you it wasn't clear. C'mon let's go. *(To Michael.)* Don't worry. We'll fix it.

(Session #7)

Michael:	Your dialogue is good. It's very realistic, and I can really hear the voices.
Student #1:	*(Her whole face is smiling.)* That's what we worked on the most.
Michael:	And it shows. The problem is the plot. *(The students' shoulders drop and their mouths open in surprise.)*
Student #2:	There's something wrong with the plot?
Michael:	Yes. There isn't one.
Student #1:	No plot?
Michael:	It's not that there isn't any plot. It's that there isn't one plot. Your play goes in four or five different directions. I think that you might have finished telling all of these stories in your head. You just didn't get them finished on paper, and when you did put something on paper you ended up with more than one story. Please understand. Having more than one plot in the play isn't as big a problem as not completing at least one of them.
Student #2:	The real problem is that I wrote my part at home and she wrote her part at home and then we crammed them together. I think that's what you want to say.
Michael:	Yes. That's another way of looking at the same problem.

(Session 12)

Michael:	This is pretty good.
Student #1:	But what?
Michael:	Pardon me?
Student #1:	I heard a great big BUT in there.
Michael:	Yes. Well, I do have one question. Who's telling the story?
Student #2:	We are.
Michael:	No. I mean which of your characters is telling the story?
Student #1:	You mean that point of view thing?
Michael:	That's the one.
Student #2:	I don't get it. We're telling the story.
Student #1:	*(Gathers up the pages of the script.)* Don't worry, I'll explain it to him.
Michael:	Are you sure you understand?
Student #1:	Consider it done, Dude! We're out of here. *(He exits with a bewildered partner following behind.)*

Eventually, the deadline came and all scripts were turned in. It was fascinating to see nineteen scripts written by students who had never written a script before. They were good scripts. I believe they were good because the process was kept simple, experiential, and the material that they were writing about was familiar to them.

I took the completed scripts and did some minor editing, wrote an introduction and epilogue, as well as some transition bridges. I put nine of the completed scripts together and created a two-act production, a series of small plays, stories, and vignettes about the lives of the elders of the community.

In addition to writing plays, we decided to perform the work in a readers' theater format. To help each of the students better understand a readers' theater approach, an expert readers' theater director joined us as a guest artist during the residency and spent one intensive day of teaching. This new learning about readers' theater was supported and followed up by the encouragement and guidance of the students' teacher and myself.

Students from the art department helped with the set decoration, and students from the typing classes typed all final scripts. I returned the completed scripts to the students and we went about the task of casting the roles. The teacher was able to secure a community theater for the presentation of the work. And then the cast went into rehearsals, which were primarily supervised by the teacher on site at the high school. I came in as often as possible to polish their readers' theater presentational approach. As the performance time approached, the students became more excited, and interest grew in the community. At performance night there was a full house. The students performed work that they had written, work based upon the stories of their families and friends, their elders. The students honored the elders of their community with their work.

> Michael: *(Sits quietly alone backstage listening to students perform plays they have written. In the darkness he can hear the laughter, the quiet tension, the sniffling. As the lights fade out at the end of the play, he can hear the roar of the applause. He speaks quietly to himself.)* I guess it worked.

The End

[Note: Two of the scripts Michael's students produced may be found in Section II of this book, pages 108–116.]

Blood In the Valley

Michael McGee London

> *(The scene opens with Piper slowly pacing around a small area center stage. There is an old straight-back chair center stage facing the audience. Piper is in the imaginary office of the pastor of a country church. Piper is about nineteen. He has straight dark brown hair and is a gangly 5' 10". He is wearing a white shirt buttoned to the collar with no tie, an old dark brown suit jacket that is well worn, and old dark blue trousers with a belt that shows how the pants are too big for him in the waist and too short for his high-top brown shoes. His white socks show when he sits.*
>
> *Suddenly Piper turns stage left and pulls his hands out of his pockets as he watches an imaginary preacher walk into the office and sit where the audience is, opposite the chair. There is a small table next to Piper's chair and it is the only piece of furniture or scenery on stage save the chair that Piper sits in. Piper nods to the imaginary preacher and sits in the chair.)*
>
> Piper: Thank you, sir. *(Pause. He is nervous.)* Yes, sir. I'm comfortable. Would you mind if I have a cigarette, sir? *(Pause)* Thank you, sir. *(Pause)* Well, yes sir, there was one other thing. *(Beat)* Do I have to sit down all the time we're talking? *(Pause)* Well, no this chair's real comfortable. I don't mean that. I mean ya gots a real nice office here, but uh, I mean sometimes I just, uh, I don't like to sit all

the time. I mean come lately I gits a little edgy and I like to move around a little bit, if you don't mind sir? *(Beat)* Thank you, sir. *(Pause)* Well, I was about fourteen when it happened. *(Pause)* Well, yeah. I always knew what papa did to s'port us an' everythin', 'cept, well, but I never, I mean I helped out with the chores on the farm an' all like that, but he never wanted.

(Beat. He lights a cigarette.)

I mean I never went 'round the butcher shed nor the smoke house nor nuthin' like that. But I helped feed the pigs an' I helped with some of the gardenin', an' I fed the chickens an', I mean I did my chores an' all but I just never went 'round the butcher shed, nor nuthin' like that. *(Pause)* Well, I don't rightly know but I have an idea. *(Beat. He stands and begins to move around the office.)* Well, Papa . . . . Now, I don't rightly know that this is what it was. But sometimes I used to think that Papa never wanted me to be a pig butcher like he was. I think he was just hopin' I'd be a farmer. I really don't know why for a long time but I speculated 'bout it. *(Pause)* Well, I never really knew what it was all about over in the butcher shed. I mean I knew what he was doin', but. . . .

(He becomes very animated, acting out his story.)

I guess I was 'bout 'leven years old one time, an' Papa, he came into the house for dinner. An' he had, he was, well, he was a mess. He had mud all over him an' he was a mess. He had all kinds of stuff, not like normal. He had blood all over him. In his face, an' his hair, just everywhere. He smelled normally, from the pigs an' all, but he never smelled that bad. He always used to clean up in one of the barns before he came in t' dinner, an' he always came in 'bout six-thirty. *(Beat)* Momma always had dinner late. You could tell it bothered Momma, but she didn't yell at him nor nuthin' like that. Momma always had a way 'bout her. I mean the way she didn't talk a lot, but she could be real firm like. I mean when she said somethin' you always listed up t' what she had t' say. Anyhow, she just looked at Papa an' she said, "Arny," she said, "Arny, you're a good man, but ya done fergot to clean yerself up before ya come t' dinner." That's all Momma said. An' Papa just looked at her real confused there fer a minute. An' then he looked a little shamed, cause he must have realized he'd just forgotten all about it, an' weren't thinkin'. He just looked at her, an' you could tell he was apologizin', but he never said anythin'. Then he looked over at me with a funny half smile, like, well Papa made a mistake here an' I guess it's OK for Papa t' make a mistake onced in a while too, you know. Well, he didn't say nuthin'. He just went out and cleaned up an all. But I think that's the first time that I really realized what Papa had to contend with. I mean it was really not pleasant, what he had to do. I mean it was all over him, an' you could see that it weren't no pleasant thing t' have t' deal with. *(Pause)* Well, yeah I guess it made me think about other things too. *(Pause)* Well, like everybody in the town nearby an' everybody in the valley, they all respected Papa an' they liked Papa, but Papa didn't seem t' have a whole lots a real close friends. Now, I just knew it's 'cause a what he did. I mean, a man smell like that, being 'round them pigs all the time an' everythin', ain't nobody gonna wanna really be near him, 'cept the people that really love him. *(Beat)* I guess I thought about that later, and I guess I felt sorry for Papa a little bit, you know. *(Pause)* 'Cause of what he did. People didn't want to be around him. I mean, like now at the church on Sunday an' everythin', everybody was real polite. You could tell, now, you could tell that everybody really respected him. And they all liked him too. But people didn't invite Momma and Papa out to their homes a lot, you know. An' they didn't come out to visit neither, oh, mebey once on a Sunday, but not very often or for very long. *(Beat)* Every once in a while they would ask Momma over, and to bring me. They would say, "Now, Elizabeth, why don't you bring Piper and come on over and visit a spell one of these days." And Papa would be standing right there. Now, I always thought that was really rude, but I know they didn't mean Papa no harm. 'Cause you could tell they really liked him, they really respected him. And Momma would say, "Well, when Arny and Piper an' I get free a spell, why we'd be real happy to come on over an' visit, all three of us." She'd say that an' they'd say nuthin' more 'bout it. Course we never went. Momma wasn't gonna go without Papa. An' we knew it was just cause what Papa did an' all. *(Beat)* People just funny that way. *(Pause)* No, I never got really involved with it. I mean I fed the pigs an' all. An' then Papa gave me one. An' I took her to the county fair, my own sow. An' Papa let me take her to the fair. An' we won a blue ribbon, now, I mean we won a Blue Ribbon. *(Pause)* Betsy, Papa let me name her. An' she's the best, I mean now she's just the best. That's all there is to it. She's the best *(Pause)* Well, things started to get real tight. One day Papa told me, he said, "Piper, things ain't been real good lately, an' Betsy ain't gonna be able to stay around a long time." Much longer, I think he said. He didn't have to tell me, I knew what he meant. But we just didn't talk about it for a long time. *(Beat)* Well, one night I got t' crying and everythin'. I mean Betsy was my pig. She weren't no butcher sow. I knew things were tight, an' I felt sorry for Papa an' all, but Betsy was mine. Anyhow, Papa came to my room, an' he said he was sorry, an' he knew how I felt an' if it could have been any other way he wouldn't want this, but that it just couldn't be. Things were too tight. *(Pause)* Well, I didn't say nuthin'. I mean, what could I say? *(Pause)* No, well yeah, well, no I didn't quit cryin'. *(Beat)* Papa held me. I pretended like I quit cryin', but I didn't really. *(Beat)* Papa told me that he thought I should go visit Aunt Meg. I hadn't seen Aunt Meg in a long time. But I didn't really wanna go see Aunt Meg. I mean, I like Aunt Meg, but I had the summer an' I didn't have to go to school an' all. I really wanted to stay home an'. . . . Anyhow, he thought it would be best for everybody, an' I knew what he meant *(Pause)* Well, he meant that when I got back Betsy wasn't gonna be there no more. *(Beat)* I told him I would go. And I did. . . .

(His voice begins to shake a little, gradually increasing toward the end of the speech.)

. . . Well, one day Aunt Meg called me into the house. I was out weedin' one of the gardens. An' I come up to the house an' we sat on the porch, an' she said "Now, I want you to listen to me real good, boy." She said, "I got some news fer ya that's gonna make ya real happy." I said, "What is it, Aunt Meg?" She said, "Now, Piper, ya goin' home. An' when ya git home your Betsy's gonna be there waitin' fer ya." Well, I almost cried, I mean I was so happy. An' I ask Aunt Meg what'd happened. Why'd Papa change his mind? An' she said, "Well, now we're gonna let yer Momma answer the rest of yer questions." *(Beat)* I think I knew then. Maybe I didn't, but that's what I remember now. *(Beat)* Anyhow, she said that I was gonna leave that day an' go back with Mr. Bartlett, an' that she was going with me. I just knew somethin' weren't right, 'cause I always went back with Mr. Bartlett by myself. So we went on back. On the way Aunt Meg got real thirsty, we all was wantin' a drink. We just left so quick that Aunt Meg forgot the lemonade she always fixes fer my trip home. So we stopped off in Pennlyville fer some water. An' I saw Aunt Meg talkin' to this man. I'd seen him at church once or twiced but I didn't recollect his name. An' I thought it was real strange that she knew him, 'cause she didn't go to the same church as we did. They was talkin' real low an' real serious-like. An' just afore he walked away I heard him say, "Well, Mam, we'll smell no hog blood in the valley today." He walked away an' Aunt Meg stood there with the tears wellin' up in her eyes. An', *(Beat)* An' I guess that's when I knew fer sure. That's when I knew why Betsy was gonna be there to see me when I got home. *(Beat)* You know, Papa was such a good man. I wish'd I'd, I mean, I was only fourteen at the time. I just wish'd I'd been able to love him more, love him more when we had each other. That's all. *(Pause)* I guess I tried to make it up to Momma. Just love her as much all the time so's to be with her an' all. *(Pause)* I guess I don't, I just, I guess that's why I'm here, Reverend. Momma's gone now too an' I don't understand, Reverend. *(Beat)* Don't you see, I really did love them. I loved them whole bunches, I did. But they're gone. *(Beat)*

(He stares into the reverend's face, the audience.)

And I don't understand.

(He stares down at the floor crying as the lights dim out.)

The End

Just across the Street: The Story of a Teacher-Based Residency

Lynn Powell

Across the street from my house is my daughter's elementary school. From the playground, students can see me running after my daughter with her forgotten lunch box, bearing cupcakes across the street on her birthday, or coming out on my porch in stocking feet to check my mailbox. I'm sure no kid ever wondered what I did in those hours when my daughter was at school. I'm sure they had never noticed how one upstairs room lit up at my house when all the morning's commotion moved to the other side of the street.

Before moving to Ohio, I had worked professionally in hundreds of classrooms in New Jersey as a Writer-in-the-Schools. When my daughter entered first grade in Oberlin, I offered to come in every Wednesday as a parent volunteer to her combined first- and second-grade class. The teachers scheduled my visits during Writing Workshop, and most weeks I helped individual children brainstorm and edit the writings they were already working on. Some weeks the teachers invited me to bring in poems and suggest poetry writing possibilities for the class. I was a parent, like many other parents, coming into the school to share something I love. This was already a poetry-friendly classroom, with a rich collection of poetry books, teachers who relished poetry in their own lives, and students who were encouraged to use poetry as a natural response to a variety of experiences and assignments. I became their casual poet-in-residence.

It was clear how this poetry-rich environment affected the children's writing over time. Children were choosing to write poetry spontaneously, and they were refreshingly free of the clichéd notions about poetry that afflict many elementary students. Their poems were not pat and sing-songy, sacrificing sense for an easy rhyme. Rather, these students were learning to welcome into their written language the associative leaps natural to their imaginations and to their talk. Without knowing it, they were beginning to employ assonance and alliteration, making more varied music with words than the usual predictable rhymes. By listening to poetry, they were absorbing the power of the image to suggest what isn't said, and in turn, they were letting images resonate in their own poems. Their writing—even when it was only a few sentences long—was becoming vivid and true.

Several teachers in the school (which is grades K–2) began to express an interest in bringing more poetry into their own classrooms. A group of teachers proposed to the Ohio Arts Council's Arts in Education program that I work as poet-in-residence for all of Eastwood School, with a handful of visits to each classroom and with the teachers singled out for more intensive work and designated as a core group. In their proposal, the teachers wrote of the difficulty of finding time for their own intellectual growth. By building into the residency protected teacher workshop time, they hoped to create an environment where teachers could explore the reading and writing of poetry more deeply and gain confidence in their ability to integrate poetry into their curricula. One of their main goals was to ensure that teachers were equipped to extend the work of the residency after the poet had gone back home across the street. We all agreed that each teacher needed to be equipped with confidence, eagerness, and the bracing pleasures of poetry itself.

When poetry is absent in a classroom or is taught only as fill-in-the-blank structures in a contained "poetry unit," it is usually because teachers feel on uncertain ground. Either their own poetry education instilled in them Fear and Trembling, or they have absorbed our loud culture's indifference to poetry's quieter gifts. Students in these classes absorb their teachers' timidity or resistance to poetry. To change students' minds, it's important to change teachers' minds.

So a teacher workshop must be fun, unthreatening, applicable to the next day's teaching, and clear about the *how* and *why* of poetry in the classroom. I began the first Eastwood teachers' workshop by reading to the teachers a charming picture book by Claudia Long entitled *Albert's Story*. Albert has a story he wants to tell his older sister Mildred. When she agrees to listen, Albert says with evident pride, "He put the thing on his back." Mildred is incredulous that Albert considers *that* a story, and Albert is chagrined, wishing he'd never told his story. Then Mildred asks Albert a question: "Who is he?" Albert thinks for a minute, then describes a little boy down the street. Mildred asks more and more questions which Albert answers more and more imaginatively until a story rich in detail is elaborated out of that first dull sentence. "We need to be Mildreds," I told the teachers. "By simply asking our students questions, we can encourage their imaginations and language to come alive, we can help them discover the poems hiding in their hearts."

In that first workshop we then discussed how I had "been a Mildred" in their classrooms during that week, especially during the group writing I always do with the students before turning them loose on their own poems. In several classes, I had read the students Native American rain chants. Then, since it was January and there hadn't been nearly enough snow days, we wrote snow chants modeled on what we had learned about Native American poetry. Because I wanted to encourage the children to think imagistically, I said to them, "Like the Native Americans, you must speak directly to the snow. And you must really flatter the snow if you want to persuade it to come down and be with you." I encouraged children to think about how snow looked and tasted and felt. A kindergartner version of Albert raised his hand and suggested we begin our poem with, "Snow, you are white!"

I said, "Oh, yes, snow *is* white! But white like what?"

"Like paper."

"Yes, paper's white and what else is white? What's white the way snow is white—fluffy and soft? Who can help him?"

"Fur!" "Cottonballs!" "Feathers!"

"The feathers of which bird? Certainly not a crow or a peacock, right?"

"Swans! Write down 'Snow, you are white as swans' feathers!'"

We agreed that the snow would like that idea, and I promptly wrote the line up on the board as the beginning of our poem.

I told the teachers that by "Mildreding" the class during a group writing exercise, I am modeling what poets do for themselves as they write. When writing my own poems, the first lines I write down are often clichéd and general. Like Albert, I have a vague notion of my story and am groping towards it. It's only by Mildreding my own lines that my poems come alive, full of detail and life.

In the first two teacher workshops, I concentrated on skills the teachers needed to guide the students into writing. I conducted group and individual writing exercises with them that they could use "as is" in class the next day. With Valentine's Day coming up, for example, I brought in playful poems about friendship and love that inspired hilarious, romantic, or racy poems by the teachers but were also just right for eliciting sprightly poems from children. In one poem, the poet imagines she could become any animal in the world, and she speculates on what new things she would be able to do for her loved one. One teacher wrote a poem for her husband which began:

> If I were a blue and yellow butterfly
> I'd flutter around your hair
> Like a halo of flowers.
>
> If I were a dark brown mink,
> I'd slip around your shoulders
> Quietly to keep you warm . . .
>
> If I were a gossamer dragonfly,
> I'd hover in your gaze
> And sweetly hum over and over
> I love you, I love you, I love you . . .

When she later gave the poem to her husband as a gift, he was so impressed he didn't at first believe she wrote it! A number of the teachers tried this exercise with their students the next day. The results were so delightful that in many classes students made their own handmade valentines for their classmates with their own poems on them. Happily, Hallmark sales were slightly down in Oberlin that February!

At the last two teacher workshops I moved beyond playful lesson plans into more serious writing. I began to treat the teachers as writers, bringing to them poetry that addressed their own lives and experiences, and inviting them into more challenging writing exercises. For example, after reading and talking about Adrienne Rich's "Song," a poem about loneliness, they wrote of their own feelings. The teachers took risks and surprised themselves with crisp images like these from three different poems:

> Perplexed, my latest stage
> In this my aquamarine year—neither
> blue nor green like the old 1957 Chevy I once drove . . .
>
> If only I didn't feel so helpless.
> Helpless as a gray coyote caught in a snare,
> As a shimmering aria sung against the power of crashing waves . . .
>
> Today I feel discouraged,
> discouraged as the sun in a futile attempt
> to break through the gray, overcast sky,
> discouraged as thyme gone flat with age . . .

An interesting benefit of the teacher workshops was the sense of community and mutual respect that began to develop between teachers of differing styles and pedagogies. In creating group poems, teachers collaborated tentatively at first, then with gusto, wit, and a sense of shared experience. On the day that teachers wrote in response to the Adrienne Rich poem, many teachers wrote about frustration and helplessness, using the poetry, as it turns out, as a means of grappling with a difficult situation within the school. A kindergarten teacher left that workshop and didn't return because, I thought, she was avoiding the writing assignment. It turns out that she was weeping in the next room in response to the poem's stark evocation of loneliness. The next day she told me she had stayed up half the night writing poetry, and in her evaluation letter she wrote:

> I have written endlessly since working with you, and it's been a helpful vehicle to release some emotions, or perhaps better focus on the ones that really exist. I have found writing to be one of the most valuable tools I have, and your reintroduction to poetry was a gift.

The teacher workshops provided a place for an ongoing dialogue about the hows and whys of teaching poetry. One teacher who was ambitious for her first- and second-grade writers was disappointed when "nothing moved her" in the poems they wrote during my first visit to her classroom. I had been pleased by their writing, and the difference in our reactions gave us the opportunity to talk about the *cumulative* effect of a rich poetry environment. During my next visit to her class, we wrote poems based on Christina Rossetti's poem "A Birthday." The teacher came to me with tears in her eyes and handed me the poem of an "at-risk" child:

> When I am sad, my heart feels
> like a star with no wishes.
> It stands alone in the dark night
> and no one will wish on it.
> But when I am happy,
> my heart feels like a shooting star
> going so fast it will race me
> and it is going to win.

Now the teacher was astonished that such fine poetry could come out of a seven-year-old child so readily.

In the workshops and in my visits to their classes, I tried to suggest to teachers the relevance of poetry to every "subject" they study, that poetry is not an ornament to a curriculum but a way of going deeper into any inquiry into the world. In an Eastwood class studying the water cycle, we read Langston Hughes's poem "April Rain Song" and imagined where we would fall if we were raindrops, what we would kiss or beat against. In a class studying ocean life, we read a poem from Africa in which the poet assumes the persona of a fish, then we listened to whale songs and imagined what those songs would be able to tell us if we could only understand. In a kindergarten class full of children with loose teeth, I threw away my lesson plan, and we wrote a poem about the tooth fairy, imagining what she does with all the teeth she gathers! In a class interrupted by a scary tornado drill, we came back and wrote a fierce chant to scare away tornadoes (and our terror).

Poetry can help any part of the curriculum move from "school subject" into experience. And in a culture and educational system grappling with "a loss of values," poetry is vital: it can help us enter the perspective of other lives, give voice to the tangles of feeling that knot inside us, and teach us not to be complacent with the clichéd thought or judgment but to revise toward something more true. Poetry should not be contained within "a unit" any more than wonder, feeling, or imagination should be.

During the residency I tried to help teachers find poetry in the work they were already doing in their classrooms. The music teacher asked me to collaborate with her on a poem for the children to recite during the annual music program. The theme of the program this year was "Around the Campfire." I suggested that the children create a chant in the Native American tradition in which they would ask the fire to burn brightly and the earth and sky to give their night gifts. I visited the music class of each first- and second-grade team. Each team created one section of the poem, which they later recited at the beginning of the music program:

> Fire, please come, burn higher!
> Your sunly power spreads your fire colors.
> Your torch makes a path of light
> through the tunnel of woods.
>
> Sky, please bring out your sparkling, glittering jewels.
> Bring us your moon like a huge pearl.
> Night, please dress yourself in black
> and bring us your treasures.
> Fly your night rainbow of shooting stars over us.
> Moon, bring out your smiley face.
>
> Fire, please come, burn higher!
> Lightning, take your silver streaks somewhere else!
> Thunder, take your booming drums away from us!
> Rain, go to a dry land tonight, the desert needs you.
> Bear, take your silver claws and white teeth somewhere else!
> You have honey waiting at home for you . . . You don't need my
>   meat!
> Wolf, you have your mate waiting at home for you with your two
>   little cubs.

Run there with your fast legs!
Mosquitoes, stay away from here! We have fire and smoke!
Take your sucking mouths to another town!

Fire, please come, burn higher!

Night, please bring us your beautiful sounds.
Make the fire crackle.
Make your sound quiet and peaceful . . .
Make the owls hoot, the cricket chirp, and the frog ribet.
Make the lightning bugs twinkle like dancing stars.
Make our voices clear as water as we sing.
Night, please bring us your beautiful sounds.

Fire, please come, burn higher!

In her evaluation later the music teacher commented on the brainstorming and Mildreding techniques I had used with the children as they wrote this poem, and how observing those techniques had altered her interactions with her students:

> . . . Especially helpful for me was helping without halting the creative ideas of the students. In the past, I would have been quicker to "jump in" and offer a word or idea. Now I am more careful to try and draw out the students' ideas without putting words in their mouths. . . . After the fire chant experience, the students seemed more willing to try something different. They are more comfortable with different ideas and join in quicker than before. . . .

The greatest challenge of the residency for me was the collaboration with the art teacher. We planned six classes together (three different lessons). We had many constraints, principally the constraint of time—we had only forty minutes to introduce and complete a lesson that included poetry and drawing or painting, plus suiting up twenty-five kids in smocks and hosing them down at the end! The making of poetry and visual art *simultaneously* was a first-time experiment for both of us.

Our first two lessons were disappointments. The first lesson produced nice enough poems and nice enough paintings, but the connection between the two seemed artificial, concocted. (First we wrote poems to spring, inviting its blues and yellows and greens to come. The art lesson then was to mix blue and yellow to make green in fold-over paintings.)

The second lesson was well-conceived and interesting, but too ambitious for the short time we had to work with. Taking as our model a whimsical Paul Klee painting that has four lines of make-believe hieroglyphics, we invited the children (after significant discussion) to make their own visual "poems" in their own invented visual language. The brightest children seized the idea and did wonderful work, but for the majority the idea was too complicated to grasp in such a short time, and their work was less successful. The art teacher was in despair after this class, frustrated by the inferior work the kids had done, and stumped, along with me, about how to make this art-poetry collaboration work in an organic way in a short time.

The final lesson was a triumph. The art teacher showed the kindergartners two paintings of geese flying: *Flying Geese* by Max Ernst and *On the Wing* by Koson. As the children were looking at and discussing the painting, I read them this haiku by Issa: "Wild goose, Wild goose/At what age did you make/your first journey?" Then we started thinking about the questions we'd like to ask the geese in the paintings and thinking of the answers the geese might give us. As the students were engaged in this dialogue, I quietly wrote on the blackboard their "poem" which was being "composed" as they discussed the painting:

> Wild goose, wild goose, what is it like to float on the water?
> It's like you're on a cloud flying you everywhere.
> Wild goose, wild goose, why do you fly at night?
> So I can ride on the pretty moon. . . .

After the discussion, we became geese with long necks and graceful wings and flew about the room, landing and folding ourselves back onto the water. Then the kindergartners went to their seats and drew (on red paper with chalk) stunning pictures of geese—in flight or floating on water or flying on the pretty moon.

The art teacher and I were both thrilled at this natural integration of poetry, visual art, and movement. She wrote in her self-evaluation:

> It was one of those "teaching moments" when a teacher's learning curve zooms upward. . . . Until that moment, the realization of how to connect the art work to poetry composition had evaded us. The questioning [of the geese] dovetailed directly into solving a difficulty I have in teaching aesthetics to young children. It expanded the instructional possibilities. . . . I believe that we were just only beginning to understand the possibilities that exist for a poetry/art collaboration. Painting pictures with words and composing metaphors with paint is a perfect union. . . .

What I learned in my collaboration with the art teacher I put to immediate use in my last official visit to my daughter's classroom. Her teachers were just about to turn their classroom into an artist's studio for the last six weeks of school, during which time the children would paint and draw in the styles of Picasso, Monet, Van Gogh, O'Keeffe, Cassatt, and other great artists. I was looking for a bridge from our weeks of poetry into their weeks of painting.

In my bedroom hangs a poster from the 1990 Geraldine R. Dodge Poetry Festival—a large Georgia O'Keeffe painting of a white orchid paired with Basho's famous haiku:

> The temple bell stops.
> But the sound keeps coming
> out of the flowers.

I brought the poster to class and read the children the poem. Then I asked them why they thought the people who made the poster decided to put the painting and poem together. What followed was a wonderful discussion full of aesthetic insights worthy of much older students. The children clearly understood and felt both the poem and the painting more fully because of their juxtaposition.

Several teachers used the poetry the children had written during the residency as an inspiration for visual art. The teacher of the kindergartners who wrote the tooth fairy poem asked each of her students to draw what the tooth fairy looked like. In one first-grade class, the children had written a poem with me based on their experience with the "I Dream a World" photographs exhibited in the school. The teacher then helped the children create a quilt which incorporated and illustrated their poem. In my daughter's class at the end of their Art and Artists study, each child illustrated one of his or her poems in the style of a favorite artist. The poems and paintings were hung in the classroom's Museum of Art, which had a gala opening one weekday during lunch for parents and friends.

During the last two days of the residency, I brought in as a visiting artist a dancer and choreographer who is experienced as an artist in the schools. We wanted to explore the possibilities of combining poetry and movement with children. Because her time at the school was brief, she was only able to visit each class one time. In each class she took one of the class's group poems and helped the children improvise movement to their own words. The children were enthusiastic dancers, and the teachers and I saw enormous potential for using movement and poetry to inform and create each other. It was clear that movement gave some children an expressiveness they hadn't had before in the classroom. One teacher commented:

> Like the writing of poetry itself, the expression of feeling through dance gave children the opportunity to reach inside themselves to tap into a response. Once again, it was clear as teachers observed the classes that we were reaching children whom traditional methods alone had not fully reached. It was a magical experience. . . .

By the end of the residency, I believe minds *were* changed. In their evaluations, the teachers spoke of new confidence in the teaching and writing of poetry and of pleasure in discovering "a creative side" to themselves. A number of teachers, like these below, voiced new insights into their own students:

> There are still times that children amaze me. Since we began writing poetry in the classroom, some of the most hardened students, those who give the impression that they couldn't care less, have started coming up to me with their journals to show me POEMS they have written. This time with poetry has touched their souls. . . .

> It was the line of a poem ("To my loneliness I say, 'Get out of my face.'") that provided a window into the deep feelings of a child who appears to be quite impassive. . . .

> The poetry residency has . . . reinforced my thinking about how powerful a tool poetry writing can be. For months, R. wrote the least amount he could get away with writing. Then, after hearing Bert Kitchen's poem, R. started spending hours at the computer every day adding more and more lines to his "Somewhere Today" poem. He wanted to share it with all the visitors to our room because he was so proud of it. It has made me think differently about some of the kids in our room. Many of the children surprised me by the poetic imagery they were able to use. A.'s poem about herself, or C.'s haiku were revelations to me, as well as to the children themselves. . . .

The art teacher, who sees each class for only forty minutes each week, commented in her self-evaluation:

> I learned more about my students. Students who have rarely spoken in my room became at ease. Poetic words and/or phrases tumbling from them. One kindergartner, whose only words in class had declared almost every week, "I'm being good, Mrs. B.," suddenly was blossoming. My assessment of her was altered as she changed before my eyes. Another student who has caused many class disruptions and usually chose to chat during discussions came forth with wonderful ideas. I saw appreciation for her skills in her fellow students' eyes. The weekly publication of the children's poetry [in the local newspaper] illuminated another side of students hidden from me. . . . When I begin to appreciate and understand my students better, I am able to instruct at a more meaningful level. . . .

On the next-to-last day of school, the school invited me back for an assembly to present me with a copy of the anthology the students and teachers had edited and produced. Among the other gifts the children and teachers gave me was a book that almost every first and second grader had contributed a page to. The students had been asked to write down what they thought a poem or a poet was. Their joyful definitions are the clearest sign that poetry in the classroom matters:

> A poet is someone who lets her feelings dance.
> A poem is something that opens your imagination when you think you don't have any.
> A poet is someone who sings the good song.
> A poem is like a single drop of rain on a rosebud.
> A poet is someone who takes you for an adventure.
> A poet is someone who makes a beautiful feeling in your mind.
> A poet is someone who makes us feel happy and the day feel happy.
> A poet is someone who has an imagination and is sort of like a sorcerer.
> A poem is a sign of happiness to me.

Since the residency, I now have three hundred new friends about town. They grin and wave at me at the supermarket, at the drugstore, at the library. When I'm out in the yard, they stop and talk to me as they walk home from school. "Hey, you're the poet!" they sometimes announce, running up to me, beaming with revelation. "I remember that poem we wrote—the one about the feathery snow!" a snaggle-toothed kid said to me on the hottest day in July, the poem blowing back over me, refreshing me with its cool lines. "My daughter wrote a poem about the moon and she wants me to mail it to you," the pleased mother of a kindergartner told me at the gasoline pump in August. A gaggle of kids dragging backpacks and lunchboxes stopped on the sidewalk as I raked the last leaves falling from our maples last month. "Is that where you write *your* poems?" one child asked, pointing to my upstairs room.

I am hopeful that the poetry residency left two impressions on the students and teachers of Eastwood School: that poets live across the street, buy Brussels sprouts and toothpaste, check out books, pump gas, rake leaves—and that poems can "open your imagination when you think you don't have any" and "make your feelings dance." After hearing the Basho haiku, one first grader wrote this poem, which I like to think of as the residency's last word:

> Lynn stopped talking,
> But poems still rang in our ears.

Translytics: Creative Writing Derived from Foreign Language Texts

Nick Muska

I walk up to the blackboard and chalk up the following poem by Salvatore Quasimodo:

Ed e subito sera

Oguno sta solo sul cuor della terra
Trafitto da un raggio di sole
Ed e subito sera

This short piece whose brevity emphasizes its content—the magnificent transient moment of life, each of us illuminated by the sun's brilliance, before the sudden onset of evening—is a miniature masterwork of modern Italian literature. But for the kids in my classroom it will serve a much different purpose.

"What's that?" "Huh?" "I don't know any Spanish."

I tell them it is a poem and yes, I do know what it "means" in Italian, but that I want them to sound out the poem as best as they can, pretending they know what the words signify. I take volunteers. The first is hesitant, piecing together the puzzle of sounds awkwardly. I thank her. The next reads with a good deal more fluidity as he accurately renders many more phonetic elements of the text. The third, though eliding a sound or two, performs the poem theatrically, complete with emotional inflection and hand gestures. We laugh in delight. "Okay," I say, "because you paid attention to all these chalk marks on the blackboard and sounded out the letters they make, pretty much as you would sound out English words, you have learned to speak a poem in a language not your own. Also, you now know that part of the poem which is its sound without having to know what the poem 'means.'"[1]

"But now," I say, "Let's pretend we can understand this *Ed e subito sera* poem. There are several ways we can do this. We can start by creating a vocabulary for it. Are there any words here that look or sound like words in your own language, which is some midwestern variety of late twentieth century North American English?" Hands go up. I write down their suggestions beneath the Italian words. We do not do this in any particular order—*raggio* is sometimes interpreted before *cuor* as we try to make some sort of poetic sense from this cryptogram. Typically, we fill the board with connections such as these:

> *Ed* = Ed, a boy's name. Likewise, Edward, Eddie (Ed e)
>
> *subito* = submarine, sub sandwich, subway, submit, substitute
>
> *sera* = Sarah, a girl's name
>
> *Ognuno* = oregano, oranges
>
> *Sta* = stays, states, stale
>
> *solo* = alone, musical solo, one
>
> *cuor* = choir, (apple) core, queer, cure
>
> *della* = Della, a girl's name; delicatessen, delta
>
> *terra* = terrace, terror, terrorist, tear
>
> *Trafitto* = traffic
>
> *da* = Dad
>
> *raggio* = Ragu spaghetti sauce, a Reggie Bar, rags, raggedy, reggae music
>
> *sole* = soul, shoesole, fish

Other possibilities occur as we work with this word-by-word method, but I suggest another. "Try saying some of the Italian words quickly, maybe mumbling them a little, or try saying a group of them while running their sounds together like we sometimes do when we talk to each other." Thus, *Ognuno* becomes, "Oh, you know," *solo,* "so low," and *di sole,* "diesel." "Now, let's play with some of these words and see if we can find other words hidden in them. We can turn some words inside out if we want to." In this way, *subito* reveals "bit" and "toe" and, by reversing *sub* we find "bus." Now a student waves his hand. "My title for this poem is 'Eddie Bit Sarah's Toe on the Bus!'" "Good," I say, "We write that down. Anyone else have a suggestion for the title?"

Several more are offered, some fairly obvious, like "Ed Substitutes for Sarah," "Ed's Substitute Sister," or "Eddie Eats a Sub Sandwich;" others not so: "She Sings to Her Soul," and "End in Complete Silence." These I praise particularly since they reveal creative associations beyond straightforward acoustic or visual recognitions. Intrigued, I ask the young woman who proposed "She Sings to Her Soul" who the "she" is.

"Do you mean 'Sarah?'"

"No," she responds, "the old nun."

"What 'old nun?'"

"The one in the first line, see—OgNUNo—*Og* is like 'old.'"

Another student raises his hand. "That could mean 'ugly nun,' too."

"Yes," I agree, "or maybe her name is 'Sister Ogo.'"

Yet another chimes in, "And she could be fat, since *Og* looks like 'hog.'"

"I think you all have the idea," I say. "We pretended we could understand this foreign language poem and tried several ways of inventing our own words for it. I bet now you are ready to make some kind of sense out of it, so go ahead and write a piece that plays off this Italian one. You don't have to use every word of the original poem for your own associations—though you can if you like—but please use some of them. Once you have made your own vocabulary connections, feel free to manipulate those words as you see fit, juggling them until they make some sort of grammatical sense, if that seems appropriate to you. And finally, don't be afraid if some of the lines you write sound unusual or weird. The purpose of this kind of playing with foreign languages is to encourage you to create 'a new thing made out of words,' which, by the way, is my definition of a poem."

I began using this technique with student creative writers about five years ago and have repeatedly been amazed at the poems they have spun off in response to foreign language texts. The writing that results is called a *translytic*, or *translitic*, the term invented by poet Joel Lipman to distinguish this sort of creative language work from translation. Although originally spelled *translitic*, I prefer the variant since the word *sly* appears at its heart, thus suggesting a cunningly clever way of working with foreign language texts. Joel Lipman provides the following partly specious etymology: "*trans* (across) *lytic* or *litic* (to cut, loosen, to loose); therefore, 'to cut across the word lines' or 'to slip the knots of the language barrier.'" A suggestive poetic definition, indeed. Poet Sibyl James uses an almost identical gloss to introduce her translitics of Louise Labe's sonnets. The pun here is on "slit," that is, "to cut," or, as Lipman has it rhymed in his mixed metaphor, "slip." (How does a "language barrier" have "knots"?) Yet, etymologically accurate or not, his definition serves well as a guide to the translytic process.[2]

Here is a sampling of translytics based on *Ed e subito sera:*

She Sings to Her Soul

An old nun lays stale on her back singing sadly,
Softly to her lost soul. Then she boards a train.
This train blocks traffic day after day.

The old nun then droops her raggy head till dawn.
In her dreams she sings to her soul.

Lindsey Gorman, 6th grade

Eddie Eats a Sub Sandwich

Under the bitter toe of a sea serpent
Sister "O" playing Uno starved and alone sold coral at Dilly's—
  terrified.
"Get out of the way, Dad, a rag doll died."
They played soul music at the funeral.

Brian Shepler, 10th grade

Eddie's Substitute Sister

Gregory Adeler, jail inmate Hello to you, Lonely Star, hardcore
  daughter of earth.
Terrific, yes, a ragged dead soul.
You are Eddie's substitute sister.

And, finally, this wonderful response to the four lines of Italian:

Sister Ogo Seen as a Fat Submarine in the Sahara

Sister Ogo is as fat as a submarine in the Sahara
Sister Ogo could stop a train
Sister Ogo plays Uno in a way that would terrify you
Sister Ogo eats Fritos all day long alone
Sister Ogo would need the whole sun to get a burn
Sister Ogo would scare any old terrorist and stop a war
Sister Ogo must not have taken Phys Ed
Sister Ogo's weight is unknown, but who would have the courage
  to ask her?
In fact, it is unknown where she originated
Sister Ogo listens to rock 'n' roll on the radio
Sister Ogo sleeps at night with a Raggedy Ann doll
Sister Ogo's corpse would not fit into a casket the size of a
  stadium
So, Sister Ogo, you will have to get used to heaven wearing an
  oversized submarine.

Amy Louden, 11th grade

You might notice that when I introduced this poem as an exercise, I first asked that it be sounded out syllable by syllable until the class felt comfortable with it as a language construct before I asked that individual Italian words be glossed to fabricate its vocabulary. This is to assure that all the glyphs (a *glyph* is any mark or series of marks that records an element of language, "letters" in this instance) of the foreign text are noted, even if every word is not used as a source for the student's final translytic rendering. In some instances, however, the foreign text cannot be pronounced by a monolingual English speaker, as is the case with hieroglyphs, pictograms, or texts in Greek, Cyrillic, or Sanskrit alphabets. In such cases the writer must depend solely upon visual recognitions to "tell the story of the picture," or attempt to identify words in the foreign alphabet that bear a resemblance to English. Let us take a closer look at the work of two fifth-grade students and get an idea of how they responded to unpronounceable texts:

After a Navajo Drawing

A cactus rising with the sun
With a man running very fast.
There's the enchanted castle.
At the castle there's a magic mirror
with a 4-eyed 3-nosed block of cheese
With mice all around it!

A cat's tongue licking a pineapple under the moon.
7 switches in a cellar flipping on and off.
A lady holding potatoes upstairs.
Two people cartwheel down a hill.

The cactus is dying now.
Now, the man is going up a hill fast.
There's a crown by the mirror.
A nine eyed potato.
There's a man jumping off a plane into a pool.

A manhole in the ground
The cactus is wearing a hat.
A potato in the trash.
A boy whistling while holding a ball.
Two people doing cartwheels again.
But now around a river.

Kristin Couts

By examining the Navajo pictogram and comparing it to its translytic, we can identify a number of the connections made by Kristin: In the first line: glyph 1, cactus; glyph 2, a rising sun; glyph 3, a man running; glyph 4, a castle; glyph 5, a mirror; glyph 6, a block of cheese; glyph 7, mice. Kristin, of course, not only identifies these things, but invents all the details, actions, and relationships among them. Note also in line three, the first glyph is rendered as "The cactus is dying now," doubtless since in line one the figure had five branches; and here, only two, such diminution indicating a move toward death. Further, glyph 3 on the first line, rendered as "There's the enchanted castle" is, when darkened along with glyph 4 in line three, is interpreted as "There's a crown by the mirror." The glyphs, though similar, need not be interpreted identically. Also notice the action realized from glyph 3 in line two, a rectangle with seven dots in it, which is read as "7 switches in a cellar flipping on and off." Sometimes, however, the connections a student makes are much more complex:

Three People Went Sailing

Three people went sailing. The sun set. Bird flew from water.
His eye poked out 44 times.
Bird dived from the bottom of the water.
He put headphones on and
Grandma played golf.
By accident she hit 4 beehives and 3 more.
So hit 7 in all.
There was a basket on a table.
They didn't know what was there.
And he stood on one foot.
Backwards questionmark,
eXes,
upside down E.

Ashley Robinson

In Ashley Robinson's translytic based on a short passage of hieroglyphs, many of the connections are not linear—we cannot easily follow this text from left to right and make consistent one-to-one connections. Several of the glyphs serve double duty, it seems, and much invention takes place among them. The first glyph resembles a sail, the ninth and tenth are identical but are interpreted as "44 times." In the second line, the first and third glyphs are again identical but here, taken as "eXes," although the reference might be to the "X" figure above in the first line. Glyph 5 does resemble elongated "headphones" and glyph 7 is "Grandma playing golf." She "hit 4 beehives" (Again the "4" or sail figure!) "and 3 more," must refer to glyph 11, three horizontal dashes. Glyph 14 could be the "beehive" or "a basket on the table" or both. What we have here, actually, is several versions of the same text, read from left to right and then shuffled. "Bird flew from water" and "Bird dived from the bottom of the water," clearly devolve from glyph 8, a birdlike figure under a wiggly line that can be taken as waves of the sea; also "They didn't know what was there" could be glyph 13, a kind of stick figure with hands out in a gesture of "search me" or "I don't know" taken in conjunction with the last glyph in the line, a "Backwards questionmark." Glyph 13 is obviously "And he stood on one foot." Glyphs 4 and 6 might be seen as eyes, one of which is an "X," thus "poked out," but at this point I won't guess at further correspondences. I can only marvel at the writer's complex response to the text. I must mention, however, that this translytic was used as a performance piece, Ashley Robinson reciting it with appropriate hand gestures as if it were a cheerleading routine or some sort of esoteric hand jive, each of her movements mirrored by the twenty fifth-grade classmates seated behind her.

If a student creates a piece, like the two examples above, that manages to gloss every part of the foreign text, the result is a *strict translytic*. In most cases, however, only a portion of the original foreign words are used to start vocabulary associations so a *loose translytic* results. By and large, I have found that most alphabetic texts produce loose translytics, the writer necessarily ignoring a portion of the original text to arrive at an intelligible result. But when the text provides unpronounceable visual prompts, as we have seen with Egyptian hieroglyphs and Navajo pictograms, the translytic often accounts for every glyph. Further, the writing usually makes pretty good syntactic sense, since a "story of the pictures" is rendered, rather than an associative sounding out of alphabetic cues that can all too easily result in wrenched syntax and language fragments.

To get a better handle on this process, attempt a translytic of the passage below. Pretend you understand the foreign text, invent vocabulary correspondences for some of its words, then try a rendition of the four lines.

> Vajon mi er? vajon mi torenik velem?
> Sejtek, s e sejtelem, ez olyan rettento.
> Ugy ranatozik, ugy ugrandozik szivem
> Mikent a porban a levagott emberfo

You do not have to account for all of the foreign words and can skip as many as you wish. It may help if you first copy the passage by hand to get a feel for the foreign words. If you get stuck, try some of the techniques mentioned above to get your words flowing. Following is a roughed-out piece sketched beneath the original lines and a couple of completed translytics based on this portion of a Hungarian poem taken from the work of Petofi Sandor.

Vajon mi er? vajon mi torenik velem?
What's wrong with my hair? What's wrong with this torn neck
  venom?
Sejtek, s e sejtelem, ez olyan rettento.
He's dead, yes he's dead and already rotten
Ugy ranatozik, ugy ugrandozik szivem
Ugly rattlesnake, ugly sainted grandmother
Mikent a porban a levegott emberfo
Monkeys on probation, a goat lover gives birth

A voyage in your ear? A voyage in my turtleneck sweater?
The surgeon went to Jerusalem to get an oily red lion
An ugly ranch house, an ugly slimey doorknob.
"George, please wake up our son."

John Owens, 11th grade

Am I an arrogant vagabond? They speckle my nose like a villain.
(or: They speculate my cross is a villain's)
Should I send a message to the retired ambassador?
As the ugly kangaroo is boogying down the highway
That imbecile Mike goes to the latrine.

Anonymous high school student

I must also add that the translytic process does occasionally produce complete gibberish. Usually this can be remedied by reviewing the foreign text, or by rewriting and editing the translytic without reference to the original. The student can be encouraged to edit this draft, altering or eliminating words derived from the text and adding any which help give the translytic the "feel" of poetry. Since the ultimate purpose of this exercise is to encourage the creation of "new things made out of words," the student should be free to depart from the foreign text whenever his or her feelings dictate. After all, the objective is to use the foreign text as a stimulus to creative writing and need not be strictly followed word by word, glyph by glyph. The creative mechanism at work here, it seems to me, responds to the original text as a language puzzle, a cryptogram which the writer attempts to solve by inventing or modifying whatever language is required to achieve a coherent solution for it.

There are times, also, when "the die is cast" effect takes place. Once the first line or two of a foreign text is successfully rendered as a translytic, those which follow will be bent to the theme it strikes. Once this central idea is established, or a keynote image struck, its development will strongly influence vocabulary choices as the translytic finds completion.

Whatever the result of your or your students' first workings with a text, consider for a moment the purpose of a translytic exercise. In the first place it is an end in itself that, at the very least, provides an interesting kernel of language for future germination. Second, it requires the writer to pay close attention to language, to study the text. Further, it helps break suppositions about what "poetry" is. Most important, however, it encourages young writers not to fear foreign languages, but to embrace them as the stuff of art.

Notes

1. Sometimes I digress here to talk about American audiences in the 1960s who listened to Yevgeny Yevtuschenko read in Russian though they didn't know a single word of his language; or the instance of Kenneth Rexroth reading in Tokyo, with his voice piped outdoors to the overflow crowds of Japanese who could not fit into the packed auditorium. In both instances the audience wanted to experience the "music" of the poet's speech, although they had no or very little purchase on the literal content of his poems.

2. A Part of History. In late 1978, I got an excited phone call from Joel Lipman with whom I partnered in our management of the Toledo Poets Center. He read me three pieces he had "winged" from the Spanish of Cuban poet Julian Del Casals. They had the feel of Latin American passion and a defiant revolutionary spirit along with the window dressing of blood and bulls and sand. All this despite Joel's total ignorance of any Romance language. What was brought across from the original texts had to do with an assumed theme, mood, or central image based on the poet's presumptions about what the text *might* mean. Very little of this, however, is conscious, but rather stems from cultural presuppositions. In the same way Joel responded to Spanish, my own mindset about Egyptian hieroglyphics affected how I treated them. I assumed they would be occult records and, if spoken aloud, would doubtless be in the stage accent of Lon Chaney in the vintage Hollywood movie, *The Mummy.* My piece, "Mystic Egyptian Football" (See Appendix I) reveals as much. Because of Joel's translytics of Del Casals, I became intrigued with his method, so went back to working with foreign texts afresh. I had, however, experimented somewhat along these lines earlier on.

My first real translytics, around 1968, were accidental. I had been translating from a surrealist anthology and when the vocabulary became densely unfamiliar, I began to invent whatever words I needed to complete a phrase or line, basing my connections on the text's visual appearance, the sound of the words spoken aloud in a poor French accent, as well as on their immediate context. Inaccurate but fascinating results came of this. Also, my readings in Louis and Celia Zukofsky's *Catullus,* Jack Spicer's *After Lorca,* and a few chance lines by Alden Van Buskirk convinced me there were far more fruitful ways of experimenting with foreign works than careful translation or poetic version. For example, the Zukofskys in their effort to bring across the sound, rhythm, and syntax of Catullus's Latin, in effect "read his lips" so the reader can "breathe with him." ("Translating Catullus," *Kulchur* 2.5 (Spring 1962), note 5, pp. 47–49.) The result is a kind of Latin jivetalk which completely sidesteps Latin/English dictionary meanings to achieve results such as this:

Carmina XLI	**41**
Ameana puella defututa	Ameana pulling, a foot touted high,
tota milia me decem poposcit,	touched me for all of ten thousand:
	and popped scut
ista turpiculo puella naso,	is the tour-pickled, low-puling
	long nosed, ah
decoctoris amica Formiani.	decocted heiress of the milked
	Formiani.
propinqui, quibus, est	
* puella curae,*	Propinquity, quick buss this fuel,
	cure eye,
amicos, mediosque convocate:	amigos, medicos, call convocations:
non est sana puella,	
* nec rogare*	no nest, she is nuts, pulls her
	neck, rogue harried,
qualis sit solet aes	
imaginosum.	what lies sit solid ice imagine o
	some.

Appendix I: Examples

Here are some translytics from a variety of texts. Examine them to see if you can determine how the writer made particular language connections with the originals.

No Te Veo	**No T.V.**
Pedro Salinas	Scott Noel
	(Translytic based on "No Te Veo" by
	Pedro Salinas)
No te veo. Bien sé	No T.V. what a bad sight
que estás aquí, detrás	Can you imagine no "Aqua Desers."
de una frágil pared	No "Doomed Fragile Couple,"
de ladrillos y cal, bien	
al alcance	No "Lady Lords Your Turn
	To call Them"?
de mi voz, si llamara.	All insane
Pero no llamaré.	No "Micahel Von Sir Ilama"?
Te llamaré mañana,	Please, no radio
cuando, al no verte ya	Tell Mom now!
me imagine que sigues	I can do nothing. Al will never
aquí cerca, a mi lado,	watch a "Verne" show again!
y que hasta hoy la voz	I try to imagine living with no T.V.
que ayer no quise dar.	And get nowhere, a pity on me.
Mañana . . .cuando estés	You guessed it: "Boston Hay Lover"
allá detrás de una	is on Channel 13.
frágil pared de vientos,	Again no trivia games
de cielos y de años.	Oh man, who did this?

(Presagios. 1923)

All a dirty joke, huh?!
Fragile cord you are now alive.
This is the way to watch
my soap Boperas.

Espace

Pierre Reverdy

L'étoile échappée
L'astre est dans la lampe
L'a main
tient la nuit
par un fil
 Le ciel
 s'est couché
 contres les épines

Des gouttes de sang
 claquent sur le mur
Et le vent du soir
sort d'une poitrine

Escape

Shelley Spriggs

Lay tile each by each
The ashtray is dancing with the lamp.
The main tent with nuts was
 partially unfilled.
The seal stops at the couch,
controlless in spines.
The donuts sang while being served more.
At the event they soar, sort of like
 dumb portraits.

Storm

Plotsligt moter vandaren har den gamla

jatteeken, liken fortenad alg med

milavid krona framfor septemberhavets

 svartgrona fastning
Nordlig storm. Det ar I den tid nar
rennsbar-

klavar mognar. Vaken I morket hor man

stjarnbilderna stampa I sina spiltor

 hogt over tradet.

Storm

Becky Banks

Plot lit terror deep in a
gambling hall
just taken, like algae
from medicine.
Vivid chrome from
September
starts growing fast.

It ignores the
storm.
Details are indentations
of the rose.
Clever Mongols make
market men.
Still ajar from earnest
Stampedes of sin, slice
 through the trade.

Sixth Grade Poems Based on Mayan Glyphs

Getting a Bathtub

There it is, the faucet
O, I really like it
Even my dog likes it. It even has a soap holder
and towel holder

and comes with a big towel
and a pretty knob to turn it.
Let's have a party in it
and wear bow ties.

Carol Riedel

Backwards torch with a handle
A bucktooth Indian man with a cone head.
A dog dancing in an Indian tribe—all dressed up.
A Chinese woman dancing, also to music.
A cob of corn that's very wide, and has a hollow hole in it.
An Egyptian man in the desert looking through a telescope.
A planet with deformed rings on top of it.
A fat girl over in Africa walking home from school with
a backpack on.
A scarecrow with a snake as the pole.

Matt Weaver

Mystic Egyptian Football
(based on three "lines" of hieroglyphs)

Ran about 20 yards/
Fell through manhole, lost the crutch.
there the offal stank, though I kneeled to it at dawn.
Offering the warmth of my lamp.
Called Safe, cornered the maze, one eye popping, the
other blurred.
A mudhole by the beehive, spearmint ascending
My eye pops again at the parachutist, swinging at me.

Like a jackrabbit over rough ground,
Like a duck leaping waves
Tongue goes "yuck!" over cold offal.
Mouth puckers at sour kid's jack
I'm astonished, limp.
Fancy milkshakes others would gladly have,
Are walking bores to me.
Angrily throwing the lamp away, I consider desert
But my third eye is stupefied,
I have nothing more to cast away.
I ascend from the manhole at nightfall

Glaring, scared of the regal serpent.
The first evening wind and light rain
A dash of ten—then

The length of the field for a touchdown!

Nick Muska

Appendix II: Foreign Language Texts

Finally, here is a sampling of foreign language texts and glyphs that you may photocopy for your own translytic workshop.

Lumière

Pierre Reverdy

Midi
La glace brille
Le soleil à la main
    Une femme regarde
ses yeux
    Et son chagrin
le mur d'en face est dépoli
Les rides que le vent fait aux rideaux du lit
    Ce qui tremble
On peut regarder dans la chambre
    Et l'image s'évanouit
    Un nuage passe
    La pluie

Motivo

Cecília Meireles

    Eu canto porque o instante existe
e a minha vida está completa.
Não sou alegre nem sou triste:
sou poeta.

    Irmão das coisas fugidias,
não sinto gôzo nem tormento.
Atravesso noites e dias
no vento.

Se desmorono ou edifico,
se permaneço ou me desfaço,
—não sei, não sei. Não sei se fico
ou passo.

    Sei qu canto. E a canção é tudo.
Tem sangue eterno e asa ritmada.
E um dia sei que estarei mudo:
—mais nada.

Excerpt from Virgil's *Aeneid:*

CHOMMODA dicebat, si quando commoda uellet
    dicere, et insidias Arrius hinsidias,
et tum mirifice sperabat se esse locutum,
    cum quantum poterat dixerat hinsidias.
credo, sic mater, sic liber auunculus eius,
    sic maternus auus dixerat atque auia.

Hojas Secas

José Juan Tablada

El jardín está lleno de hojas secas;
nunca vi tantas hojas en sus árboles
verdes, en primavera.

En el invierno sombrío
junto al río,
esponjado de frío
llora su nombre el tildío.

So
lo
estoy
con mi
frasco
de vino
bajo un
árbol en flor
Llovió toda la noche
Y no acaban de peinar sus plumas
Al sol, los zopilotes.

Llovió toda la noche
Y no acaban de peinar sus plumas
Al sol, los zopilotes.

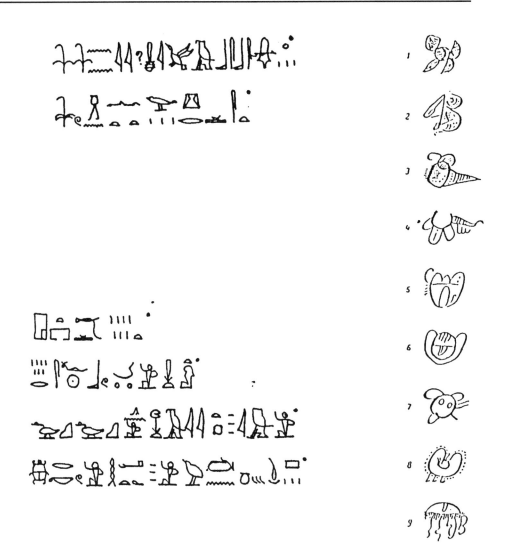

How to Do a Poetry Night Hike

Terry Hermsen

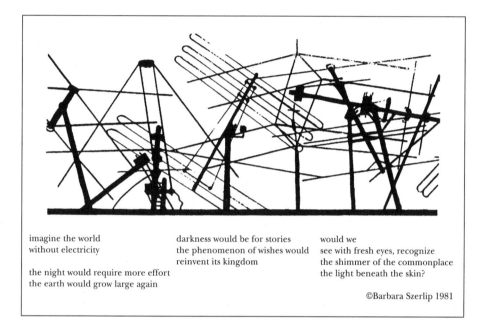

imagine the world
without electricity

the night would require more effort
the earth would grow large again

darkness would be for stories
the phenomenon of wishes would
reinvent its kingdom

would we
see with fresh eyes, recognize
the shimmer of the commonplace
the light beneath the skin?

©Barbara Szerlip 1981

Someone handed me the above postcard years ago. Almost without thinking, I tucked it in a folder. Now it resurrects itself from time to time, falling out of a book where I'm hunting for another poem and in which I've used it for a marker, sliding out of a stack of old cards I sometimes tape to the kitchen cabinet door. (Right now our cat thinks it a distraction as he rolls around on top of it trying to keep me from reading it as I type.) It reminds me of how, from ancient times, the night has been for stories, myths spun from embers or stars.

Here's one:

I am doing a poetry residency at Cloverleaf Junior High School, a gray-brown, featureless, moderately new building set in the midst of north central Ohio farmland. One evening after a long day at school, Jann

Gallagher, a CJHS English teacher, takes me for a tour of the school's land lab, a wooded area sloping down to a small creek and its steep embankment, all wonderfully restful after the crowded halls, all within a literal stone's throw from a major four-lane truck route. On the way back, walking through the upper meadow, I let slip the words, "Hey, we could do a poetry night hike here. . . ."

Little did I know what a *poetry* night hike was. My wife Carla had conducted several environmental night hikes at outdoor education camps in Ohio, though I'd never gone on one. But I underestimated the person I was speaking with—an energetic teacher always looking for a way to spark students' love of language and the world, the only member of the faculty (I found out later) to make consistent use of this natural resource with her classes. Within three days, she'd arranged the hike, talked three teachers and nearly twenty-five students, along with her own nine-year-old daughter, into participating, and we were set for the following Wednesday. But what exactly were we going to do?

At least I had the weekend to think about it. If writing residencies were really a place for experimentation and if poetry was to meet these kids' lives outside the desk-bound classroom, here was a chance to prove it. On the long drive home I began composing ideas.

Years, and several such excursions later—including night hikes in Vermont, California, and two Ohio state parks—here's what I think a poetry night hike can be: a cross between the fourteenth-century Japanese tradition of writing group *renga* (where participants build a long poem together over the course of an evening) and a typical American outdoor education camp's Thursday evening activity where students explore the mysteries of the unlit half of the world. I believe poetry night hikes are most of all a blend of silence and words. Using that creative opposition, it's up to the planners to structure an event which mixes those two elements in interactive ways. On the language side, one might include some writing of poems, individually or as a group, on paper or out loud, along with the reciting or reading of poems by one or more members, with the others gathered around in the darkness, testing how the twists of the words find their way up through the pines like quickly vanishing smoke; but these verbal projections can be alternated with plenty of receptive time, walks done in silence, owl calls, the gathering of objects, games for awakening our often brittle (because unused) night senses, particularly touch and hearing. Whatever mix is chosen, any "plan" will of course be adjusted to the nature of the group and the terrain to be covered. The progression should be slow, gradually letting the senses open wider, the way the rods in our eyes find their own way of gathering in the light. Each hike is different, even in the same terrain. The feel of the night at hand should influence the outline. The idea is not to follow any set formula. Rather, it is to find spaces within earth's "dark skirts," as Mary Oliver puts it, to listen.

On that first hike we improvised. Late dusk, we gathered in that same meadow on the hillside above the school woods. From a song by John Denver with the lines "Some days are diamonds, some days are stones," I created an exercise where each participant contributes a line beginning with, "Some nights are . . . ," followed with a metaphor. "Some nights are hollow secrets/Some nights are suspended webs. . . ." Not exactly new lyrics for the radio, but hints of what we might find down there in the woods. (Are all poems a kind of preparation?) Next, we walked in a line down the small slope, forming a group "caterpillar": placing our hands on the shoulders of the one in front of us, we closed our eyes, all except the leader, who led us down the hill any way but straight. Giggles. Twists. Stumbles. Holding on, tripping into each other's shoes, we came down into the now much darker forest. Had our eyes adjusted so quickly? We broke into small groups—and with the aid of two teachers trained in outdoor education techniques, we investigated the small areas around us, "washing our hands in the leaves," matching the shapes of those on the ground with the ones still in the trees.

Later, at a small amphitheater of seats down by the creek, the students listened while I recited a few poems about the night. In my planning, I'd been surprised when I realized how many of the poems I'd memorized over the years had to do with night. William Stafford's "Traveling through the Dark," Mary Oliver's "Sleeping in the Forest," Robert Frost's "Acquainted with the Night," and the Spanish poet José Luis Hidalgo's "Shore of Night," among others. What is it about night that draws poets to it? Perhaps a heightened sense that just as in a poem there are yet to be uncovered layers, as Robert Bly says, "waves breaking on shores/just over the hill." Like language, night is there and present every day of our lives, a polar presence to our claims of mastery and understanding, and yet we are often so removed from it. The poem hopes to bring us closer.

Listen to these stanzas:

> All of the night on this earth
> is running out between my hands
> like water trying to run away
> between bulrushes and birds.
>
>   José Luis Hidalgo, "Shore of Night"

> Whatever it was I lost, whatever I wept for
> Was a wild, gentle thing, the small dark eyes
> Loving me in secret.
>
> James Wright, "Milkweed"

> I thought the earth
> remembered me, she
> took me back so tenderly, arranging
> her dark skirts, her pockets
> full of lichens and seeds.
>
> Mary Oliver, "Sleeping in the Forest"

> The car aimed ahead its lowered parking lights;
> under the hood purred the steady engine.
> I stood in the glare of the warm exhaust turning red;
> around our group I could hear the wilderness listen.
>
> William Stafford, "Traveling through the Dark"

Quietly, then, we moved up the last trail toward the school. I'd asked the group to remain in full silence and explained that we would be doing what is known as a Seton Watch before we left the woods. For this, each would be positioned ten feet away from anyone else and asked to sit in silence on the trail, simply paying attention to where they were, listening and watching. Because we would be within ready reach of the group, we would be perfectly safe, but because we were far enough away so that we couldn't see anyone else, we would get a chance to feel what it's like to be "alone in the night." Would we be able to shut down the little voices of worries that run through our heads continually? I tried not to sound melodramatic here. It was a simple thing we would be doing: spending ten minutes watching one of the most basic phenomena on earth, the ritual passage from light to dark, as people have done across all cultures for millennia. And yet I knew the experience was odd to us, something we seem to remember only distantly.

Back at the room, we got—among others—this poem from Bill:

Trapped

Trapped,
In my brain,

Misty,
I see words floating
Around in my brain,
All school related
Words.
All of a sudden
The walls start
To close together.

As if they didn't
Want me.

A door
Flies open,
I jump out.
I keep falling,
Falling
Down,
Stairs all around
Until I almost
Hit bottom.
Then,
A truck roars by,
With its horn blasting,

Waking me out of a trance,
Until I am back
Under the tree
Gazing into the sky.

    Bill Simmerman, 7th grade

Clearly this was no run-of-the-mill experience for Bill. (He'd told me on the way back of a sense that his mind really wanted to close up, wanted him gone.) Notice, however, that it's not only the strange vision which counts in the end, but how the sky has cleared and he's back under the tree, watching. There is nothing more that a night hike can hope to accomplish, if it helps one student see the world more closely.

There have been other hikes—and other variations.

A few years later, at a two-day encampment with Jann's students at Mohican State Park, it rained steadily. When time came for our scheduled night hike, the ground was soaked, the trees hung heavy, and we wondered if the students would balk at going out again into the soggy, now-dark world. She had spent six months preparing them for these two days, giving them exercises in description and metaphor, having visitors speak on local history and the interaction between writing and art, as well as writing and study of the natural world. We met on the wet stoop after dinner and laughed at each other's drenched clothes.

"They're having a great time," she said. "Did you see Brenda and Amy climb out on that trunk over the river?"

"Like vultures in the rain," I replied, ever hunting for dark images.

"No, like wide-eyed children again."

The optimist won out. We knew we had to do it.

We gathered the kids, with ponchos and candles, and stood in a circle beside the river. I said, "If every night is something of an oracle, maybe this one has something to teach us as well." Their good spirits were encouraging; they weren't half as worried or bothered by the rain as we were. In their regular lives, they would never have ventured outside of their houses in this weather—but here at Mohican it seemed quite natural.

Following much the same procedure as our first night hike, we made up a group poem, explored certain trails, listened to poems, did a Seton Watch (this time along the river on the opposite side from our cabins, watching an eerie light form from out of nowhere on the river as the rain fell), walked back in silence. Back in the warmth of the cabins, we gathered and wrote. Many found the use of a repeated line helpful, based on an example from the anthology *Roots & Wings*, a poem called "Growing Toward the Earth" by Luis Rosales:

> When the night comes in and the darkness becomes a staff,
> when the night comes in perhaps the sea will have been asleep,
> perhaps all of its strength will not help it to move a single pebble,
> or to change the face of a smile,
> and perhaps among the waves a child could be born,
> when the night comes in,
> when the night comes in and truth becomes just another word . . .

At night poems seem to take on a strength of sound which competes with imagery. And perhaps that's where poems originate, in the voice, or as a "sentence sound," to quote Robert Frost, a ramble in the head that seeks out the possible phrases, sorts the too simple from the overly ornate, the cliché from the strongly felt—and begins. The seventh-grade students wrote . . .

> All patterns go slowly
> Hide as trees, as the gods
> In their place stands a
> cloud like light
> Rain talking to water . . .
>
> > Kristi Dorland

> When the night falls the trees stick
> like arrows in the ground
> When the night falls you're hiding in the
> darkness
> When the night falls droplets
> of nothing come from the skies
> When the night falls
> the images of sorrow pass through
> the trees
> All is quiet but the raindrops
> on your head and in your heart
>
> > Annette Palmer

When the rain falls down
all the green seems to turn the blue
everything turns when the rain falls

Mike Heider

Years later something valuable still shines through their words: the experience of those two days in the rain. Both Jann and I have each run into students from that group in other locations, other cities: one as she is doing her student teaching in a Columbus elementary school, another buying a dulcimer—because of the afternoons we spent at Mohican learning that Appalachian instrument, each one mentioning first, almost proudly, "We went to Mohican."

With another class, I used a more complex challenge. When we created the group poem, I asked that each student make up an image for night using an incomplete sentence. As we sat around in a circle, I gave them this definition of imagery as a variation on metaphor: the juxtaposition of unlike things. For example, I gave them these phrases from Robert Bly's "Surprised by Evening," "the asylum of the waters" and "the tissues of the grass," suggesting they look for some unfamiliar pairing of words. We composed our lines and phrases in our heads, then combined them into the following spontaneous poem, spoken as we went around the circle:

The hours of pines
Green moss, waterfalls
Darkness choking you like a hand
The rocks are like days
Naked trees; dead leaves
Stream rolling through the valley

The logs like bulldozers
A flash of moon
Flight of winds
Trails like branches
The brittleness of leaves

Hidden sunlight weaving
Owls stand like sentries
Run away into the whispering wind
Night comes
Like a tiger on its prey

7th grade Challenge class

The weather being dry this time, we lay down in the leaves, our heads touching at the center of a circle, and spoke our thoughts as we gazed up through the trees. One student noticed how if you blink your eyes quickly, the effect of the light at night creates a kind of flickering movie. Soon all our eyes were in rapid motion before the black and white reel unfolding above us.

It's often helpful to have blindfolds along, particularly for opening activities before full dark arrives. On one hike, done at the school guidance counselor's ten-acre woods, there stood an acre of fifty or so beech and walnut trees of different heights and intriguing shapes. We blindfolded half the group and had each blind member led by a partner through circuitous routes to one of the trees. He or she was then asked to "memorize" the tree by touch, getting to know it so well that when they were led away—again by a deceptive route—they would be able to find it once the blindfold was removed. The only problem with this activity was that we had trouble getting them to re-focus for the rest of the hike; they wanted to repeat it over and over.

One poet I know passes out chocolate on her night hikes, claiming she's helping them expand their senses (she claims that chocolate tastes different in the dark). Christy Dixon, an environmental specialist with whom I planned a night hike for adults at George Rogers Clark State Park, asked us at one point to find an interesting stick in the area around us. She then gathered us in a circle and asked us to get to know the stick, without relying on sight, noting its peculiar feel and ridges. After two minutes she took the sticks away, shuffled them and passed them around the circle at random. We were to carefully touch each one till we knew the familiar feel of ours. It was oddly satisfying to come back to the familiar "first stick," as if we'd found home again, or it had found us.

Much as a heightened awareness of our senses helps to guide us back to the night world, our sense of memory can help add meaning to a night hike, particularly for adults. After asking us to look up at the shapes between the leaves above us, noting the relationships and spaces *between* the trees as much as the trees themselves, Christy had us think back into our past and see if there was a tree we remembered well. I thought of the willow I'd climbed so often as a kid. If you got up high enough, you were supposed to see all the way to downtown Chicago. Several remembered trees which had since been cut down. And one man said he hadn't thought of *his* tree in maybe twenty-five years: a huge beech with knobs on its upper trunk. He used to go out and stand in its presence as a kid, feeling hidden and safe.

Borrowing Christy's idea, I wanted some storytelling on the night hike I planned for a group of writers at Chapters & Verse, the first national Poetry in the Schools conference held in San Rafael, California, in 1990. My sign taped to the cafeteria door brought fifteen writers together at the base of the mountain behind the Dominican College campus. Much as we were there to talk about teaching in the schools, I thought that this was a time for experiencing the night ourselves, just as we might ask a group of kids to do.

Fortunately, I had help. This night hike in particular felt like a joint adventure. We had writers from all over the country—two poets from Iowa, fiction writers from Minnesota and New York, and several Californians. There was John Oliver Simon, who had led poetry writing tours in the Museum of Natural History in Mexico City. And Ruth Gensler who would, the very next year, go on to edit *Changing Light,* an anthology of poems about night and day. And Daryl Chinn from near Fresno, whose poetry weaves a balance between his Chinese heritage and his American upbringing. Many were more familiar with the landscape we would be traveling than I was. I had climbed twice to the top, exploring routes and trails: some ended in impossibly tangled gullies and dropoffs, others circled down into residential backyards. Finally, one branched off onto a fire road and led high up to a huge meadow above the Pacific. It would be a perfect place to write at dusk and to watch the night come in over the bay, I thought.

Little did I know how cold it would be. By the time our group got up there at dusk, the wind was coming in strong off the ocean. My midwestern naiveté was being tested. If night were to be a source for poetry, it would have to be tasted in all its ferocity here.

Nearing the top, with the sound of the wind above us, we all felt more than a physical shiver. Yet John, well versed in this landscape (he'd been pointing out bay leaves, eucalyptus, manzanita bushes along the way) assured us we'd be okay. "We don't have storms up here in August," he said. Half our worries were gone. We put on our jackets. Up above, the dusk was as magical as I'd hoped. . . .

Every night hike asks that we adapt ourselves to where we are. In this case, we needed to spend not too long out in the open, so I suggested that people spread out and find spots of shelter in which to write. It's often difficult to pinpoint the arrival of the dark (the official time of sunset as listed in most papers doesn't indicate when full darkness will arrive), so we were a little early and had plenty of time to settle in. In fact, when it was time to move on, people were reluctant to leave their cozy spaces inside bushes, behind rocks, down the leeward side of a slope. We gathered under a huge spreading California oak, one fifty-foot-long limb lightly bobbing just above our heads as we talked about the night. Unable in the dark to read what we'd just written, several of the writers recited poems of their own, and we got to experience how any poem sounds different when said out into the night to faces that could be no more than huge pinecones at the edge of the circle. We listened . . . we could have used a fire . . . we shivered . . . we finished with stories from our memories of other nights.

One told the story of staying in a cabin at Lake Okoboji in northern Iowa, going out for a swim at midnight with her sisters and mother. Another spoke of watching the moon over the Atlantic with two friends just before graduation from high school. Daryl told simply of feeling the warmth from the stove pour into the unheated bedroom he shared with his brother when his grandmother opened the door. No words to say goodnight, just that caring gesture to take away the chill. It was hard not to make the connection to our present situation. We'd shivered long enough; we started back down the path. In the comfort of the lounge, John read to us from his notes scribbled on the mountain:

> Far below, the flocks of cars
> measure the night
> along a path of expectation.
> May feet know the moves of earth
> even in imperfect darkness.
> This breath, this other breath
> a name for bright red fingers,
> manzanita, formed to scratch the dark
> and patterned soft for deer
> as soft as I
> rev up & climb the grade
> past the last clouds of evening . . .

As if to echo him, Michael Carey from Iowa read from a poem he'd titled, "Night Falls on Tamalpais":

> Your back bends
> like the morning eucalyptus
> yet you keep your promise
> not to break the silence
> you step on.
> Shriveled bark flakes
> like the skin
> you step out of . . .
>
> Without wings
> your body rises,
> each step a breath
> each breath
> a short but willing walk
> into the dark mountain.

I thought of Frederick Church, Martin Heade, and Asher Durand on their painting expeditions into the American wildernesses of the

1840s, taking their art to the out-of-doors, testing them against the light of storms and night and sunrises. It felt just a bit like that, as if we strangers might return writing to the world again.

Often we do not venture out at night beyond the seeming safety of city lights and streets. Unlike the amateur naturalist Chris Ferris who, because of insomnia, found a real love of taking walks at night through the English countryside (her book *The Darkness Is Light Enough* provides a fascinating account of her discoveries), most of us won't go out there alone. But under the umbrella of a "sanctioned" night hike, we can address more directly the other half of the world.

Perhaps night hikes are most important for adolescents, who in our time have become increasingly stuck in homes, malls, and automobiles, from whose isolation the fears of the night world and all it can represent, are heightened. In the van on their way to a poetry night hike at Cooper's Woods one spring in Ohio, a group of ninth graders found some rather real fears arising behind their laughter. "Night is evil," one said. While some objected, others had to admit they had that feeling. There had been some controversy at school over a group of students who had taken to wearing all black. Was the color black itself evil? The administration had hinted as much. These all-white students from rural Ohio had too little experience to guess what age-old prejudices they were dipping into here, a history of Eurocentric racism well detailed by Nathaniel Hawthorne and others. All they knew was that this night hike field trip was raising feelings they hadn't counted on. When they met me at the cabin across the field from the woods, they had stirred themselves into a mild controversy. Though I only found this out from the teacher the next day, I could sense something odd about the mood of these students, all of whom had written well over the past two weeks during my residency at the school and who had volunteered for this evening.

Fortunately, a lot of the tension was broken by humor. Just off the bus, Fred, one of the "nuttier" kids, announced that he wanted us to perform a "poem," and proceeded to show us how to pantomime a little ditty about "Four Chartreuse Buzzards" who flew one by one "a-a-away" ("what a-a-a shame") until oh-so-sadly there were none. . . . We all had to act out the motions, as if we were back in kindergarten. Ice broken, we threaded our way silently down the path toward the night.

Midway across the meadow (in all directions encompassed by forest) we stopped to consider our purpose for the evening. I talked about night and its history in literature, how the earliest stories began around the fire, and about the need to integrate all areas of learning. I knew that several of the students were more inclined toward science than poetry, so I gave them Kabir's poem "The Clay Jug":

Inside this clay jug there are canyons and pine mountains,
and the maker of canyons and pine mountains!
All seven oceans are inside, and hundreds of millions of stars.
The acid that tests gold is there, and the one who judges jewels.
And the music from the strings that no hand touches, and the
    source of all waters . . .

(translated by Robert Bly)

How similar is this fourteenth-century mystic's thought to the insights of some twentieth-century physicists who have claimed that the structure of the universe may be reflected in an atom, each small part, like the clay jug, holding something of the whole? Going out into the night, I suggested, is a way of putting ourselves back into closer touch with *possibility*, with the mysteries of the world that lie so close around us and go unnoticed in the flatlands of Ohio.

Because we had improvisational musician Bill Walker with us, we next staged a little experiment in choral voices. He assigned students individual lines and phrases from the poem to play with verbally, singing them, chanting them, adding staccato or slurred lines, increasing and decreasing volume, all under his direction. "Canyons and pine mountains . . . All seven oceans . . . Hundreds of millions of stars. . . ."

Quiet once more, we turned our backs to the circle we'd formed, and stepped out along invisible spokes, seventy yards or more, to the point where our individual radius met with the edge of the woods. All tied together by our imaginary circle, yet unable to see much beyond our little niches inside the edge of the woods, we wrote poems. Wanting to keep things as simple as possible, this time I'd suggested they write about the feeling of night—without mentioning the word. Or, since they'd been studying mythology, I said they might think of the night as an oracle and write a poem expressing what this night had to tell them.

While we wrote, the thickness of the night arrived. We entered a kind of untimed stasis, it seemed, where words and silence, light and dusk, branches and sky merged. Were we floating? At a prepared signal, Bill gave a kind of wavery call out over the darkened meadow and from all their spots around the periphery of darkness, invisible figures emerged.

We walked on, found stones beside the river, heard poems recited while the students lay on their backs to watch the stars, and finally read their poems back (and sang) around a fire that Mr. Cooper had prepared back at the cabin. In the end I don't think any of us wanted to leave. The students' poems reflected in many cases the emotional and philosophical struggles they originally brought to the woods, but these had been inverted, transformed, seen now in a rather new light. Let the last words be theirs:

I see a dream fly over
my head hastening to someone's
sleeping form

I see your half-
closed eye
your silver form
taunting me about the
dreams I cannot reach
The silver-maned lions
that cling with dew
They seem to know so much
they seem to be miniature
moons

The dance of joining
is not interrupted by my presence
by the light of the moon
so graceful I wish to
join yet I am hindered by
mortality

a dying pine
this dying tree

Jessica Funk, 9th grade

Dark,
like a blanket with holes it descends upon me
Why,
Did it have to happen to me, I've been good
When
Will it end, when will I be able to see light again
How
Will you cure this blindness
*
Alone I was,
When it hit
In my bedroom
Doing, I don't know what
But it just came
Without a sound
As soon as
The sun left
*
The sky is not black at night
It happens to be a deep dark blue
Black is not evil I don't know why you would
think such a thing
It just happens that any color is evil—
you just have to look for it

Steve Carlson, 9th grade

I see softly something that day cannot bring.
I hear sounds that touch deep inside me.
The droplets of moonlight caress my face.
The darkness I feel is that of many years gone by.
Any sounds I hear are of a world
I dare not travel.
For in my world, the night, silence is
just something to make up for the mistakes of sound.
And sound just pushes silence
further into my world.
For when a bird flies he doesn't
fly toward sound, he flies toward silence.

Missy DeLaney, 9th grade

Appendix I: References about the Night

Chris Ferris, *The Darkness Is Light Enough: Field Journal of a Night Naturalist* (Ecco, 1986)
Journals of walks at night through the English countryside—especially with animal observations.

Ruth Gensler, *Changing Light: The Eternal Cycle of Night and Day* (HarperCollins, 1991)
Selection of myths and poems about sunset/night/dawn/day and twilight.

Diana Kappel-Smith, *Night Life: Nature from Dawn to Dusk* (Little Brown, 1990)
More explorations of night from a lay-scientist's perspective.

Donald Keene, *Seeds in the Heart: Japanese Literature from the Times to the Late Sixteenth Century* (Henry Holt, 1993)
See especially the chapter on the *Renga* tradition (Chapter 24, pages 921–70).

Chet Raymo, *The Soul of the Night: An Astronomical Pilgrimage* (Prentice-Hall, 1985)
Scientific speculations about the night—in lay terminology.

Steve Van Matre, *Acclimatizing: A Personal and Reflective Approach to a Natural Relationship* (American Camping Association, 1974)
Exercises for exploring the natural world (see especially pages 17–58).

Appendix II: Poems for the Night

Margaret Atwood, "The Planters"
Amiri Baraka, "Preface to a Twenty Volume Suicide Note"
Robert Bly, "After Drinking All Night With a Friend, We Go Out in a Boat at Dawn to See Who Can Write the Best Poem"
    "Surprised By Evening"
    "Snowfall in the Afternoon"
Louise Bogan, "To Be Sung on the Water"

Italo Calvino, from *Invisible Cities:*
　　"Cities & the Sky #3"
Robert Frost, "Acquainted with the Night"
　　"The Secret"
Edward Hirsch, "In Spite of Everything, The Stars"
Langston Hughes, "Dream Variations"
　　"Georgia Dusk"
　　"The Negro Speaks of Rivers"
Ted Hughes, "The Thought-Fox"
Randall Jarrell, from *The Bat Poet:*
　　"A bat is born"
　　"A shadow is floating through moonlight" (and others)
Lu Yu, "I Walk Out into the Country at Night"
Osip Mandelstam, "How dark it gets along the Kama"
Mary Oliver, from *Twelve Moons:*
　　"Buck Moon"—From the "Field Guide to Insects"
　　"Sleeping in the Forest"
　　"Wolf Moon" (and others)
Sylvia Plath, "Crossing the Water"
Theodore Roethke, "Night Crow"
　　"Night Journey"
Richard Shelton, "Requiem for Sonora"
Gary Snyder, "Mid-August at Sourdough Mountain Lookout"
　　"Piute Creek"
William Stafford, "Traveling Through the Dark"
Hardie St. Martin, ed., *Roots & Wings: Poetry from Spain:*
　　José Luis Hidalgo, "Shore of Night"
　　Luis Rosales, "Growing Toward the Earth"
Jean Toomer, "Beehive"
Georg Trakl, "Summer"
Tomas Transtromer, "The Name"
Tu Fu, "Written on the Wall at Chang's Hermitage"
James Wright, "Lying in a Hammock at William Duffy's Pond in Pine Island, Minnesota"
　　"Milkweed"

Reaching to a Sky of Soba

David Hassler

I worried about what I would say to the fifth-grade class at St. Sebastian School. They were my first assignment for the Ohio Arts Council as a poet in the schools. I assumed they were growing up with electronic teaching aids, interactive computers, their lives immersed in the media. Would they be wired differently? Would we speak the same language, be able to listen and respond to each other? I feared I wouldn't have an experience with these kids that would begin to measure up to my memory of fifth grade.

My fifth-grade teacher, Mrs. Kouba, had the softest voice I'd heard. She told us listening was a skill—it was something we needed to learn. She sat us in a circle with our eyes closed, and we took turns walking around tapping the heads of those we loved. I remember hearing her footsteps, waiting for her to come to me. I realize now she must have tapped all our heads. She told us she kept a tape recorder by her bed at night in case she awoke with an idea or dream she wanted to record. Every Thursday was ecology club. After school, we went to the university where college students taught us about water filtration and led us on trips along the river to identify plants and collect bags of trash. We ended our day eating dinner at the university cafeteria, sitting together at long tables, as if we were college students ourselves.

Every week, Mrs. Kouba assigned us personification essays. She told us to clear our desks, get out pen and paper, and write as if we were a scratched table top or blackboard. Write about what it feels like to be a pencil, wind, trees, or grass. She deepened our empathic nerves, taught us to escape into the world, to see through other eyes, to expand ourselves. She taught us not just to know, but to feel the world around us and to care for it. Knowledge came like a tap on the head, something we felt with our eyes closed. It came from silence, attention, and respect.

In our circle, the tap traveled down my spine, like the pulse I felt on my fishing line those afternoons I sat by the river waiting to pull out bluegill and sunfish, too small to keep. I'd feel the fish alive, then throw it back into the water, the slow, perceptible current that was the pace of life itself.

That's what I remember, the thrill of my fifth-grade year—the smile and bright eyes, the dark, nested hair of Mrs. Kouba, almost old-woman-ish, though she must have been in her mid-thirties—inextricably connected to my memory of childhood, that storehouse of feeling that will nourish me the rest of my life, so difficult to deplete because it's not a quantity, but a structure, the wiring and circuitry of impulses, influencing my responses to the world.

A while ago, a friend who teaches kindergarten told me that at her school teachers are advised not to touch their students, either to discipline, or to show affection. Any contact would make them liable for charges of abuse. I was appalled and frightened to think of a generation growing up without being touched. How much is conveyed in a hug, in the touch of a hand! What knowledge is really valuable that isn't filtered through the personality of a real human being?

So when I walked into Ms. Brown's fifth-grade class, I was afraid I wouldn't be able to touch these kids; or worse, they wouldn't respond to it. But, immediately, they ran up to me and nudged their bodies against mine. They wanted to know how tall I was and if my hair was real. They asked the important questions. Was I real? How big was I? I followed my impulse to hold their shoulders, pull them into me, put my hands in their hair. I captured their attention by being real and playful. I said I was eight feet tall. "Wow!" one boy said, "The tallest man in the world is only eight six!" I paused and knew he believed me. "Well," I said, "he's my father." He frowned, pulled back, and then smiled.

I'd reflected back to him his own wonder and imagination. I had lied, but I hadn't lost his trust; I'd given him an "emotional truth" in keeping with his wonder. We all need emotional truths, especially when we are children, to nourish our soul and imagination. This is also the realm of poetry. In William Stafford's poem, "With Kit, Age 7, at the Beach," his daughter looks out at the ocean and says, "'how far could you swim, Daddy/in such a storm?'/'As far as was needed,' I said,/and as I talked, I swam."

Swimming without realizing it, I'd set the tone I'd wanted in class, one of trust, respect, and playfulness, a feeling between us, what the Japanese call good *kimochi*. Before I read them poems about my experience teaching English and living in Japan, I asked them if anyone knew any foreign words. Many kids raised their hands. I asked them to say their words without telling the class their meanings. We practiced pronouncing the words, feeling the way they shaped our mouths, then guessed at what they meant, sometimes agreeing that the sound conveyed the meaning. Then I took the words "ugly" and "beautiful," and asked them to say the words in a way opposite of their meaning. I demonstrated. They laughed and giggled, wooing each other: "You're so uuugly!"

We were exercising our mouths and ears, our imagination and humor. We were doing mental calisthenics, stretching out, becoming limber, receptive, aware. I was having fun. They knew that and were having fun, too. Children, less intellectual than adults, make better divining rods. You cannot fake having fun with them. We were making discoveries, real as my hair. And real discovery is fun.

Before I read my poem about eating soba, they tried to guess what soba was. I explained it was a long noodle in a big bowl of broth; when you ate it you could slurp as loud as you wanted, and the air cooled the noodle between your lips. The louder you slurped, I said, the greater compliment it was to the chef. They giggled again. We practiced slurping.

I told them a raw egg in a bowl of soba was called a "Full Moon," because it looked like the full moon reflected in water. And if you wanted an egg in your soup, you ordered a "Full Moon Soba." I said the Japanese language was full of such beautiful images and expressions. Then a girl raised her hand: "But in our country we order our eggs, 'sunny-side up.'" "That's great," I said, laughing at myself for being deaf all these years to that phrase. For a moment she held the magic wand, the star dust, that opens others' eyes. I told them that when I arrived in Japan, I couldn't speak Japanese, but when I ate soba, I felt fluent. Then I read my poem, "Eating Soba."

> I speak your language when I eat—
> the silence of steam and scent
> rising to me; red pepper, ginger, and soy.
> This bowl's heat in my hands.
> I snap apart chopsticks,
> break the yoke of the raw egg
> they call Full Moon that drifts
> in the center as though in a pond.
> I pull the soba noodles to my mouth,
> un-making their long strings
> and hiss. This is the sound
> of eating soba, sucking in air,
> loud and energetic.
> I hear wood rasp and tap

inside the bowls as they are drained
and clacked down on the counter empty.
Customers come and go through
the heat and steam of these small
kitchen shops, ordering soba,
"soba o-kudasai!"

I bow over your bowl
your body, your broth.
These are my hands that hold you.
This is the sound of my lips, warm
breathing you in
saying soba!

When I finished, a boy, who the teacher told me later never spoke in class, raised his hand: "Could you say the sky is a bowl of soba?" I heard his question. He was asking me for permission. I was thrilled. "Yeah!" I said, not expecting him to go on. But he did: "Then the sun is a raw egg floating in it!" There was an audible gasp. Another boy shot up his hand, squirming in his seat, impatient to release his idea. "And trees are chopsticks!" he shouted. Another gasp. Some turned to look out the window, then looked back at me.

It was the Big Bang in one period. One student spoke at a time, waiting to be called upon. They wanted to hear each other, one idea sparking another, building, elaborating, revising. They were all natural, respectful critics, applauding lines they knew felt good.

At one point I said: "Do you guys know you're making incredible metaphors?!" They didn't care. "Yeah, we know we're making metaphors," one boy said. It didn't matter what it was called. They weren't concerned about a literary term, which audience received it. They were in the moment, fishing the lower layers of consciousness, courting the muse. They didn't try to see what was down there before they pulled it up. Bluegill or sunfish. It tugged on their lines and their hands shot up. "Oh, oh, oh!" All period, they renamed the universe in terms of eating soba, creating their own cosmology, making the world their own. This is the poem they dictated that I wrote on the board:

Reaching to a Sky of Soba

The sky is a bowl of soba.
The sun is a raw egg floating in it.
Trees are chopsticks.
And clouds are the steam rising above.
Planets are onions.
The moon is a bump at the bottom of the bowl.
Stars are spices.
The Milky Way is a row of bowls.

Earthquakes break up the noodles,
their rumbling is slurping.
Our mouths are Black Holes breathing it in.
God is the chef.
Meteors are coins we throw down to pay.
The universe is a giant bowl of soba.
We continue to eat it until the final explosion.
When the universe ends, our bowl is empty.

Ms. Brown's 5-A English class
St. Sebastian School, 1995

The period ended. They didn't want to leave, and neither did I, one boy pleading, "I have two! I have two!" In the hallway the next class was waiting to come in. The room was a forcefield, its energy palpable. Feeling the tap on their heads, they were inspired, the universe inexhaustible. The touch I, myself, had received from so many teachers they were accepting now, feeling as large within as they imagined the universe without. They were not reducing the world to what was known, but enlarging it to what could be felt and imagined. When we rose from our seats, all of us that day stood eight feet tall.

II Returning to the Source: Poems, Stories and Plays from Ohio Schools

A s rivers return to their sources, the water that has flowed on through its seven-year journey to the sea and beyond winding its way back, so does writing. And no book about the teaching of writing would be complete without the works of those-who-are-taught. Often, as we know, the students are the ones who teach us, who show us how metaphor and image, invention and drama, story and dream, might still be alive in our time. They carry us back to the sources we all begin with.

As Hale Chatfield, a veteran of school residencies puts it, "the home of poetry is childhood: delight in words, in feelings for their sweet or sorrowful sake, in playfulness. Aging adults love the arts partly for their childishness. In art we and our children are equals, equally healthy and undamaged."

In the same way that any of us as teachers might read a poem or a story by an adult and get a new idea for a writing lesson, so we can read these student works and mentally reconstruct how such a piece might come about. Rather than guess some definitive "how-to" procedure, we can let the writing trigger our own ideas for model writing and approaches which might get at the same theme(s). Reading second grader Daniel Takacs's haiku, for instance, we might be inclined to open up Basho all over again, just as after reading the Oberlin students' chants to snow, we might re-explore the possibilities in Native American literature. The process can work in reverse as well: browsing through the 811 (poetry) section of the library, we can find poem after poem which might connect with the discoveries of the students in these pages.

The stories, poems, and plays in this section are arranged by age, from kindergarten to twelfth grade. They represent only a few of the residencies done in Ohio recently and are intended as a sampling of various styles and genres. As you read them, please note how many of the poems take us back not only to a delight in words, as Hale puts it, but also to the elemental substances which compose our world. Water. Stars. Mirrors. Pepsi cans. Fear. Wisdom. Wonder. Others, especially in the older grades, explore stories passed down (or sometimes hidden) over generations. It's as if the writers and the students had collectively set a goal of recovering the basics of life, as Pablo Neruda did in his "Elemental Odes." See if they don't change the way you look at the simplest things in the world around us, or for that matter, the inside of any classroom.

Returning to the Source

I. Eastwood Elementary/Oberlin
Lynn Powell, resident poet

Kindergarten

What Is the Rain?

A waterfall is falling off the edge of the clouds.
The water the cloud-like lambs drink is falling.
A man in the sky hammers water out of the clouds.
The man in the moon is trying to get water out of his bucket.
The rain is a present the moon and the stars opened.
A white dragon flying through the air is crying.
Water is falling from inside the sun.

Mrs. Johnson's morning kindergarten

WHY IS THE WIND SO COLD?
The clouds are hiccuping!
WHAT ARE THE STARS?
Lots of white grapes growing on an invisible tree.
Or a golden necklace a magic person gave to the sky
for the whole world to wear.

Miss Fridenstine's morning kindergarten

First Grade

If I were a butterfly, I would
land on your head and
tickle you with my soft feelers.

Sarah Peacock

The book was closed,
but the story was still alive.
Lynn stopped talking,
but poems still rang in our ears.

James Jaffee

Second Grade

Poem in the Manner of the Japanese Poet Basho

The rain has stopped.
But there isn't enough light
for the prisms of the rainbow.

Daniel Takacs

A tornado is a wild dog that spins around
and around when he's mad.
And he bites everything up.

Kerry Johnson

The sunset is God's finest silk on the floor.

Evan Poirson

When I am sad
My heart feels like a star
With no wishes.
It stands alone
In the dark night
And no one will wish on it.
When I am happy my heart
Feels like a shooting star
Going so fast
It will race me
And it is going to win.

Amanda Wojciechowski

Fox

Fox in the desert,
Hot sun
and the fox,
the fox blends
in the sand.

Emily Erwin

Scorpion

If I were a scorpion,
I would remove my venom
so my powerful sting
wouldn't hurt you.

Daniel Takacs

If I Were . . .

If I were a lizard,
I would stick out my tongue
and grab your heart away,
and give you mine.

Alice Mathews

II. Glendale-Feilbach Elementary/Toledo
Ellen Behrens, resident fiction writer

Stories from Kindergarten

[Note: In order to show how beginning writers often feel their way into the nature of words, the original spelling has been retained in the following two pieces.]

The Balloons
Leyna

The balloons are house diving. They almost cashed in to the nine house is. Thair is meny hills. It is Sumer time.

"I Toc to Bug"
Eric Gerhardinger

I can't bulev I'm tocing to an inseked in the Bathroom O no I for got that if my mom fines out she will. get mad and if she get mad. I'm in trubl and if I'm in trubl My Brane got me in trubl.

Jessie the Baseball Elephant
Mrs. Braun's afternoon class

Jessie the Baseball Elephant was chasing the ball when he tripped and flew up and fell in the mud. "Strike zero," he said. That meant he got to start over.

He swung his bat and missed the ball. He tripped and fell again, this time into a deep hole. "Strike two," he said.

So when he tried the third time, he got on a horse to hit the ball. This time he hit it. It went up in the air, over a fence, and broke the house's roof and window. "Homerun!" he said. The score was then 22. He ran around the bases but slipped in the snow and wrecked a snowhouse in the middle of the baseball diamond. He got back on the horse and the horse fell in the snow! The horse said, "Help me up," so Jessie did.

Jessie the Baseball Elephant won the game by 522.

Kate E., 4th grade

Beth wanted to go swimming but she had to clean her room. She hated to clean her room. She was a Pisces! It was her destiny to swim. She went to her room, sat on her junk covered bed, along with everything else. She stared at the mess with her silver eyes. Suddenly the mess was gone. She could make things disappear by looking at them. Beth got on her swimsuit and swam for the rest of the day.

III. O. R. Edgington Elementary/Englewood Lynne Hugo, resident poet

Shooting Stars

The shooting stars are
Like a running child's silver scarf lost,
Floating in the sky very
Fast.
    The sea is
Like a blue diamond
Of a queen, sitting
On her finger.

      The desert is like a
Never ending road of boxes
That a worker left there
during his job.
    The caves are
Like a room with no lights
    Lit and the child is
Dreaming.

        Aubree Brown, 3rd grade

Bird Songs

Birds on wires
    look like scattered
    notes shooting their
    sounds into the night.

a flock of soaring
    boomerangs from the
    black nights.

    Todd Blair, 3rd grade

Breath Mint

I would get put in a wrapper and
shipped to a store. Someone would come
take me off the shelf. I would get thrown
into a bag. Later on, someone would take
me out of the wrapper and stick me
in their mouth and start chewing on
me. I would hate that, I would love

getting sucked on, I like making
people's breath smell good, even though
I get smaller and smaller and smaller
until I disappear.

Casey Davis, 3rd grade

Icicles

Icicles are little
stockings for little
fairies in the winter.

Sarah Powell, 4th grade

A Perfect Weekend

A perfect weekend finds me
in the cool of this
room
soft-cushioned with
a hint of recline,
popcorn drizzled
with hot butter,
voices in happy,
hushed whispers,
lights dim
slightly, gently
Shh
the movie is about to begin.

Genna Duberstein, 4th grade

IV. Duxberry Park Elementary/Columbus
Gretel Young Hickman, resident poet

Snake Transformation

Part 1
Summer Vacation,
hot like a car on a warm day.
I'm a sloth,
lying around doing nothing,
sitting on the front steps,
a snake basking in the sun.

Part 2
My skin is cold, clammy, hard.
I reach to feel it,
but I have no limbs.
Everything goes blurry,
my mouth is very wet.
I'm a water snake in a pond.

Part 3
I'm human again . . .
warm, tired, amazed.
I miss the cool of the water,
the way I slithered through the water
and the way it felt,
like sticking your hands
in a bowl of jello.

Max Eberle, 5th grade

V. Kyle Elementary/Troy
Diane Kendig, resident poet

The Love in Grandpa's eyes

Sitting in the cabin
waiting for the snow to fall,
staring, waiting,
Dad comes in with a grin on his face.
There's someone behind him
Long blue bibs on
gray hair
medium tall
he comes in and stomps his boots
it's Grandpa
he wipes my face from the charcoal of the fire
he smells like waterfalls of lemons
with the twinkles in his eye he winks at me
with the wrinkles on his cheeks he laughs at me
then he says, let's go somewhere.

Alyshia DeBoard, 5th grade

The Nolochucky

Up and down
we go racing through
the water
The rocks changing
the dark water
white as an
old woman's
hair.

Dannon Schweser, 4th grade

My Grandpa

My grandpa smelled like
tobacco, and he looked like
rags. He never looked too good,
but he never looked too bad.

But then he got ill,
and his head felt so hot,
he looked like boiling water,
and he had spots.
Then one day he died,
right when I got to know him,
and I'll never forget
that smell,
the smell of tobacco.

> Joshua Gates, 5th grade

The Poet

Oh, what would it be like
if there were not any more poets
to bring joy and wonder
of shadows and toasters
with the colors for all the little people?

> But the little people
> are coming out, so wouldn't it be shameful
> for a child never to see
> a poet, a color

> And always live in black and white?
> But that would never happen
> because more bright people
> are coming out to write the world.

> Samantha Lewis, 5th grade

VI. Glendale-Feilbach Elementary/Toledo
Ellen Behrens, resident fiction writer

Core Group Stories

[Note: The following two stories were written by adult community members who were part of the core group.]

My Disappointing Day
Alice Welch

Mother didn't have to call us twice. My brothers and I were dressed, and seated at the breakfast table long before she had finished making up our toast and pouring our juice.

"I can't believe this is the day we're going to see the Lone Ranger!" exclaimed Billy.

"Yeah! I've never been in a broadcasting studio before. I can't wait to tell all my friends," answered Bob.

Taking one last look in the mirror, I made sure my big red hair ribbon was just right. I wanted to look perfect for my hero. I hurried out to the car, noticing the boys had each taken seats by the window. I didn't even stop to fight with them. Nothing was going to spoil my day.

I hated riding in the elevator. Oh well, if the Lone Ranger could ride unafraid through the dark mountains into the unknown, I too would try to be brave. I'd not panic when the doors slammed shut, and we lurched up through the tall building.

Hearing the sound of distant hoof beats and a hearty, "Hi O Silver Away," I moved to the edge of my seat, waiting to see the Lone Ranger and his trusty steed come galloping across the stage. Where is he? Something is terribly wrong! I can't believe my eyes! I see a man reading from a paper. He doesn't even have a mask. Looking more closely, I see two men with wooden blocks rapping on a washboard. Slumping in my seat, I cover my ears, and close my eyes. All my dreams are shattered. I want no part of this. I wish I'd never come.

For once, Bill and Bob didn't tease me as I listened to my mother trying to explain how radio programs are produced. Tears streaming down my face, I vowed I would never listen to that traitor, The Lone Ranger, again.

The Lights
Susan Cray

She lay in her bed, half awake, half asleep, watching the tiny blinking lights dance around the dark bedroom. Jessica could hear the grandfather clock chiming 2 a.m., and Mom snoring in the next room. But other than that, the house was quiet. Jessie reached across to her sister and gently tapped Sarah.

"Wake up," she whispered. "Wake up, Sarah."

"Leave me alone," yawned Sarah. "It's dark. It's not time to get up yet."

"Sarah, will you wake up. Look at the lights."

"What lights? It's dark."

"Just open your eyes and look," said Jessica softly as she continued to nudge her sister.

"Oh! What are they?" asked Sarah, when she finally opened her eyes and spotted the dancing lights.

"I don't know. But aren't they awesome?"

Suddenly, a high pitched scream pierced the darkness. Instantly, lights came on all over the house. Everyone was up and running to the spare bedroom, the source of the scream. Sarah was the first to reach it and turned on the lights.

Sarah and Jessica's mouths dropped open as they looked at Aunt Milly. She was standing in the middle of the bed, with pink gunk on her face, a chin strap, and plastic blue rollers in her hair. Aunt Milly was waving her arms frantically and screaming.

"Get them off of me! Get them off of me!" she shrieked hysterically.

Bill gave his wife, Terry, a questioning glance. She looked at Bill and shrugged her shoulders. Terry didn't know what his Aunt's problem was.

"Dad, look at the ceiling," exclaimed Jessica as she pointed to the lightning bugs. There seemed to be hundreds of them.

"What the heck. Where did they come from?" he asked.

"Never mind where they came from," said Terry. "Let's get your Aunt out of here. With all that screaming the neighbors will soon be calling the police."

"I didn't mean to," Sarah explained as she pulled on her mother's nightgown. "They're my lightning bugs. I put the jar in my bedroom. The lid must have come off."

Terry and Bill looked at each other and started to laugh. Realizing their parents weren't angry, the girls joined in. Aunt Milly, thinking they were laughing at her, jumped off the bed and left the room in a huff.

"The excitement's over," said Dad. "Go on back to bed."

Jessica took her sister's hand and walked down the hall to their bedroom. They passed Aunt Milly on the phone. She was yelling at their Uncle John. Aunt Milly wanted him to come and get her right away. She wouldn't spend another night in this house.

Baldy
Sean Heil, 4th grade

Baldy was a kid that had cancer. Baldy's real name was Mike. Baldy or Mike was the only kid that had cancer in the hospital. Therefore everybody made fun of him and called him names.

One day Paul was walking down the hallway to the lunchroom. Paul was the bully of the hospital. Paul especially hated Mike. Paul was the one that gave Mike his awful nickname Baldy.

At the lunchroom the kids were misbehaving and had to have assigned seats. John next to Kate. Danny next to Ben. Mike . . . Suddenly everything became quiet. Nobody wanted to sit next to Mike. But Mike was excited. Until . . . Paul next to Mike. And the assigned seats were for one whole month! Paul was so unhappy that he was about to cry! And

Mike hated that idea also. Mike and Paul looked each other in the eyes. Everything was quiet until . . .

"Everybody cross your fingers or you'll get Baldy germs and lose all your hair!" Paul said.

Mikes eyes opened wide. Mike yelled out, "Don't listen to him. My disease is not catchable."

Paul shouted out, "Aaaaa! I have to sit next to someone that has diseases!"

Mike's eyes filled with tears. Mike ran into the hallway and cried.

Mike's best friend came to make him feel better. Mike's best friend's name was Joe. Joe was handicapped. Because Joe was handicapped a lot of people made fun of him also. And there were other handicaps in the hospital. A lot of the handicaps got made fun of also. Joe was Mike's best friend because Joe was the only friend Mike had. But Joe had more friends than just Mike. Joe had Mike, the other handicaps, and some other kids liked him also.

"Mike I know how you feel. When I first came here everybody made fun of me," Joe said, feeling sorry for Mike.

"But you don't know how I feel," Mike said. "Come on . . . let's go back into the lunchroom and show those guys."

Joe said, "Hey! You're right! I'll go back into the lunchroom and show them." As soon as Mike's face appeared, everybody made an awful face. Mike sat in his seat next to Paul. Paul moved over a seat but his teacher saw him and sent him back to his real seat.

"I'll teach you a lesson!" Mike said angrily.

"Ha! Ha! Ha! I am the toughest kid here and I always will be," Paul said.

Mike said angrily, "Well, we'll see about that!" Baammm! Mike punched Paul right square in the stomach! Paul fell right to the floor. Paul pushed himself up with a smile of his face.

"I like your style. Say . . . do you want to be buddies?"

"Sure . . . that would be great! I wish you really meant it," Mike said.

"But I really think we should be friends," Paul said.

"Do you really think so?" asked Mike.

"Sure we should be friends. Hey Baldy!" said Paul.

"But I thought you are my friend," Mike said with a puzzled face.

"I am still your friend but I made you a different nickname. As the matter of a fact I made you two new names."

"That's nice but could you just call me Mike?"

"Sure. So Mike, when is your birthday? No wait. I want to guess it. Is it September 14? No. O-kay . . . Is it April 11? No. I give up."

"It is tomorrow," Mike said smiling. "Well it's time to go to bed. I'll see you tomorrow," Mike said.

The next afternoon after lunch was Mike's birthday party. Happy Birthday Mike! Let's open the presents now! The first one is from Adam. Rip! Rip! Rip! Wow a new toy car! A blue one. "Blue is my favorite color," Mike said. After opening all the presents the kids were going to eat cake. Wait Mike! There's one more! But Mike didn't see anything. Under the table. Mike looked under the table there was a little box. "Wow! It's from everybody! Wow! It's a brown wig. Thanks Paul."

"Well don't just thank me. We all put some money in it for it."

Suddenly a car drove up to the main entrance and beeped its horn three times. Beep! Beep! Beep!

"O no! It's my mom!" said Paul. "So what's so bad about your mom," D.J. asked.

"She is coming to pick me up! To leave for good!"

"To leave for good where?" Shawn asked.

"To North Carolina!"

And right now we are in California. "Gee" Tim said, "that's all the way across the United States!"

"Do you think we will ever see each other again?" Mike asked.

"I doubt it," Paul said. "Well, we can write letters to each other," Paul said.

"But that just wouldn't be the same," Mike said.

"Telephone calls," Paul said.

"But it still won't be the same," Mike said. "And besides my family doesn't have one," Mike said.

"Well I guess this is goodbye," Paul said.

Beep! Beep! The car horn honked two more times.

"Well I have to go now," Paul said.

Vroom! Vroom! The car was gone. Mike went to his room.

"What's the matter?" Mike's nurse asked.

"Well my friend just left," Mike said.

"Aaaa yes, the kid that left after lunch today," Mike's nurse said.

"Yah, his name was Paul," Mike said.

"I was his nurse until you came here. So I became your nurse and Ms. Widlow became Paul's nurse," Mike's nurse said.

"Paul was great," Mike said.

"Paul was a very fine man except for his problem," Mike's nurse said.

"What problem?" Mike asked.

"His problem of making fun of disabled or handicapped people, or other things like that," Mike's nurse said.

"He doesn't have that problem anymore," Mike said.

"That's good to hear. Here is your dinner, and you have a visitor," Mike's nurse said.

"Who is it?" Mike asked.

"Joe," Mike's nurse said.

"Hi Joe," Mike said. "What are you doing here? It's dinner time and almost time to go to bed," Mike said.

"I am already finished with dinner. My nurse Ms. Zarves gave me my dinner earlier just so I could come here and see you," Joe said.

"But why are you here?" Mike asked.

"I just wanted to cheer you up, but I guess you're fine so I will just leave," Joe said.

"I'll see you tomorrow," Mike said.

That next morning while Mike and Joe were eating breakfast, when suddenly.

"Ouch!" yelled Mike.

"What's the matter?" Joe asked.

"I don't know, let's just keep on eating," Mike said.

"Well, if you're sure," Joe said.

"Hey Joe," Mike said.

"Ya," Joe answered.

"After we are done eating breakfast do you want to go into my room and help me with my model airplane?" Mike asked.

"What model airplane?" Joe asked.

"That's right, I forgot to tell you about my new model airplane," Mike said.

"Well I'm already done," Joe said.

"I just have to finish my toast. There done. Let's go now," Mike said.

"I like models and I like airplanes too," Joe said.

"Finally we are all done," Mike said.

"Wow, that sure is neat," Joe said.

"Hey Joe," Mike said.

"Ya," Joe said.

"Before you leave I want to give you something," Mike said.

"What is it?" Joe asked.

"My model airplane," Mike said.

"No it's all right, and besides you probably spent a fortune on it," Joe said.

"No really, take it," Mike said.

"Wow, thanks," Joe said smiling.

"Bye," Mike said.

About a hour later Mike started to hurt.

"Ouch! I hurt all over. Nurse Mary! Nurse Mary," yelled Mike with an awful look on his face.

"What! What!" she yelled.

"Never mind. I had a pain all over, but it's gone now. I must have just . . . Well I don't know. I think that I'll just lie down and take a nice long nap," Mike said.

"Well . . . if you insist. Good night," said Nurse Mary.

By the time that Mike woke up it was 8:30! It was 8:30! Time for Mike to do his homework. So Mike started to do his homework. All that he had that night was math. He started his first page.

48 + 21 = 69.

He was on his fourth problem on the second page when suddenly someone knocked.

Knock! Knock! Knock!

"Who is it," Mike asked?

"It's me, Nurse Mary. I have your dinner," she said.

"Come in. You can just leave it in here. I have to finish my homework," Mike said.

"Why don't you go ahead and eat your dinner first so it doesn't get cold," Nurse Mary said. "Well . . . all right," Mike said.

That night Mike finished his homework and ate his dinner.

That next morning Mike woke up at eight-thirty.

"Time for breakfast already!" Mike said.

So Mike quickly got dressed and went to the lunchroom. He sat next to Alan and Kristin.

As soon as Mike finished breakfast Nurse Mary brought Mike his vitamins. He had one vitamin C and one animal-shaped vitamin.

"I like the animal vitamin, but the vitamin C is sour," Mike said.

At recess Mike played tetherball and then he watched the sixth graders play football.

After school Mike went outside and played with Joe. Mike beat Joe in a game of tetherball. Then Mike came inside and watched his favorite show *Beetlejuice*. Mike thought Beetlejuice's jokes were funny.

That night when Mike went to bed he started to hurt all over. He tried to go to sleep but he couldn't with that pain. About a half hour later it hurt so bad that he started to scream! His nurse came running up the stairs. Mike's disease started to fight back! Mike couldn't do that much. About two years later Mike died.

And that's the story of Baldy.

VII. Maumee Valley Country Day School/Toledo
Debra Conner, resident poet

Dear Guilt
Beth Young, 8th grade

Dear Guilt,
You would probably think Wisdom is an old man with a long white beard, right? Wrong! He is really a middle-aged man with a wife, Sadness, and his nervous wreck of a daughter, Panic. He lives in an apartment on the corner of Main and Glendale. He is incredibly fat, so fat they had to get a ground floor apartment because he can't fit in the elevator.

So if you see a large man in a plaid shirt and jeans, driving a beat up old pick-up, you will know exactly who he is.

Your friend,
Anger
P.S. If you see Wisdom, tell him I said, "Hi!"

Leather Bombers

So much depends upon
a black leather bomber
so soft, like a horse without hair.
I can feel its warmth,
as I stand outside
in the cold,
watching the snow fall
all around me.

Tami Ducat, 7th grade

Poem

So much depends
upon

some dissolved
caffeine

washed down with carbonated
sugar water

from a green
aluminum can

Peter Tubbs, 7th grade

Woods

chipmunk	bullfrog	riverbed	bluegrass
hilltop	waterfall	fallenleaves	topsoil
bigtree	underfoot	babytrees	mousehole

evergreen	treebranch	deertrack	molehill
raindrop	thunderstorm	fallentree	treemoss
rainbow	dewdrop	sunset	sunrise

Jacob Selman, 7th grade

VIII. Ladyfield Elementary/Toledo
Debra Conner, resident poet

The White Weasel

This morning
the weasel rose
out from under
the rocks.

Scampered over
the light snow.
With the cold air
behind him, rustling.

He is like a snowman
white and small.
That always stands
on his hinds.

It has a ferret's body,
a head like a baby bear.
Its legs like an anteater.

And I said: remember
this is not like a snowstorm,
but heaven's fist full of life and love.
Then it leapt over each rock
and it turned into
an arrow which quivered
across the snow.

Tony Lucarelli, 5th grade

Radio Man

I'm like a radio, like a radio that plays sad songs.
Often I'm happy like a radio that plays happy songs.
Sometimes I feel lazy and laid back like
I don't have anything to worry about.
And again the radio has just the right
song. Sometimes I'm on the run
going fast and nothing can stop
me, a fast moving,
grooving song. Even though I don't look like
a radio, deep down inside where nobody but
me looks, that same moving,

grooving, slow relaxed radio's inside me, deep inside me
that little radio is alive and playing that same
smooth song.

Vidall Long, 6th grade

IX. Fort Loramie Middle School/Fort Loramie
Debra Conner, resident poet

Trashcan

I am dirty, but loving.
I accept all things unwanted.
I am not prejudiced or picky.
People handle me carelessly,
but I handle every rejected object with care.

I am smelly, but thoughtful.
I am a patron saint,
a temporary home for the rejected,
until the large, grumbling noise comes,
and takes my children away.

Gina Bensman, 7th grade

Fog

I am thick and visible,
yet I have no shape.
Whatever I touch, I engulf,
yet I cannot be caught.
I am fallen clouds.
Most of the time I cause trouble.
Water and air form me.
I think I am made to darken the sky,
for I reduce vision and
increase blind danger.

Kevin Meeker, 7th grade

Larry Bird, A Basketball Legend

From the Boston Gardens, I hear the fans
cheering me on as I sink my fifth
straight three, the ball a sinking rock
in a puddle of water.
My light breathing keeps me on the floor
for our second straight title.
I hold my head high on the floor
as I hear my name in the background
Larry, Larry.

I go and gather my clothes,
I hear the writers, their mouths moving

like the basketball I just dribbled.
I leave them as my father and mother left
me many years ago. What difference could it
make it they knew I made the N.B.A.
What would they say now?

> Bryan Winemiller, 7th grade

X. Solon Middle School/Solon
Lynne Hugo, resident poet

Bees

The boys were armed
Ready
The beehive a good target
The beehive in the backyard
Hanging there
Ready to fall
Fall hard to the ground
that was their mission

Firing only sticks
Stones and firecrackers
The enemy
Armed with sharp
Sharp stingers
Unsuspecting
Unprepared for the fight

The counter-attack
With stingers ready
Comes
After a minute
Going only after Doug

Stinging in revenge
Wherever possible
Stinging
Stinging

> Chris Mulcahy, 7th grade

The Experiment

The Christmas of 1918 I got a lot of presents,
But my favorite was a chemistry set.
Right away I started on the experiments,
Then I soon got bored and needed a challenge.
I went to the library and looked up the making of gun powder.
Afterward, I went home to make the mixture,
And later smashed it.
The sound was that of the dropping of pots onto the floor;

It reverberated off the walls and through the apartment.
Then I sensed the true danger of it.

Outside my apartment building,
Were silver rails of a streetcar track.
They were Moses parting the Red Sea.
This gave me an idea.

On a summer day I made the mixture,
I then spooned it into an envelope.
When there was no one out on the street,
I quickly snuck to the tracks.
There I laid the envelope, out on the tracks,
And casually walked back.
And waited.

Finally a streetcar came,
The envelope lashed out with sparks, and thunder
Loud as though it were just about to storm.
In the background I heard screeching of metal against pavement,
And then the whining of police sirens.
I knew it was time to go inside the apartment building;
It was time to hide.

Matthew Consolo, 7th grade

This Place Was Mine

It always made me happy,
But I can never go back.
Outside are gardens with yellow tulips
That rise in the spring shade
And white lilies of the valley.
A short sidewalk leads up to the door
with a plaque saying "Speth's."
On the side where a basketball hoop
hangs in hope. Near a two car garage
The back is wide open welcome
with a homemade wooden playground.

This place was mine

There is a deck with a picnic table where
I used to get peanut butter sandwiches
And bees dive bombed my Koolaid in the summer.
I can smell the blue grass;
The lawnmower is whining its way around the perimeter.
I used to ride my three wheeler with my brother

This place was mine

Kellie Speth, 7th grade

Sirens

I hear them wail
and I wonder
who next?
How many people?
Why did it happen?
People hear me and think I worry
too much. I tell them in my
defense that I'm just
concerned.
Concerned about what the future
has in store for us all.
They should be concerned too
but they're not.
That is what is so frightening.

Melissa Hudak, 7th grade

Irritation

The gritty,
Trashy,
Messy,
Ugly,
Filthy,
Nasty,
Gross,
Disgusting,
Pitiful,
Way my brother
Keeps his room.

Melissa Hudak, 7th grade

A Ghost Town

the colors weren't so drab,
once they were bright;
    but the sun is strong,
and colors fade,

the tools they used aren't new;
once they were,
    but time wears on,
and things stay the same,

long ago the things the children were taught,
to read and write,
to find a trait;
things aren't taught that way now,

    an old wooden globe
sits quietly in the window,

an old mattress spring
waits quietly in the dump,
        old bottles on the saloon walls
wait silently for people,
when no one comes these things will wait,

many times a floor has been retiled,
as recent fire shows it through;
coffins are seen through the window of an old gray house,
a wooden cemetery lies near,
with words carved in charcoal,
and bricks outlining a baby's bed,

an old cardinal's bird cage is open,
one side of the mountain is closed off,
but once men labored here,
old donkey trails are still engraved

where beautiful flower beds once laid,
my ears will pop,
the elevation is so high,
in my favorite place,
where many people once walked,
        but now I walk alone,
        in my favorite place,
in Bodie.

Sara Martin, 7th grade

At Night

floating, twirling, swishing, gliding,
sometimes late at night my soul leaves me,
I don't call it back,
I help it get away,

it goes dancing in gardens late at night,
swinging on wooden swings in old graveyards,
swimming in small murky ponds,
but it always comes back to me by morning,

harmony is always playing in the background,
there is no melody,
and violas rule the orchestra,
only strings can be heard,

if it gets caught in the undertow of music,
I will go to heaven,
but only for a visit,

always late at night,
in the deepest of my slumbers,
my soul sometimes leaves me.

Sara Martin, 7th grade

Homeless: A Portrait

A man holds an empty bottle,
once full of whiskey.
His ragged hat lays over his face
His gray shirt is torn to shreds,
and the wool gloves that he wears
are worn through,
his fingers hang lifelessly out of them
in the cold fall air.
His arms are overlapping one another
as he embraces himself
trying to keep warm.
He is sitting in a wheelchair
that looks ancient like an old grandma.
One of his legs is limply hanging over
the wheelchair.
I can't say much about the other,
for it is only half there.
His pants are a smoky brown color.
He uses a giant silver safety pin
to secure his pant leg.
On the other,
a crease mark is left
from sitting too long.
His tan colored tennis shoes
have holes at the toes;
The laces are untied.
Next to him
there is a sign
with bright pink letters painted:
"WILL WORK FOR FOOD."
The sign is held up by a wooden easel with a red bucket hanging
from it. The bottom of the bucket
has a smattering of dimes and pennies
like glistening drops of rain
The fall wind makes the bucket
sway back and forth.

Carrie Layman, 7th grade

XI. Pleasant Run Middle School/Cincinnati
Nick Muska, resident poet

Allora

ALLORA . . . in a tempo assai lunge
felice fui molto; non ora:
ma quanta dolcezza mi giunge
de tanta delcezza d'allora!

Quell'anno! per anni che poi
fuggirono, che fuggiranno,
non puoi, mio penises, non puoi,
portare con te, che quell'anno!

Un giorno fu quello, ch'è senza
compagno, ch'è senza ritorno;
la vita fu van parvenza
sì prima sì dopo quel giorno!

Un punto! . . . così passeggero,
che in vero passò non raggiunto,
ma bello così, che molto ero
felice, felice, quel punto!

Giovanni Pascoli

Gee Vinnie, Pass the Cola

Flowers in a casino lounge.
Fettuccini, moldy non-okra
My daddy doesn't like me, gee, Luna
I want to be a dolphin named Amy!

My piano! And my chia pet.
Fettuccini and more fettuccini
No pools, more pools, non-pools.
Paintings got wet, so call mama!

Uncle George fell quickly, should I send
champagne, or should I send rotini?
The van broke by his parachute.
See, Luna, see, dolphins do ignore me!

The piano! It costs money,
Luna isn't a ragamuffin.
My jell-o costs lots of money.
Lice, lice, please no lice!

Eleanor Willen, 7th grade

Les Deux Bonnes Soeurs

La Débauche et la Mort sont deux aimables filles,
Prodigues de baisers et riches de santé,
Dont le flanc toujours vierge et drapé de guenilles
Sous l'éternel labeur n'a jamais enfanté.

Au poète sinistre, ennemi des familles,
Favori de l'enfer, courtisan mal renté,
Tombeaux et lupanars montrent sous leurs charmilles
Un lit que le remords n'a jamais fréquenté.

Quand veux-tu m'enterrer, Débauche aux bras immondes?
O Mort, quand viendras-tu, sa rivale en attraits,
Sur ses myrtes infects enter tes noirs cyprès!

Et la bière et l'alcove en blasphèmes fécondes
Nous offrent tourlà tour, comme deux bonnes soeurs,
De terribles plaisirs et d'affreuses douceurs.

Charles Baudelaire

The Dark Bone Sizzles

The dumb barbequer, Mort, burnt the dark fillets,
Bob the barber made the rich sauce,
Don't let Frank take over the hot grill,
So Ethel won't lose her PJ's in the flame.

Five potatoes simmer, and Emily ate them all,
"My favorite!" said Emily as she ate the mailman,
Timbuctu ate leopards and the charcoal,
Until Regies' PJ's caught fire.

Quadro entertained dumb Bob with immense bras,
O, Mort, Quadro said, Heraldo Rivera is on,
Serve the insects inside the noisy Cypress.

Eat the bear, eat the clover, and eat the biosphere for seconds,
Noel offered a tour of the bones and sauces,
A terrible plaster storm covered the barbeque.

Group poem (Chris/Travis/Matt/Richard), 7th grade

La Musica

De pronto, surtidor
de un pecho que se parte,
el chorro apasionado rompe
la sombra—como una mujer
que abriera los balcones sollazando,
desnuda, a las estrellas, con afán
de un morirse sin causa,
que fuera loca vida inmensa—
Y ya no vuelve nunca más,
—mujer o agua—
aunque queda en nosotros, estallando,
real e inexistente,
sin poderse parar.

Juan Ramón Jiménez

The Music

The problem searched at the door,
the unpeach went to the party to tell the chorus
    about passion and romance,
And to tell some bra to come and sing music.
The ape lost the balconies in the tornado,
The nude went to Las Vegas to buy a fan.
Nuns cause sin with morsels,

And he fueled local video games immensely
    and said,
"You have no value, and nuns like Christmas, so
    don't argue!"
Mannequins question the nostrils of tall tuxedoes,
They are real and exist with sin pondering the
    stars!

XII. Miami Valley East High School/Miami County
Michael London, resident playwright

The Soccer Field
Rob Janssen and Steve Wright

> (Music transition)

Narrator: Sometimes they told us stories from far away.

Tommy: I will never forget that day, soon after my tenth birthday. I lived in a little town with my mother and aunt. My father was somewhere, fighting in the war. Our village was a place where they kept the Polish captives. About two hundred of them lived at one side of our town. Some of the Nazis lived there to oversee the prisoners.

> My friends and I always wanted to be wherever something was happening and one day we got our chance. Every day we met at the edge of town, and walked together through the woods to the clearing where we always played soccer. One day I was late.

Jimmy: Hey guys, did you see this sign over here?

John: What sign? What's it say?

Jimmy: The Nazis wrote it. It says we can't go to the forest tomorrow.

Bill: Why can't we go to the forest? We always go to the forest. Where are we going to play soccer?

John: Okay. Forget it. We'll find another place to play. We won't get to play at all if Tommy doesn't get here soon.

Bill: I'm sick of waiting. Let's just leave without him.

John: He's my cousin. We've gotta wait for him . . .

Bill: No we don't!

John: Oh, here he comes.

Tommy: Guys, guys. Guess what I heard!

Bill: Nobody cares. You're late.

Tommy: I was on my way here and I dropped the soccer ball behind a tree. I ran back to find it. While I was looking for it, I heard two soldiers talking as they passed the tree. They were talking about one of the captives. He tried to escape and he got caught.

Bill: That's not true. He's just a kid. He doesn't know!

Tommy: That's what they said. I heard them.

Jimmy: So that's why we can't go to the forest tomorrow.

John: What do you mean that's why? Do you know something we don't? 'Cause if you do, tell us.

Bill: Yeah, Mr. Know-It-All! Let's hear it.

Jimmy: Well, what do you think is going to happen to him? He's a Polish captive who got caught trying to escape a Nazi camp. They're sure to punish him in some way.

Bill: But why in the forest?

John: Maybe they don't want anyone to know.

Bill: What'd ya think they'll do?

Jimmy: Only one way to find out.

John: I don't know, Jimmy. Our parents might find out and punish us.

Bill: What if the Nazis find out and catch us?

Jimmy: Are you gonna be a momma's boy all your life?

Bill: I'm not a momma's boy, you . . . jerk!

Jimmy: Well, then, what'd ya say? Are you in or out?

Bill: Alright, I'm in.

Tommy: I want to go, too, John!

John: No, you can't go, and I'm not either.

Jimmy: C'mon John. I don't want to go if you don't.

Tommy: Why can't I go? If Bill's going, I should be able to go.

John: Alright, I guess we'll go. But if something happens don't blame me.

Jimmy: Alright, we'll meet here tomorrow, same time.

John: Alright, we'll see you tomorrow. Oh, and don't say anything to anybody. We can't let anybody find out.

Bill: And don't be late, *pipsqueek!*

Jimmy: Shut up, leave him alone.

Narrator: We met at the same time the next day to go to the forest, but we ran into trouble on the way there.

Tommy: Look, there's a Black Shirt guarding the entrance to the forest.

John: Let's go around the side of the woods and go in there.

Jimmy: He saw us.

SS Officer: Hey! You kids aren't supposed to be around here. Can't you read the signs? Now get outta here and don't come back.

Boys: Yes sir.

(Music transition)

Narrator: The only possible way to get into the forest was to go in the side entrance. We sneaked around the guards so that they couldn't see us. We had just entered the brush when I fell behind the older kids.

Tommy: Guys! Wait up, guys. I'm stuck.

John: What now, dang it?

Tommy: My foot's stuck in this darn hole.

Bill: Maybe we should turn back anyway, guys. What if we get caught?

John: Quit whining. You get scared when your mom turns out the lights at bedtime.

Tommy: I don't either get scared of the dark.

Bill: Oh yeah? Why'd you cry for a week, then, when your mom threw away your teddy bear?

Tommy: Hey, that's not true.

Jimmy: Alright, both of you guys shut up. Come on, I think I hear something.

John: Quick, get down.

Tommy: What is it, John?

John: Nothing. Be quiet.

Tommy: But I can't see.

John: Alright, get up here, but stay down and be quiet.

Bill: What is it? What's going on?

Jimmy: Ssh! Don't say anything. Oh my God!

John: It's an SS officer.

Tommy: What's he doing?

Bill: That guy, he's got a rope around his neck. They're gonna hang him.

Tommy: Who is it?

Jimmy:	It's the Pole, the one they caught trying to escape.
John:	Look, the SS officer. Oh God, he . . .
Tommy:	What? I couldn't see! What'd he do?
John:	Nothing, don't worry about it. Just stay down.
Jimmy:	It's the Pole, he's on a barrel, and . . .
Tommy:	What, and what?
John:	The SS officer . . . he's kicking the barrel off balance.
Tommy:	What's he gonna do?
Bill:	You think he'll kick it? Will he hang him?
Jimmy:	He's doing it again. He's kicking it.
John:	Oh God!
Tommy:	He . . . he . . . he hung him.
Bill:	He's still moving around.
Jimmy:	His legs are jerking. Look!
John:	The SS officer spit on him.
Jimmy:	C'mon Tommy, quit crying.
Tommy:	But he killed him. Why'd he have to kill him?
Bill:	He's not dead yet. He's still jerking around. Look! His head's twitching!
Jimmy:	Shh! Be quiet. The SS is saying something to the other Poles.
John:	He hit her; he hit that lady because she wouldn't watch.
Jimmy:	He's sick. If I had a gun, I'd kill him myself.
John:	Oh God! Get down! Get down!
Jimmy:	He's looking right at us.
Bill:	He saw us. Let's get out of here.
John:	No, he didn't. Stay where you are. Don't make any noise. If we move now, he might see us. Stay put until I tell you it's okay and we'll all go at the same time.
Jimmy:	He's turning away. Let's go now.
John:	Okay, let's go. Now!
Tommy:	Wait guys. I can't run that fast.
Jimmy:	Hurry! Do you want us to get caught?
John:	Let's go!
Narrator:	When we reached the edge of the forest everything was quiet. No one said a word. None of us could believe what had happened. Then I broke the silence . . .

Tommy: I can't believe it!

Bill: Shut up! Don't talk about it!

Jimmy: I can't wait to get home.

John: Hey you guys, don't breathe a word of this to your parents. If you guys do, it could mean big trouble.

Tommy: (Quietly.) I can't believe they just hung him . . .

Bill: I told you to shut up!

Tommy: Ouch!

John: You ever hit him again and I'll kill ya!

Jimmy: Hold up, hold up! We need to calm down. Just be quiet until we get home and try to forget it.

Tommy: We just can't forget about it!

John: Listen Tommy, if we keep talking about it, we're just going to make things worse than they already are.

Tommy: How could it get worse than it is right now?

Jimmy: It can! Remember when David used to live here. Every time I ask mom about it she says he just moved, but all of their furniture is still in the house and no one has moved in yet.

John: They even tell us where we can and can't play. We used to play in those woods whenever we wanted to. Now we can only go at certain times during the week.

Jimmy: Okay, we're here Tom. Go inside and don't say anything, understand?

Tommy: Don't worry, I won't!

Narrator: When I got home that evening, I didn't dare say a word to my mother and my aunt. It wasn't until years later when our children asked about my memories of the war, that I said anything. I had thought about it nearly every day since and my dreams were filled with pictures of the man on the barrel and the officer kicking it.

(Music transition)

In the Still of the Night
Nicole Demmit and Julie Easterling

Narrator: And sometimes they gave us a good laugh.

(Music: duelling banjos.)

Geraldine: Little Nubbie! How many times have I told you not to go and be eating dirt! You go wash your hands and round up them sisters of yours. It's time for our dinner! Hurry up now! I don't want to hafta tell you twice child!

Nubbie: Aahh Momma. Why don't you go and find 'em and I'll go get Poppa. I think he's out in the woods again with ol' Cecil McGrew! Speaking of that old Cecil, why's him and Pa always back in the woods? He's always got that brown bag . . .

Geraldine: Now Nubbie, don't you be nosin' in your Pa's business! And you know you're not to go near them woods. Pa will be in when him and Cecil finish their work out there! Run along and get your sisters like I told ya!

(Music transition)

Bessie: Hmmm Momma! These biscuits sure taste good. May I have another?

Geraldine: Bessie, we need to save a few for your Poppa—he's been working hard all day.

Ursie: Momma, why do you make excuses for him? Us kids know that him and Cecil are cookin' whiskey back in our woods. They just sit around all day testing their concoction and watching the steam roll off that still.

Geraldine: Ursinne Kaye! Now you hush your mouth. I don't ever want to hear you speak about your father's going-ons again. You know what he's doing is illegal and if he gets caught, he'll end up in jail just like Jessie down the road did.

Nubbie: Pa, you're just in time to get some biscuits before Bessie eats 'em all!

Ces: What's goin' on here? Geraldine, have them girls been giving you a hard time?

Nubbie: Nope, she wasn't givin' Momma a hard time. She just said we all know that you and Cecil got a still hid in them woods.

Ces: Now that may very well be so, but I suggest that you kids keep quiet or we all will catch hell!

Geraldine: Speaking of which, Ces, I heard old Jessie spilled his guts and turned in everyone who's been cooking.

Ces: Yeah, I know—we spent all day dismantling the still and find hiding places for all the whiskey. There is still a couple of gallon jugs we need to get rid of, but right now I'm hungry and tired, so let's drop this subject and let me eat my dinner in peace.

(Music transition)

Sheriff: I knew sooner or later Jessie would start talking. He was bound and determined not to go down alone.

Benasal: Hey, Sheriff, who we raiding tonight?

Sheriff: Well, son, we are going to be mightly busy tonight. We're gonna pay a visit to several people. We got to check out ol' Ces Mooney to see if Jessie's telling the truth or feeding us a line of bull.

Deputy: The key to a good raid is gettin' 'em when they least expect it. That's why we're waitin' till late tonight, when they're all warm in their beds and can't get rid of their stash.

(Music transition)

Geraldine: Ces, it's gettin' late. We best be turnin' in. But first, why don't you and I go out and fetch them last few jugs and put them up in Ursie's room? You know them feds would never think of lookin' in her room.

Ces: That's a damn good idea for now, but we can't leave 'em up there for long. We'll have to think of a better place later. Let's get done and get some rest. All this talk of gettin' caught gots me beat.

(Music transition)

Geraldine: Ces! Ces! Get up! Somebody's trying to knock down the door.

Sheriff: Ces! We know you're in there! Open up! It's the sheriff! We got a search warrant!

Ces: Shit!

Geraldine: Go down and stall 'em, and I'll try and get rid of the whiskey!

Ces: What's the meaning of this? I ain't got nothing you boys are looking for.

Sheriff: Well, we will be the judge of that! Benasal, start looking in the back and the Deputy will be looking in the front.

Ces: Now, you can't just go and bust into my house in the middle of the night . . .

Sheriff: Like I said, we got a warrant and this little piece of paper let's us do whatever we want!

Geraldine: Ces, what's happening? The girls are scared and little Nubbie's cryin'!

Sheriff: Don't mean to upset ya, ma'am. Our business will be through here shortly after we find what we're looking for . . .

(Music transition)

Ursie:	Bessie! Wake up! You gotta help me quick!
Bessie:	What's going on?
Ursie:	Ma and Pa hid jugs of whiskey in our room this evening and now the sheriff's raiding the house and we've got to get rid of it somehow!
Bessie:	What are we going to do?
Ursie:	Hurry up! Let's start pouring it out the window! And for God's sake—be quiet!
Bessie:	Oh God! We're gonna get caught. I just know we are!
Ursie:	Quit running off at the mouth and pray that they can't hear what we're doing!

(Music transition)

Sheriff:	Well, did you find anything so far?
Deputy:	Nope—so far both Benasal and I have come up with nothing.
Sheriff:	If you're done down here, you can start on the upstairs!
Deputy:	I'll start in the parents' room. Benasal, you go check out the kids' room. You never know where Ces might be hiding stuff.
Benasal:	Sir, do you smell something? I could've sworn I smell whiskey.
Deputy:	Well, now that you mention it, I am getting a strong whiff of something. Where is it coming from? You go check it out while I run and get the sheriff.
Benasal:	I can't just go a-barging in there. His girls might be in the room in their skivvies.
Deputy:	Oh, hell, Benasal! You act like you ain't never seen a girl in her underclothes before. You got yourself a warrant—just go on in!

(Music transition)

Ursie:	We've got one more to pour out Bessie. Hurry up. I can hear 'em coming.
Bessie:	I'm pouring as fast as I can! Why in the world would Pa ever want to hide these in our room in the first place?
Ursie:	Who cares why he did it! He did and now it's up to us to get rid of it.

Bessie: Okay, that's the last one. Hurry up and hop back in bed and act like they just woke us up.

Ursie: Sshh, they are right outside the door!

Benasal: You girls had better be decent, 'cause I'm coming in!

Ursie: Who are you and what are ya doing?

Benasal: I've got a search warrant here! Your daddy's been making whiskey and we are here to catch him red-handed!

Deputy: Benasal! You find anything yet?

Benasal: No sir! I can smell it, but I can't find any!

Bessie: Poppa!

Ces: Now, you had better not have laid a hand on my girls!

Deputy: Calm down, Ces! Benasal just came in here to look for whiskey, not to look at your daughters!

Benasal: Over here, sir! I've found some jugs!—Oh shit, they're empty!

Deputy: Ces, you care to tell us what those jugs are doing in your daughters' room and what was in them?

Ces: How in the hell am I supposed to know? It's probably just piss!

Deputy: Since when does piss smell like whiskey? Well, Ces, we know what you've been up to. We may not have found anything tonight, but we will be back!

Ces: Don't waste your time, you'll come up empty like you did tonight. Goodbye Sheriff.

(Music transition)

Geraldine: Your brewing days are over, Ces. Do you hear me?

Ces: Now, sweetheart.

Geraldine: Don't sweetheart me. I'll take the girls and I'll leave you. I love ya, but I'll leave ya if'n ya don't quit.

Ces: I'll never brew another drop, I swear.

Ursie: And you know, he never did.

(Music, end of scene)

Appendix: Publishing Student Work

Nothing affirms student writers more than having their work published. Despite all the new technologies, the printed word still carries power and authority. We recall the fifth-grade boy who bicycled from his suburban school to downtown Toledo, where his mother worked as a hairdresser, with a copy of our statewide anthology containing his poem. Publishing, or making student work public, can include broadcast (sowing words like seeds through the school and out into the community) and electronic publication, as well as print media. What works best depends on your particular community.

We see a number of school literary publications which appear semi-annually or annually. They are usually printed professionally, with money from English or language arts departments, PTAs, school supply stores, and coffee shops. However, if your school doesn't yet have such resources, the increasing availability of personal computers and sophisticated photocopiers make neat as well as innovative productions possible. Collaborate with the art teacher and involve art students in providing illustrations and design. If your district has a technical school, it may have a print shop that can do as good a job as a commercial printer, but remember that they will need a lot of advance time to schedule the work. Such a partnership can help a community see itself as a whole.

No matter how you produce a publication—mimeograph, ditto, photocopy, or offset—put a price on it, whether or not you actually sell copies. People should know that books, regardless of authorship or format, have monetary value. If you can sell copies, all the better.

Here are a number of ideas that can augment or substitute for a regular, schoolwide publication:

- Write regularly with your students and publish their best work by classroom. Use mimeograph, ditto, photocopying—whatever means are most accessible. Students will be glad to do their own typing.

- Hold a reading (coffeehouse style or more formal) to celebrate publication—in the school or public library, or other public spaces, inviting parents, district staff, school board members—and share your own work, too. Use a microphone so that those with soft voices can be heard (see MaryAnn Titus's essay, p. 121).

- Have students read on the school public address system on a regular basis—same time every day or week, e.g., Monday or Friday mornings just after the principal's announcements.

- Arrange for students to read regularly on local radio, or in response to a special event—a significant anniversary in the town, a national holiday, etc. Be creative and avoid the usual holidays which lend themselves to cliched themes.

- Post student poems, stories and essays on the walls outside your classroom or in a school display case, an effective opportunity for demonstrating the relationship of writing to reading.

- In Susanne Rubenstein's book *Go Public! Encouraging Student Writers to Publish,* consult the lists of publications and contests that welcome submissions from students.

- In lower grades, or with reluctant readers, make illustrated books. Picture books provide excellent examples—illustrated text is as old as writing itself.

- Display student books in the town as well as in school—in the public library, a bank lobby, a senior center. Host a reception, too.

- Ask your local newspaper to set aside space for student work. Maybe they'll let you and your colleagues edit a regular column (refer to Lynn Powell's experience in Oberlin, p. 37).

- If your school has online computers, publish electronically. Create a bulletin board where students can post their work. Schools within a district may share, or you may create a network with other districts. Reach out into your state or region or beyond. Create a writers' workshop with a nearby or distant sister school.

Publishing beyond your school can let the community know that creative writing is not a frill, something to be taken as an elective, but that it embodies the essence of the writing process.

III When Teachers Become Writers: Essays from Participants in The Experience of Writing

The following essays are all written by teachers who have attended The Experience of Writing jointly sponsored by the Ohio Arts Council and Wright State University (see Bob Fox's essay, p. xiii, for the background of this teachers' institute). These narratives range from MaryAnn Titus's experiments with introducing the works of William Blake, Samuel Taylor Coleridge, and other poets to her third-grade students, to Carl Krauskopf's bravery in writing stories along *with* his high school students; from Mary Noble's reflections on how she changed her whole curriculum to include creative writing alongside the writing of expository themes, to Janice Gallagher's and Barry Peters's essays on how their own writing changed as a result of these weeks in the summer (with examples of their work).

As Barry points out, perhaps the most important gift they gave themselves during those weeks was *time*. Throughout the school year, there is so little opportunity to build our own work—to follow out an image in a poem, a possible character in a story, or a strand of thought in an essay. But during the institutes, such rarely-tasted luxuries of our "regular" lives became the main meal. Writing slows down the world. We become more patient with our own minds, more insistent on "getting the phrase right" (or rather, on letting the piece of writing find its own ear and direction), more aware of the beauty and possibilities in the language of others, more ready to explore new directions. In short, we become students again.

Teachers at The Experience of Writing went out to gather images from the towns, the fields, and people passing by. They interviewed each other and recorded their own best/worst memories. They listened for the tone and nuances of dialogue around them in restaurants. They set writing goals and projects for themselves and stayed up late at night (or got up early in the morning) to exchange ideas or complete a last draft. They became—in the words of William Stafford, "ready to read or speak or write or listen with an ear for surprise." And in the fall, they brought this new readiness to their students.

When Spirit Moves, Children Sing

MaryAnn Titus

In the Beginning

> In the beginning there was an ant.
> His name was Andy Ant.
> In the beginning there was a broken down tree.
> In the beginning there was a fish who swallowed money.
> In the beginning there was a book with no pictures.
>
> —Eric Dipzinski

I read Eric's poem aloud and asked, "How did he know?"

How did he know the tree was broken-down? How did he know too many prunings, too many freezes, too many names carved into its bark—its brain—could leave it as good as dead? How could he know inside a broken-down dead tree lies a new beginning?

Only the name needed changing. It wasn't Andy Ant, but Christopher Merrill. And he's not an insect, but a writer—editor, poet, journalist, and author of several books including *Grass of Another Country* and *Watch Fire.*

I met Chris in July of 1992 at a week-long institute co-sponsored by the Ohio Arts Council and Wright State University. The Experience of Writing is a continuing institute designed to provide teachers the opportunity to develop skills as writers. For two hours each morning, Chris immersed twelve teachers in the literary worlds of John McPhee, Margaret Atwood, Wendell Berry, and others. Quoting works and relating anecdotes, he nudged us into our own eccentricities and fears. "Write truthfully and courageously," he said.

As I listened daily to writers reading their works, I realized the intimate connection between reading and writing. The command of language, the style, the nuance I heard stayed in my head. I fell in love with the particular and my work changed. My experiences took on richness unseen before. During an assignment to write a one-hundred-word sentence, I tripped over the central metaphor for what would become an extended prose poem. With Chris's encouragement I discovered the power of writing, and I was at once both terrified and exhilarated.

The following September, during morning cycles (journal writing), during author's time after woods walks, at every opportunity, our third-grade class talked. We shared how we felt, what had happened the night before, sights we saw or sounds we heard or what we hadn't. I spoke to the children as I do with adults, sometimes adding meanings of words parenthetically, sometimes filling in an analogy, and sometimes allowing the words to stand on their own.

We listened to the cadence of speech, hearing the rhythms of nature in it. Experimenting with words, we tried making the sound of a flowing stream or the crackle of autumn leaves.

I read poetry to the children daily, poems like David Waggoner's "Lost" or Wallace Stevens's "Thirteen Ways of Looking at a Blackbird." With the poets' words singing inside our heads, we wandered the beech forest behind our school, the children listing ideas as "Seventeen Ways to Look at a Stream" or "Forty-one Ways to Look at a Leaf."

Because the children were eager, I turned to *Rose, Where Did You Get That Red?* for assistance. Blake's "The Tyger" fired their hearts. The line "what immortal hand or eye could frame thy fearful symmetry" rang continuously inside our room—either whole or in part. The children wanted more. I borrowed a volume of Blake from the library and read more poems to them.

Some pieces we discussed—whenever a child had a question or whenever I found a line or image relating to a previous shared idea or experience.

Gradually, the children's work began to change.

I read Coleridge's "Kubla Khan" in an effort to encourage respect for each other's working space. When I related how a knock on the door interrupted Coleridge's work and that the poem remained unfinished, they were impressed.

The poem produced more than I had anticipated. Reveling in exotic sounds and words that could mean whatever their imaginations or experiences dictated, they wrote:

The Man in the Marbella Hat
The man in the marbella hat
calls everybody fat.

He makes us drag.

Sometimes we want to call him fat,
but he'll turn into a vampire bat.

But then he will eat us at midnight.
So we stay away from the man in the marbella hat.

Jacob Wooten

The Catog

Mountains of bones with a pet catog always fighting.
The og of the catog takes a bone from the mountain
but the cat of the catog keeps on fighting,
and the og drops his bone.

Mark Yurina

The children were hearing rhythms previously unnoticed and enjoying the sound of words whose meanings they might not know. Most
of all they were becoming comfortable with mystery in a setting where
mystery too often goes unacknowledged—school. The wonder and magic
of a pre-institution world was not only tolerated, but nurtured and prized.
Poetry became their language for conveying mystery.

Stream

Calm stream in the woods
but just a few feet away
rushing rushing waters abide with the rocks.

Mark Yurina

Silk

A piece of waving blue silk
wraps around a tree,
the wind blows the silk
into a river.

The silk hits a rock.
The silk splits in two.
Then both pieces flow down the river
in two different ways.

Mitchell Law

Fire

I see my cat sitting by the fire
the sparks are getting higher and higher
But then the light goes out
it's time for bed.
I can still see the sparks
getting higher and higher
by the light of the fire.

Andi Peterson

I used many of Chris Merrill's writing exercises with the children:
choose five words and write a poem; write a "really bad" poem; pick an

object and describe it without naming the object—use metaphor. We held Writers' Circle in the back of our room and listened to whoever wished to read a poem. Sometimes the class commented on specific parts they liked, the usage of a word, or the flow of language. We asked questions about sections unclear to us or that didn't work as well as others.

The children enjoyed this time so much that I bought a microphone. It gave added importance to their words and helped children with soft voices be heard, eliminating the problem of conversation during readings. Their confidence increased. The person with microphone in hand became the authority and was treated with new respect. (After the novelty wore off, however, even amplified readers were subjected to questions.)

As the year progressed, we added Lewis Carroll's *Alice in Wonderland* and *Through the Looking Glass* to our list of favorites. The children took note of opposites wherever they appeared and while searching for an intermediate often discovered a pattern. Comfortable with ambiguity, the paradox on the wall above our chalkboard, "Everything is different; everything is the same," was accepted on a new level. The children posted *paradox* and *oxymoron* on our Word Wall.

After our discussion of Coleridge's inability to complete "Kubla Khan," most of the children came to value silence and respect its power. My hope was that each child listen for and hear his own words. I explained words are sometimes soft and fleeting. Listening to another's voice may result in missing one's own. After the first reading of work produced in this way, the children recognized the value of silent reflection.

Blake

He gave beauty to the rose
And water to the hose,
And blue to the crystal and me,
And gave copper stingers to the bee.

Kunal Gupta

Fly

I fly so high in my little plane.
Searching for the creature of the sky.
Seeking higher and higher.
Looking for the creature
that is calling me.

Mitchell Law

We found many ways to explore ideas, but the children's hands-down favorite was writing to music. Once settled and focused, either one of the children or I would select a tape from the assortment by the recorder. R. Carlos Nakai's improvisations, George Winston's arrangements, and Ralph Vaughn Williams's "Lark Ascending" evoked lovely writings.

The Different

The tree of attention is being held.
The women of life are playing their violins and flutes in soft notes.
A flower bud with golden wings flies beneath the sky.
A world with different figures will all come to an end.

Heidi Papworth

K.M.C.

Kolliding on the air
Making metamorphic snow
Collisions on the ground spring up.

Kinds of different animals
Make magic fill the air as hope will rise.
Collecting and catching all they can as more and more fall.

Kittens purring heal the wounds
marching soldiers lose their sighs,
Children will soon leave their stage.

Kicking, shoving are just memories now,
Melodies are hummed again
Christ has reborn himself.

Katie Cox

The children were opening their eyes to other ways of seeing—ways that allowed them to know without knowing how they know. The tolerance for ambiguity carried over into other areas. In mathematics, the children showed less frustration in problem solving as their minds were better able to hold the complexities of a problem for longer periods of time. Examining problems from different perspectives, their thinking became more divergent.

The children were developing a language of images, metaphors, and analogies to understand and be understood by each other. *P.O.V.* (*point of view*) became a buzzword, so that in resolving playground differences, one child could be heard saying to another, "Well, I wouldn't worry about Sam—that's just his P.O.V. and yours is different."

One little girl reacted to my lesson on perimeter and area by writing in her composition book, as I was drawing rectangles, this poem:

Perimeter

Perimeter! Perimeter! What the heck's a perimeter?
Is it a noun? Is it brown? Does it even live in this town?
Oh! I guess I know, it's a line that goes around everything!

Stephanie Crist

When the children quoted from their classmates' poems as examples during our lessons, they were not only listening to each other's diverse voices, they were hearing them. They were understanding, too, how their own voices are distinct from others. The question most often asked a writer was "How did you go about writing this piece?" Metacognition prompted Nick, one of two brothers in our class to comment, "Hmmm, you know how Billy [his twin] draws pictures first and then just writes his poem really fast? Well, I gotta have lots of words before I can write. So I make long lists, then I go back and see which things sound right together and after a couple days I see if I like my poem . . . it's hard to know when it's done."

And so Nick, who takes great delight in methodically putting disjointed things together, wrote:

A World of Shaded Colors

A world of shaded colors,
A world of different minds,
A night with a bitter sound,
    How can this place be bound?
    With bitter minds or mighty tines?
    Shouldn't this place be found?

A world of silvery waves,
A world with orange mountains,
A river with purple sea,

And a bear with golden caves,
Whither or not Thy is Thee,
    When will this place be main?
    I wonder—by black roses and magenta skies
    And how would blue trees sound?

                    Nick Ferrin

Nick's brother Billy possesses quick impulsive energy. He wrote in five minutes:

When Pigs Fly

Black crows fly as if they were golden
and pigs on them as passengers
and a rottweiler on elephant's tusks
lays as if you were laying at the face of the ceiling
and the elephants have the pants legs of a person
and a wild animal's colors
as bright as the sun.

              Billy Ferrin

In late spring Terry Hermsen, a poet with the Ohio Arts Council and one of the faculty at The Experience of Writing, came to spend two days with us. Terry asked the children to write poems using metaphor to show what their poems meant to them.

What Poems Are Like

My poems are taking a step.
My poems are the easiest thing to do.
My poems are old, my poems are new.
I keep my poems in a net.
I keep them tight,
I make them bright,
I don't let them go.

Kunal Gupta

During another exercise Terry asked the children to choose a person and write surprising, outlandish lines about them. This activity produced several fine pieces, one of which Billy wrote about his older brother, Ryan. The reference in the next-to-last line, drawn from our study of the color wheel, revealed a wonderful surprise for Billy, Nick, and the class.

My Brother

My brother
singing row row row your boat
holding a feather over my foot
with some hot coal in his hand not even yelling

My brother
sleepwalking into my room
trying to open the wall as opening a door

My brother
walking in the window, on the roof
not responding to anybody and down the chimney.

My brother
yelling! and screaming!
You want no I want no—until we tape his mouth shut.

My brother
running around screaming
with markers in his hands paint on the walls,
paint on the walls, colors of the warm family
all over the walls.

By April the writing voices in our class were so recognizable that children would say, "That sounds like Joey" or "That's Becky's." Some children were serious and used an economy of words, some liked strong rhythm, some humor.

Talking

Talking, talking is all I do,
talking, talking, I'm talking to you.
I'm going on and on that's nothing new.
Talking at night, talking all morning,
talking 24 hours through the day.
Do I have anything else to say?
I've said everything,
I guess I'm a pest,
but talking is what I do best.

Danielle Schrider

You Won't Die Unless You Sigh

You fall but never die unless you sigh I wish to die. You fly like a
    fly but
you get swatted. You won't die unless you sigh what a stupid guy.
You spy
on a fly but you get caught and swat—you won't die unless you
    sigh, I wish
I was in the parking lot.

Joey VanHassel

Canyon of the Wolves

Canyon covered in snow
gray figures racing around the rocks,
dashing after one another.
Soon a tall brown creature enters the canyon.
One of the figures pounced on the deer.
This canyon is ruled by wolves.

Kele Waaland

In the spring we celebrated our work with the First-Ever-and-Hope-fully-Not-Only Poetry Reading. We arranged our desks as tables and covered them with pink and yellow paper. A few mothers baked cookies. I brought the punch. Jacob's mother brought the lamp from her living room. With Jacob's lamp as spotlight and my kitchen stool as stage, we read to fifty-some mothers, fathers, and grandparents. One by one the children stepped into the light, held the microphone, and read. With their words dancing off the walls of the room, several parents cried.

When one mother asked Alan if the class got ideas for poems from one another, he replied, "Well you see, we're a whole—a big giant WHOLE puzzle and each person is like a piece of the puzzle—everybody's different but everybody fits and you can't see the picture unless all the pieces are there and when Ryan left—he moved to Pickerington—he left a BIG hole but his shape is still here and we remember him. So to answer your question, yes . . . of course we do."

Alan is extraordinarily bright, and his eccentricities are sometimes misunderstood by his classmates. Yet, at that moment, I knew the irregularities of each of us are what binds us together, our differences causing us to fit snugly one to the other. Without these differences, we'd slide apart, slip off the surface and be lost.

The work the children read was honest. That night they revealed their obsessions—eight-year-old obsessions about loss of friends and death and loneliness. They acknowledged fear and spoke of acceptance, empathy and love.

Flower

Flower,
when I last saw you,
you had all your petals on you.
But now someone cried and you lost a petal.
But I still like you
just the way you are.

Becky Thomas

The Lonely Flower

Oh lonely flower,
what shall I plant beside you?
A lily? A tulip? A dandelion?
What's your choice, flower?
Mine is a friend like you.
Plant your love beside me and I'll plant mine.

Mark Yurina

Leaf

Oh leaf what is it like to hang from a tree?
What is it like to be trampled by feet?
How do you find your way to the ground?
For you have no eyes and make no sound.

Eric Echbach

By June all of us realized what we had become, and while bread and fruit molds grew in our classroom, we stumbled upon a metaphor to carry us through endings into beginnings. Returning to where we had started—Wilder Woods—we stopped before Eric's broken-down dead tree. The rotting log was crumbling. Soaked with rain water; filled with ants, termites, and other insect larvae; invaded by the mycelium of fungi, the log waited for us. The children's initial reaction was the same as their first reaction to the growth of mold spores: "Yuk!" Then they saw what was taking place inside the log.

Within its dark damp interior, life was at work taking apart a structure no longer useful, no longer able to function as once it did. Decomposition was converting energy into food needed by the seedlings and animal life that would come the following spring.

We returned to our room to view Andrew Wyeth's "Man on a Log." Sensing the inevitable, the children let their feelings about endings emerge:

Man on a Log

An old man trying to get away from his thoughts, his feelings, his life, sits in a rotting meadow sad and lonely with hands outstretched.

Your long face turns and for the first time I see the sadness in your eyes.

                                        Alison Wagner

Log

An old man
on a high
hill—

—old, poor,
homeless. A log
is becoming his friend—

—way out there
is something
or someone
coming to get
him.

An old road
he's looking at—
way out there.

The old log,

There is fungus on it—

—the log is
home for an
old man

                    Mark Yurina

We March

Everyone lay still then the music starts, soft and slow, then
louder, and louder
    a man in a coat unlike any others steps up.
    Many animals follow behind him.
Soon people start to follow him past the heavens, past Life and

Death where the fabric of life lay torn and ragged.
　　Soon they walk on top of it, mending it, healing broken
hearts and soothing wounds the world has rejoined.

　　　　　　　　　　　　　　　　　Alan Klick

Back in January, in response to a request for the children to select
five words from their spelling test and write a paragraph using the selected words, Brian asked if he could write a poem. What he wrote was
an enigmatic line that intrigued everyone for the remainder of the year.
None of us was more puzzled than Brian.

"Abandon the candy before it pops in a book on a page called
'die,'" became a favorite refrain whenever we met something we didn't
understand. So on the last day of school when rain altered our plans to
return to the stream and disperse parting words into moving water, it was
no surprise when Brian's hand shot up from his desk. "Mrs. Titus! Mrs.
Titus! I've got it! I know what it is!"

"What, Brian?" I asked. "You know what *what* is?"

"The words. 'Abandon the candy.' I know what they mean."

And at that moment Brian's eye reflected what surely seemed to
be the admiration of the entire world as he proclaimed, "The candy is
the idea—I put it into words before it pops—I leave it alone to live—and
then just like we said—our work isn't ours anymore—to us it dies, but
still it is alive."

Although some of the poems the children wrote are stronger, tech-
nically better than others, that was not the criteria for selection in this
article. I hope that the poems represented here give the reader a sense
of the many voices singing at once different songs in different rhythms,
but making this class a community. Whatever happened this year was
wonderful. I trust it will happen again. I know that whenever spirit moves,
children sing.

Appendix I

The children of this essay have come and gone. Another class took their seats.
The new class was very different: more than half were identified with special
needs. The new group was as argumentative with each other as the previous class
was cohesive. As a group they were less verbal and had a difficult time with Blake
and Dickinson. I taught metaphor and analogy in an intentional way. We worked
on revision in narrative writing, eliminating the unnecessary as I had learned
from author Lori Segal during the summer institute of 1993. Three elements
remained the same, however: the music, the silence, and letting go of control.
Following are a few examples of the work these children produced:

Morning Singers

Morning singers hiding
where you cannot see.
Copycat singers
oh where can they be.
The music comes from the west
and it comes from the east.
It gets cloudy.

All the morning singers hide.
Then all you would hear
is the ripple of the water.

                    Kevin Staats

Open Your Eyes

Open your eyes
Smell the rose
Go barefoot on your toes
Hear them blooming from their bed
Watch the world turn on its head.

                    Nichole Stambaugh

Twilight

By and by
the sun will go
knitting the light
to darkness.

          Britni Karst

Shattered Words

The shattered words are read by shattered mirrors. The shattered words lay shattered in the mind's eye. The shattered words trick us by shattering our hearts to sadness. The shattered words invite the sun to darkness.

                    Daniel Riquino

WindStrike

Stars are dancing this very night. Whirlwind curly Q's shout out their fireworks. Darkness in every way. Crooked hills and mountains. Dancing candlelight bombs its way to night. Music walks its way home and tells it goodnight. Rocking cabins creek till old. With the crayon-colored night and star-painted light, Everything and All, will be alright.

                    Rob Wiggins

Dreaminate

Dreaminate the path that leads you to a star. Up upon it you sit, yelling with no fear. Tie the twisted rope, tying it to a star, and

then to the night. When I am not in fright, I'll swoop
and sweep and dance and prance. Over the Atlantic and Pacific.
And spin around three more times and dreaminate.

Rob Wiggins

Appendix II

After working with Terry Hermsen during the 1994 institute, I pursued revision techniques with the children. We investigated line breaks, lively verbs, titles, and central metaphors—areas addressed in my own writing. We read William Carlos Williams, D. H. Lawrence, and Gerard Manley Hopkins. Still the music, the silence, and a new element: morning pages as described in Julia Cameron's *The Artist's Way*. This two-week experiment with a daily fifteen-minute unstructured writing period yielded exciting work:

My Head

All the stuff inside my head
won't come to a stop.
It seems like I lost the key
and now all the good ideas
are plunging out the back
too fast for me to know
so I'm writing
whatever I can catch in my net . . .

Andy Foley

Something to Put Down
Like a Red Wheel Barrow
(with thanks to William Carlos Williams)

so much depends on a
red wheel
barrow glazed
with rain water
beside the white
chickens
like grain
rocks
an old woman pushing
it up the mountain
when when
when
when will she
put
down
the red
wheeeeeeeelbaarooooooooww?

Evan Spurrell

Under the Sea

things swim
and
things walk
and things steal
the flesh from others

nothing survives
the horrifying
thing
called shark
but
if it wasn't for shark,
night
would last forever.

Chris Roebuck

Working

He wiggles
his fingers across
the keyboard like
a spider
walking across
its web
going to get
its prey

my dad
just sits there
hypnotized
his eyes
glued
to the computer.

Chris Roebuck

Lasers

People climbing like
purple moonbeams in the night.
Ropes like lasers.
Necklace sparkling like
soda in a glass.

Mountains in the light.

Matt Cullinan

The City That Swims

Dappled fish
    Or couple-color
Floating, crawling

who knows the color
color?
Xanadu the
city that swims.

Tiffany Price

The Banjo Lesson

They sang a sorrow song
faith blows away
forgiveness blows in
times ago their heartship awaits
dreams await
the banjo tries to find the key
gloomy sunlight shines in
unlocking unknowing
dreams are free

Erica Johnson

Understand

Understand:
when you know a math problem and
figure it out right away.

when your mom knows how you feel inside

when you hear what someone inside of you
is saying

when dreams get caught
and you understand they can't get out

Erica Johnson

Desert Lions

In the baking sand
a pride of lions observing
vultures flying overhead
a land of drought becomes
Tanzania
Tanzania
Tanzania

Evan Spurrell

The light
is like God
raising His spirited hand and saying
"Peace be on my golden shelled earth.
Love goes around one by one
and the rainbow is my eye."

Brandi Cade

Sudden Revelation: Fiction Writing in the Classroom

Carl H. Krauskopf III

Sudden revelation is the stuff of which everything is made, from soap operas to scripture. The Ohio Arts Council/Wright State University program at Antioch College during the summers of 1992 and 1993 was, for me, closer to the scriptural: The Experience of Writing has helped me improve not just how I teach writing but how I deal with students. This experience has helped me change who I am.

Big claims, eh? Well, in Yellow Springs I met some people who can say more about daily teaching than even they realize. One evening Chris Merrill said of my guru for the week and influence for as long as I teach, "Ron Carlson is the kind of writer who, if he can't make things better, at least will bear witness to them with style and dignity." In some enlightened place, that is the definition of "teacher." We try in every class to make things better. When direct sermonizing isn't the best course to take, we hope that our style of presentation will lend dignity to the point in question, be that point one of punctuation or one of clever imagery, be it one of characterization or one of political awareness.

When that works, we are truly teachers, for then we have students taking the point seriously because they believe it matters to know things instead of because there is going to be a test on it later. You don't need me to tell you that the stress level of teaching for a living—and I'm trusting that you teach for a living and not simply to pay your bills—abates considerably when our kids believe in what we are trying to do together.

One of the most rewarding moments of a recent school year involved a tenth grader telling me that one of her classmates "has better imagery than Sophocles." Okay, okay, that wouldn't take much, since we read Sophocles in translation, but my point is that here was a student so excited about another's writing that it became a class discussion about nonvisual sensory imagery. The discussion lasted two days of class, and it occurred *before* the assignment was due, so all students in the class had time—and most took the time—to reevaluate their use of imagery and to feel better about the fiction they were writing. It is, after all, the wrestling match, the process of writing, critiquing, and rewriting, that does the teaching. It is not the final grade that teaches.

Speaking of grading, however, one of the biggest barriers we build for ourselves as teachers is composed of a few words: "How do I assign a score to creative writing?" Should mechanics count? Yes, but we have to be attuned to manipulation of language for positive effect. Should a certain style be taught? Yes, but we have to be aware that the goal of the process is the growth of the students' own styles. As Lore Segal said during my second summer at Antioch, "If you get something back that doesn't fulfill the assignment but is beautiful, celebrate!"

So what could that assignment be? I have had success requiring a piece of prose of at least one thousand words to be constructed over the course of one week. This is to include at least one time manipulation: flashback to suspend time, as in "I remembered the time when Sarah . . ."; time compression, as in "The next time I saw Sarah was nearly a year later . . ."; or time expansion, as in "I felt like I was seeing Sarah clearly for the first time. . . ."

I also ask for at least one sensory image (a simile will do, but lots of kids will go beyond that) for each of the senses. You'll enjoy watching the struggle to come up with nonvisual images that say what the young writer wants to say—that "just right" phrase. Oh, and you may want to make clichés off limits. One of the by-products of this exercise is that some of your kids will thank you for helping them notice more about the world in which they live: good, bad, and neutral odors, a wider variety of tactile impressions, noises and flavors that carry emotional impact—all imaginable combinations of the above. These are all things kids already know, but there is a serene magic in seeing them find out that they know. It's that magic that wakes me up and gets me to work every morning. Probably you, too, if you're still reading this.

Time for a digression, lest you think there is too much rose tint in my glasses. For eighteen years I taught English at Northmont High School without teaching creative writing. All graded papers were expository, and creative writing was an extra-credit assignment at the end of each quarter of a year-long course. I didn't think I could evaluate, let alone teach, fiction writing. I was wrong. For three years now my kids have taught me how wrong I was. Expository writing, a major focus of my district's curriculum, improves after we write our short stories. So do reading skills, especially attention to an author's word choice—gee, I guess that's why we write fiction before we study Shakespeare, eh? Also improved are class discussion behaviors as the kids discover each other's gifts, in what areas their peers are open to suggestion, in what areas their peers will not be influenced. Life skills all, wouldn't you say? Rather like talking?

Speaking of talking, do you hear *how* people talk as well as *what* they say? And how many levels of what they mean do you hear in what they say? Of course you do, and at least several, right? These skills can be taught when you require dialogue in your students' short fiction. In the writing process, kids will read dialogue to each other, as if it were a play script, and they will tell each other, "Nobody really talks like that," or words to that effect, and learning will begin: learning to listen to others more perceptively so we can write it more realistically. Truly listening fits nicely on that list of life skills.

So how do we get started? How about asking for two hundred words on day one, at least one third of them dialogue, involving two characters in a single setting? How about the next day asking for volunteers to read and a feedback lesson? Always start the feedback session with applause for the reader. It takes courage to read your own stuff. If you don't believe me, do the assignment with your kids, but never read your own stuff first. Never. Oh, yeah, and if you think you're the best writer in your class, give up that attitude. Forever, if possible, but at least for the duration of this assignment.

Onward: at the end of day two (initial reading and responses), ask for time manipulation if it's not already in the first-step assignment, and ask for a change in point of view (take the first person out and see if the story changes) if you think it would help the young author free up more possibilities. Some of us tend to write nonfiction if we let ourselves into our fiction.

On day three, work on characterization nuances to sharpen dialogue. Remind your kids how much we say with our bodies, and let them struggle with how to put that down in words. Remind them of the fact that what we wear—clothes, jewelry, and other accessories—says a lot about who we are. So does how we interact with these objects. Remind them also that rewriting is often more painful than writing. Most of us like to believe that we do things right the first time. Ask them to add four or five touches of body language to their growing stories. Some will say, "Well, that means I have to start over." Consider smiling as you respond, "That's okay, if it's true, but you may find that what you've already written demands to be in your story. It's all a process." Again a life skill, seeing our work as a process.

Writing fiction isn't imitating life, it's being alive. Simply look into the eyes of your students during the feedback sessions, which may become heated while still being positive, and you'll know it's true: writing is living.

On day four, after more reading and response, ask for the sensory imagery discussed earlier. By now you have had the opportunity to comment on imagery that came naturally to the kids in the earlier stages. Keep reminding your students that not everyone will be good at each task (the tension of plot, dialogue, setting, time manipulation, characterization, imagery), but everyone must attempt each task as a basic requirement of the total assignment. Heck, tell them they're guaranteed at least a C if they try each one. Tell them to mark in the margin where they think they've accomplished a special olfactory, tactile, visual, saporous, and auditory image. Tell them to mark what they think is an effective time manipulation, mark what they think is the best sentence in the whole story, mark their favorite sentence. Be prepared for the "favorite sentence" mark to be the one with the off-color language in it. This too will pass.

Let them have day five to read to each other and trade ideas. Drop in on reading groups and say what you have to say. This is also a good time to remind your students that clean copy (grammar, spelling, punctuation, and neatness) makes for a better read, a more enjoyable piece of writing.

Then step back, give them the weekend to come up with a final copy in the format of your choice, and wait to see what you get.

I cannot stress enough the importance of small interactive groups and reading/feedback time in this process, but that doesn't mean you need to schedule daily classtime for such. Use your classtime to present each new task and offer examples. We have found that, once the tone of positive interaction is set on day two of the project, kids get together (and help each other become better writers) on their own time. Well, okay, what we've really found is that parents proudly complain that their kids are reading entire short stories to each other over the phone at strange hours of the night.

Uh, gee, that's what I'd call a successful assignment. When writing and sharing original writing becomes as popular as teenage gossip, maybe it's because there's no difference: both are fiction, and both are very real.

Try an assignment such as the one very vaguely outlined above, and trust yourself to know what to say when you know you must say something. Trust yourself also to know when not to say, but when to ask, "What if . . .?" What if the phone rang just as he mustered the courage to say what she thought he'd never say? What if none of the characters know what's really happening in the scene? Whoa, just like real life, eh? Obviously, it's fiction, so the possibilities are endless. What if one of the characters has superpowers?

Did I catch you by surprise there? Your kids will surprise you, too. You'll read science fiction from the young woman from whom you would have expected romance. You'll get autobiographical fiction, too, and that is also helpful for the young writer. You'll read some things you may wish you hadn't read, learn things you may wish you hadn't learned.

When the process is completed, though, you'll fall asleep one night knowing that a lot of young people benefited from your decision to require and then help create a piece of writing involving plot, characterization, dialogue, setting, time manipulation, imagery, and clean copy.

Try it, wrestle with it, and then smile about it. For some of you, as it is for me, the experience of writing fiction with your kids will be a sudden revelation.

A Year of Writing Workshop

Mary L. Noble

The Beginning: The Experience of Writing Workshop

It all began one day in the faculty dining room when I mentioned I was considering taking The Experience of Writing that summer. After I explained the program, a colleague of mine said, "Not me. That sounds too intense."

I replied, "I've decided I've got to be willing to do what I ask of my students. Besides, the cost and credit hours are too good to pass up."

Bright and early Monday morning that same colleague stuck her head in my classroom door and said with a grin, "Okay, you made me feel guilty. I've decided to take the workshop too." And so began the best workshop we've attended in years—and both of us have been happy about it ever since.

The week that I spent at Antioch that summer was incredibly intense. We wrote and discussed writing from early morning to late evening. We met with our small writing group every day, chose a new writing area to explore in the afternoon, and attended evening sessions with the workshop leaders where they read and talked about their own writing. We completed writing exercises structured by the published authors leading the small groups, and we all got over the anxiety of reading to others pretty quickly. Through their writing, I probably learned more about some of the people in my small group sessions than I know about friends I've had for years.

I frequently found myself writing far into the night because something was important to me to complete. I wrote about my father who had died ten years earlier, and dealt with the death in a whole new way. I studied strangers downtown in Yellow Springs to write a description of an activity, and developed an obsession to do a series of vignettes which would characterize the feel of the town. After an interview exercise, I wrote a character sketch and the woman involved asked me for a copy. She felt it had helped her understand something about herself a little better, and she wanted to reread it occasionally. By the end of the week, I found I really *wanted* others to read what I'd written. I was thoroughly exhausted, and yet it had been one of the best "vacations" I'd given myself in a long time. In reflecting on my experience on the last day of the workshop, I wrote:

> That first night
> I fell into it
> my prose became a poem
> emerging on the page
> took on a life of its own
> and led me where it would
>
> From that point on
> Trust
>
> Each new piece
> had taken me either
> forward or back,
> it makes no difference.
>
> Compassion, empathy, awe
> photographer, spendthrift, voyeur
> it makes no difference.
> They all are me
> and the most important me
> has reemerged

I went back to school that fall determined to convey some of that excitement to my students. Had this experience really changed my teaching? I knew it had when one of my students looked up at me about the third week of the school year and said, "Are you *sure* you're the same teacher I had last year?"

Planning the Writing Process

When I sat down to plan a change in my writing program, I isolated the aspects of the workshop I valued most and tried to translate them into student activities:

1. I'd laughed and cried at essays written by myself and other workshop participants, so meaningful content for students was important. This would come from exercises, freewrites, and modeling.

2. When one piece went absolutely "dead" on me, I was thankful I could drop it for something which was working. Therefore, students needed more "idea writes" than the required finished pieces.

3. I'd learned that some pieces just wanted to make themselves into poems even when nonfiction was expected, so students would occasionally need flexibility in choosing their genre.

4. Group readings and critiques were helpful once the initial fear faded. Students would need to work in cooperative writing groups for revision.

5. When I finished typing and assembling a portfolio of final pieces to submit at the end of the course, the feeling of accomplishment was wonderful. In my classes, we would move to a quarter system of drafts, revisions, and a quarterly portfolio of the students' best work.

6. I really enjoyed final publication of a class book with contributions from everyone. It was important for someone besides me to read the students' work; therefore, each student would contribute something to a book the class would publish at the end of the year.

The next step was to decide what other skills I wanted my students to practice. I added the following:

7. I believed reflection on their writing strengths and weaknesses, an assessment of their progress, and personal goal setting were important to the process. We would have an initial goal-setting conference at the end of the first quarter, a second conference at the end of the year, and students would be required to write a creative reflection to include in the final portfolio.

8. Students needed to develop computer and word-processing skills even though we had no computer lab for the department. They would receive bonus points for drafts and portfolios completed on word processors.

9. We would take a whole language approach to literature. Students would use their literature selections to write both literary analysis papers and personal essays. When possible we would also use our literature as a writing model.

10. I wanted real revision of their work, not just proofreading for errors in mechanics and usage. We would do our writing in three stages: (1) content/idea/message, (2) genre/organization, and (3) presentation/publication. At each stage, I would grade ONLY the goal of that stage. All portfolio pieces would have a minimum of three drafts, one for each of these stages.

A Year in the Classroom

Content/Ideas: "What do you think, feel, know, remember?"

To get students started with good material, we did two to three freewrites and/or exercises per week. These fell into several categories—one was a personal application of something from the current piece of literature; one was frequently focused around a writing technique, such as descriptive detail; and, sometimes, we'd take a current issue and respond to it.

As we worked our way into this process, I noticed some confusion among the students. What were they really supposed to do? I knew they were finally understanding when Michelle told me one day, "I was confused at first, but now the thing I like the best are the freewrites. I really feel 'free.' I can write anything in the world and get points for it. If it's great, fine. If it's a disaster, it really doesn't matter because I know we'll do lots more. The curious thing is that most of them do work."

I knew they were developing some real interest in their writing when Molly came up to my desk one day and asked to continue writing, "The rest of the period is reading time, and you know I'll read my assignment. This topic has taken over my mind; it needs to be written NOW." The next day she handed me a four-page freewrite and explained plans for the essay it would become. Concentrating on only ideas in the first stage was working.

Grading these was quite easy since they got ten points per page, and if students finished more than one page they could earn bonus points. This encouraged them to keep writing the entire time, even if they wandered off the topic, since the idea was for the students to get material which mattered to them.

Genre/Organization: "What's the best way to get this point across?"

About once every one to one-and-one-half weeks, we had writing workshop. Depending on the need, this would last for one, two, or even three days. In this workshop at least one of the freewrites from the previous week was taken to the draft stage. In order to establish a theme, when the students had made their selection they wrote a one-sentence answer to the question, "What's the point of this composition?" The first time I asked them to do this, someone actually blurted out, "You mean there's supposed to be a *point?*" Everyone laughed, but I could tell many others' initial reaction had been the same. They'd never applied the concept of theme beyond the literature they read. We then went on to a mini-lesson on organization which was applied in this draft. Sometimes a specific genre was required and, occasionally, genre was their choice with a reminder about what was required for the quarter portfolio.

When each student had a draft, we assembled in writing groups to help each other. Students needed specific guidelines for these sessions or their remarks were not very helpful. They were required to read their pieces aloud. One day as I circulated, I overheard Charlene tell her group,

"I'm changing this right now as I read it because I can 'hear' what's wrong with it. Isn't that strange?"

On another day Jason told me, "I never thought I'd say this when you first told us we'd have to read our papers to others in groups. I was scared silly, and my voice shook the first time; but now it's something I look forward to. I've helped other people with their ideas, and they've helped me. I was so afraid people would laugh at my essays; but by second quarter we realized everybody is in the same boat, and we don't dare laugh at something that isn't meant to be funny." I was finding these students helped each other as much as I helped them.

Grading of these rough drafts was only on the organizational goal of the mini-lesson. This grading was really quite fast since I had them line off or highlight sections of the paper and label what they *thought* they'd done in the left margin.

The benefits of this grading system became obvious from Sam's comment in his semester evaluation, "At first I was nervous about grading because if spelling and sentence fragments didn't matter on freewrites and rough drafts, then WHAT DID? Now I notice that I really can pay more attention to WHAT I'M SAYING without having to worry about my atrocious spelling. It's nice to get a good grade on my organization draft even if my final spelling errors drop the portfolio grade." I had found a way to get them to concentrate on revising for one major aspect at a time.

Presentation/Publication: "Does all that grammar stuff and the way the paper looks REALLY matter?"

The last stage was the portfolio, which was due at the beginning of the eighth week of each quarter. There were specific requirements for each quarter's portfolio, such as one five-paragraph essay, one poem, one narrative essay, and any student choices to equal five to eight typed pages. Students were not required to polish all pieces they had attempted as long as they met all these requirements. Assignments had been structured so that they had at least one draft of each requirement. The week before the due date we really concentrated on presentation. This included things like neatness, margins, title pages, author reflections, table of contents, covers, illustrations, and GRAMMAR and MECHANICS. For these we had a mini-lesson each day, and then did proofreading and corrections in writing groups. In his reflection at the end of the year, John commented, "I really hated all that polishing of papers the weekend before portfolios were due, but when they were done I was so proud that my papers looked as good as they read. I'm making a spot on my bookshelf for this book along with my other favorite books." An unexpected plus for me as the teacher grading these portfolios was that I noticed that mechanics and usage were actually better than I was used to getting on finished papers.

The portfolios took longer to grade; however, I found myself enjoying them. Almost every student had at least one really good example that I could comment on. I laughed aloud at several humorous essays such as Rob's character sketch of his younger brother. I found tears in my eyes as I read Jessica's wistful poem about her aging grandmother.

I used a rubric for these, but also started out marking and writing comments on each until one day my own daughter laid out all her portfolio work for her own English teacher on the dining room table and disgustedly commented, "It all looks so nice typed and clean and white, and I hate it that she's going to ruin it with ugly red marks." I found many of my students agreed with her, so I confined myself to notations on the table of contents page.

By fourth quarter the portfolio was a book of the entire year's polished pieces along with a contribution to the class publication. I remember being concerned at the beginning of the year that this emphasis on creative writing would cut down on the scholarly papers we'd written before. As we assembled the whole year's papers, I found that all it did was increase the number of papers we wrote. I was also surprised that several students chose to contribute papers on *The Scarlet Letter* or *Julius Caesar* to the class publication. When I asked why, Tony replied, "I really enjoyed my creative papers, but these literary analysis ones have been a real struggle for two years. Even you thought this one was good, and I'm so proud of it I want others to read it."

An individual book/portfolio was the other part of publication. It contained a cover, title page, table of contents, introduction, and an "About the Author" section. As I read Lisa's introduction to her book, I was pleased to find this statement, "It seems sacrilegious to call myself an author. However, I've come to realize that I am one. I may not be as good as Hemingway or Fitzgerald yet, but that's just a matter of degree. I like calling myself an author."

The Second Year

I returned a second summer to The Experience of Writing, concentrating on the poetry section of the workshop and enjoying it just as much as I enjoyed the first summer. The second year I made some changes in my curriculum to fine tune it. In order to improve students' understanding of the writing process we were using, I began occasionally reading one of my own prewrites out loud to the class. I also took several things

I'd written, labeled the various stages of the writing process, and photocopied copies for an entire class. Studying these seemed to help. Finally, I took one topic and used it to write as many different types of writing as possible—research, expository essay, poetry, and a short story. This activity accomplished much more then I'd hoped for. Not only did they start understanding that prewrites could go in many different directions, they understood genre better, many of them started to understand theme better, and some students understood purpose and audience for the first time in their lives. Third quarter that year my juniors read novels of their own choosing. The students had to choose something controversial in the novel to write a persuasive essay on, something factual to report with dialogue, something in the book to use as a catalyst to write an entertaining article, and something to use as a basis for creative writing. Several students in both sections set themselves the challenges of using the same issue for all four pieces as I had done earlier.

The first year I'd been swamped with papers and grading. I quit trying to read every prewrite they wrote. They were just writing too much to do it anymore. When a student said, "You've got to read this one," I read it. If I wasn't asked I didn't, and none of them seemed to mind. Another change was that the only place I actually *marked* errors in mechanics was on two typed pages they could submit to me during the week we did final polishing for portfolios. It was up to them to apply this information to the rest of the pages. Eventually, several of my better students actually told me they didn't need this help, so it became optional. To make drafts much quicker for me to read, I became very creative in structuring editing/revision sessions with both the whole class and peer groups. We looked for things to highlight—generalizations in green, details in pink. In creative writing we glued stars next to the parts we loved, and put question marks next to things we weren't sure we understood. In literary analysis papers we developed checklists, boxed in and labeled what we found, and highlighted missing parts on the checklist. After these activities students were free to do another rewrite before they turned the draft in for an organization grade.

Reflections

It's been an exhausting but rewarding two years, and I find it's time to remind myself of a few things:

- I must make time to grade portfolios DURING CLASS TIME.
- My students' nonfiction and poetry improved when I began to write those genres. I'm tired of reading superficial short stories,

so I may have to return to the workshop a third summer and attempt some fiction.

- I will keep copies of the class books we've made filed with my own journal of comments about the last two years. When I get discouraged, some of the wonderful work in these should help me keep going.

- Every year I will reread the message in the letter I received last fall from a former student. In this letter Shaunna reminisced about several things she remembered about my class. She recounted in some detail an essay about my grandmother I read to the class, and a freewrite about the gardens at my home and how they reflected my writing philosophy. If I ever need encouragement to keep WRITING WITH my students and SHARING what I write, this will do it.

- Finally, when I begin to doubt that what I'm doing is worth all the effort, I'll read Michael's comment: "I was so confused at the beginning of this year I didn't know what I was doing. I've never written this way in my entire life, but I've written some good stuff this year. My Dad even asked to keep a copy of one poem. Now, I hate to think of going back to the other way again next year."

I hope he doesn't have to.

Word Works: Building a Community of Writers

Janice M. Gallagher

could see patches of blue sky among the gray clouds, and the air had just a touch of coolness. Looking out the windows of Barb Slater's closed-in porch, I noticed the trees tossing their leaves in the breeze— or were the leaves tossing the tree? Drops of rain began to fall, and I wondered if the falling drops caused the breeze. I heard a cardinal's song and thought that at the cardinal's command, the breeze blew, the leaves tossed and the rain danced. I smiled inwardly at myself remembering what I had heard Lucy Calkins say at a writing conference the week before. "Writing," she said, "makes us better observers and gives us a lens to respect the richness that is in our lives." Writing had definitely done that for me.

I waited quietly for the members of Word Works to gather. The writing group had begun meeting on the first Sunday of the month to share and discuss writing. The group had developed out of a need to write and to connect with others who were writing. Committing ourselves to the group allowed us to see ourselves as writers and to take writing seriously.

The first few meetings were held at the Wayne Center for the Arts, but we switched to the comfort and interruption-free sanctuary of Barb Slater's porch. We'd come prepared today to share our papers on "barely touching," the topic that we'd agreed upon the month before.

Barb Slater began the meeting by reading her paper. Barb's piece recounted learning the Palmer style of writing in grade school. Barb explained how her teacher had told the class that their hands should "barely touch" the pencil. She described trying to cope with fear during a writing assignment. As the students labored over their writing task, Barb's teacher marched up and down the aisles randomly pulling a pencil from a student's hand to see if the student's grip was too tight. Barb had been working on her memoirs, and this piece would be part of the chapter on school days. Tim's paper focused on his courting days. He described sensual butterfly kisses that his first love gave him, barely touching her eyelashes against his cheek. Alan's paper explored the strained relationship of a father and a daughter whose spirits barely touched.

After each writer read, other members made comments or suggestions. Sometimes the author asked for specific help with endings or beginnings. We moved on from one member to another in a gentle flow that included giving thanks for the suggestions and volunteering to read next.

As a Teacher

My writing life in Word Works was so different from my life as a teacher of writing. As a teacher of writing, I held the map and the destination for my students. Often, however, I found myself caught in the eddies and pools of correcting spelling, grammar, and mechanics. As a member of the writing group, I was not the main guide, but a collaborator. I was able to share writing with adults that I could not share with my seventh-grade or ninth- grade English classes. I had taken a twisting, meandering path to this writing group.

I began my teaching career in 1966 with six classes of below-average students. My principal, as a way of protecting me from disappointment and despair, had told me gently on my first day of teaching, "Don't set your expectations too high. If you teach them how to write a complete sentence, you will have done more than any teacher in their past ten years of public schooling."

Through the years that followed, I had struggled to help my students become writers. My most successful exercise involved combining writing with art. Often I had used an art activity as a prewriting experience. Students would create the art, and then write from it. Beginning the writing with an art start insured success for my junior high school students. They generated pieces of writing that they were proud of. Their enthusiasm for writing proved to me that I could get my students to put something on the paper, and I knew that was the first and most important step. Beyond that point in writing instruction, however, I found myself very uncertain.

The Experience of Writing Summer Institute

In the spring of 1991, I received a flyer about a week-long writing workshop. I wanted to learn how others taught writing. I longed to know more about improving my own writing, too. I sent in my tuition and I committed myself to the week-long Experience of Writing.

We enjoyed busy days on the campus of Antioch College. We attended classes led by the guest writers in the morning; we wrote in the afternoon and early evening; we ate supper together, and then we attended readings spotlighting a different visiting writer each night. The writers always saved time at the end of the readings for questions. The evening readings enhanced the instruction, and the instruction enhanced the readings.

The readings gave me insight. I learned about various genres, personal writing processes, and different ways that writers found motivation and inspiration. The most important thing I learned during the six days, however, was the value of having time to write and time to revise. I kept a journal during that week, and excerpts from it accurately detail how my thinking and learning about revision took shape.

Shortly before attending the institute, I had read Alice Walker's "Everyday Use," a short story about a quilt and the conflict between two sisters over which one should own the heirloom. On the first day of the Institute I had used Walker's story as a springboard for my own draft that centered on the important things my father had left me. In my journal I wrote:

> The discussions and even the brainstorming opened so many doors for me. Instead of helping me focus on any single area, the multitude of possibilities engulfed me. . . . I am frustrated with my first draft. I have written three different versions, and I am still not happy. I am filled with absolute dread thinking about sharing this non-intellectual paper. While the instructors are emphasizing process, I am concerned with product. It is important to me to write something meaningful. . . .

How often had I engaged my students in brainstorming as a prewriting activity, convinced that it would help them find a topic, and how often had it only added to their confusion? How much was I aware of their struggle to produce something "meaningful"? I was walking in different shoes as a student expected to produce writing to be shared and critiqued, and I was nervous about the whole thing.

I shared my first draft with a small group of fellow participants. Even though they all praised my writing, I was disappointed with their response. I received no criticism—no ideas to bounce around in my head. They told me they liked my writing, but I just wasn't happy with the piece.

Finally, in a one-to-one discussion of my paper, someone gave me the kind of criticism I was looking for.

"Who do you think you are?" Jack said to me. "You think you're so great because you don't sleep past seven o'clock in the morning? Does that mean the rest of us are lazy slobs? Your piece sounds too egotistical. You learned the joy of the early morning rising from your father, and you say that is your inheritance. A habit—a way of life—is what your father left you. That's fine as far as it goes, but you need to find a way to say that without insulting those of us who find joy in sleeping through the morning. And another thing: look at your verbs. Most of them are forms of the verb *be*."

I felt a mixture of gratitude and embarrassment. Pushing aside embarrassment, I asked for more guidance.

"What do you find interesting about what I've written?" I asked. "What do you like about the piece? Is it clear how important the inheritance from my father was to me?" I listened to his answers and then I went back to my room to revise the piece.

In my journal on the second day I wrote:

> For the first time in my life, I experience real revision. I rewrite one paragraph five times and each time it is different. I try to work my way through the entire paper, but as I write, new ideas come—new directions—new connections. My mind works faster than my pen. Before I know it, it is midnight. I decide to quit. I need just a quick shower to chase the sweat from my body. After the shower, however, my energy returns. I scrap the whole page at the end—and I try again. I read the thing over! It is vastly different from attempt number one. I am still not happy—but at least I know the gnawing is silent. . . . Suddenly, I understand the addicted writer's drive. It is NOT the need to pour out pent-up emotions. It is, instead, the thrill of possibilities—the opening of new worlds that occurs in the revision. Ah! Sweet Revision.

Had a student ever breathed these words, "Ah, Sweet Revision" in *my* English class? Had I ever structured my classes in such a way that allowed my students time for revision? Had I taken them through the path that leads to the doors of possibility? Had I allowed my students to select topics for their writing that were as important to them as this one was to me? Had my assignments demanded personal investment from my students? Had I read their papers with enough thoroughness to give them what Jack had given me, specific information for improvement?

While thoughts about my own classroom instruction swirled in my brain, I continued to work on my paper about my father. I had a title now, "Tracing the Pattern." The paper described, after all, the pattern of life that my father had left me and how I had traced that pattern. On the third day of the writing institute I wrote in my journal:

> I am beginning to like my paper. The subject is important and real to me. Even though we've been placing our emphasis on the process of writing, I know that the end-product is important to me. I am glad I have spent my time and effort working toward a good end-product. . . . I continue to be amazed at how important my writing has become to me.

I learned by doing that students must "ache with caring" (Mem Fox 1993) about their writing. I learned by doing that student-selected topics present the best opportunity for successful writing. Reflecting on my teaching, I realized that I had hit the target with my art activities as prewriting because the art had provided an immediate experience from which to write. I also realized, however, that I had not hit the bull's eye on the target. Creating the art first was kind of a "care-connector." My students liked to write. I knew, however, that on proficiency tests, AP tests, and college placement tests, my students would not be able to create art before they wrote.

Part of my journal entry on the fourth day of the institute reads:

> The paper's in its "final form." Already as I review for typo's, I see things I would like to change. I ask my sixteen-year-old daughter to proofread it, and she pays me the highest compliment possible. She asks for a copy to keep.

Her appreciation of what I'd written thrilled me. I intended the paper as a record of what my father had left me. My secret wish had been to influence my children's lives the way my father had influenced mine. What my father had left me, and what I wanted to leave my children seemed more valuable to me than an object, like the quilt in Walker's story. A pattern for living would not wear away with everyday use.

> My daughter's praise surely feels good, but the real success is my understanding of the writing process and the place in that process for revision . . . my time in the writing process will be different for my students next year! I will spend more time in conferencing and more in intervention. I will spend less time writing comments, less time correcting spelling and mechanics. I will spend time discussing peer revision. I will encourage more peer revising instead of peer editing. I will remember that my goal is not to have students produce a boring, error-free paper, but a developed or developing process of thinking and writing.

> Most of all, I have learned that the little worksheets on creative problem-solving and critical thinking skills are frills. The real backbone of critical thinking and creative problem-solving can be done with writing AND the students will be enriched with a lifelong skill, instead of a finished worksheet—or worse yet—a totally unrelated project.

My journal entries contained only my thoughts about changes I wanted to make as a teacher of writing. I did not keep a journal of thoughts of myself as I developed as a writer. Just the same, a major change occurred in me at the Institute. I had absorbed the words of James Thomas, co-director of the writing institute, who said, "The best teacher of writing is the one who takes his/her own writing seriously." For the first time in my life, I was doing just that, and I was beginning to see myself as a "real" writer.

I wrote other pieces during the week that were just as important to me as the one I wrote about my father. I had written one about a student who came to me in an hour of need, and another about a student who treated a teacher with disrespect. I turned the pieces in for comments from the guest writers. The response I received from the visiting writers gave me direction for improvement, and served as a model for the kinds of criticism all writers need and deserve. Bob Fox, co-director of the Institute and writer-in-residence for the Ohio Arts Council, commented on the paper I'd written about a student who came to me in a time of need:

> I'll start with "Into the Night." It's gorgeously written. The imagery in the first paragraph is strong and confident—the nest, the stained glass lamp by the bed. The subsequent imagery is also strong—the frozen tracks of the sleet on the window, as an example. The cumulative details are also very telling. I find this piece unresolved, though. It needs not a neat wrap up, but some sort of conclusion even if only in the narrator's mind. I think that what might be preventing the conclusion is that there are really two stories here: the narrator's marriage as well as Eric's fate. The counterpoint of the husband sleeping in "undisturbed bliss" and the discovery of the article on how to keep a wife satisfied create a dual plot. Maybe this is a story you don't want to tell. It starts to add depth to Eric's story, but then neither is resolved. I hope you can get back into this and come to a resolution, for the writing is otherwise suspenseful and authoritative.

In class Pamela Painter had said, "A writer gives herself a gift when she uses detail." By the same token, Bob Fox had given me a gift when he used detail in his criticism. He did not stop with the general comment, but told me specifically what contributed to the writing's being "gorgeously written." Bob did not give me a generic criticism like "needs development" or "lacks resolution." Instead, he explained the problems in my writing. Most of all, Bob Fox took my work seriously, even suggesting at the end of the review where I might send the pieces for publishing consideration. I tucked the model away in my mind to use with my students.

When I returned to my classroom, I was determined to present opportunities to my students that mirrored the experiences I had enjoyed at the writing institute. I knew I wanted to teach writing much differently from the way I had taught in the past. I would allow my students to select their own writing topics instead of using the pre-packaged story starters from the commercial black-line masters, which were external and didn't come from the students' concerns. I would teach conferencing and I would give up the proofreader's correction marks.

Teachers as Writers

When I returned to my classroom in the fall of 1991, I discovered that three teachers in my district had attended a writing workshop. They, too, were excited about improving themselves as writers and teachers of writing. We agreed to meet to share what we had learned over the summer. We called our group "Teachers as Writers." In addition to books by Lucy Calkins, we began to read and discuss Donald Graves and his use of day books. We reminded ourselves to write to be surprised as Donald Murray advocated, and we discussed the importance that Regie Routman placed on publishing student works. In our classrooms we tried dialogue journals advocated by Nancie Atwell. The best thing about Teachers as Writers, however, was not studying theorists and practitioners. We began to write and critique each other's work.

Teachers as Writers met after school one night a month. Seated around a table in the school cafeteria, the meetings usually began with a discussion of our progress as teachers of writing. During the second part of the meeting participants shared journal entries or free writing they'd done. Others shared pieces based on a topic we'd chosen.

We were all beginning writers, and we were hesitant critics. Each of us sensed how important and personal writing could be. We treated each other gently, and like beginning teachers of writing, we corrected each other's grammar, called attention to usage of passive voice, and made suggestions for possible word choices.

Only after we had developed a level of trust were we able to say things like, "Your piece would be stronger in the child's voice" or "What about starting your piece with the ending?" Even after receiving such criticism, few members of Teachers as Writers revised their pieces. For now, what seemed to be important to us was writing and the community that the sharing of the writing offered.

My interaction in Teachers as Writers taught me the value of building a community of writers. What I had learned at the Institute about the importance of reading your work out loud to an audience, I transferred to the group. From my own writing and from the writing of other members in that group I recognized again the power of sharing writing.

Developing Lifelong Writers

I continued as a member of Teachers as Writers even after I began working on a Ph.D. in English Instruction. Early in my program I committed myself to writing a dissertation that examined how individuals developed into lifelong writers. I originally thought that I would study the members of Teachers as Writers and explore how membership in a writing group influenced effectiveness and success as teachers of writing. The course work was demanding, however, and I was forced to give up my participation in Teachers as Writers. I changed the topic of the dissertation to *Developing Lifelong Writers.*

During the first year of the field work for my dissertation, I conducted interviews with ten adults who described themselves as writers. I narrowed my study to four writers from the original ten, with whom I worked closely for another year. In addition to engaging in formal and informal interviews, these participants kept writing logs and submitted pieces of writing for critique. As I transcribed the audiotapes and sifted through the data, I became aware of emerging patterns.

The participants of my study listed three primary reasons for their development as lifelong writers. Writing brought them positive attention. Writing helped them to think and to solve problems. Writing connected them to other people and other times. The most compelling finding was the importance that community played in the development of lifelong writers.

English curricula traditionally have focused on four modes for writing: persuasion, description, exposition, and narrative. English teachers have striven valiantly to teach writing in those four modes. The writers in my study, however, stated that they began to write, and continued to write, as a way of forming and maintaining relationships. Their writings showed evidence of paying homage and tribute to people important in their lives. They wrote to remember. They wrote to define themselves.

As I examined the reasons that the four participants gave for their development as lifelong writers, I discovered that I held similar reasons for becoming a writer. I recognized that the need for positive attention, the need and the opportunity to write about things that I cared about, and the need for a community of people with whom I could share my writing were all fulfilled with my membership in collaborative writing groups.

Word Works

One of the participants in my study suggested that after the dissertation was completed we continue meeting to talk about writing. She had taken some writing courses at the college in our town, and she knew writers from other seminars she'd taken. I had experience from Teachers as Writers, and I was excited by the idea of forming a community of writers. Advertisements in the quarterly newsletter distributed by an art center attracted some members. Most of our people, however, heard about Word Works through word-of-mouth.

Members of Word Works agree on a writing topic for each month's meeting. Our topics are general and could have many different interpretations. One month, for example, Bobbie's "Come Home" paper centered on a reunion of Vietnam soldiers at The Wall. Barb wrote about a family dog that made a thirty-mile journey home; I wrote about listening to my father "come home to his childhood."

The writing process begins at the meeting when we choose a topic for the following month. I plant the topic in my mind, like a small seed, and I let it grow. In the days and weeks that follow, I pay attention to memories that flash during quiet moments when I am driving the car, waiting in the grocery line, or pulling weeds in the garden. Once the memory surfaces, I imagine different ways of making it fit the topic. The pieces I have written during the past year have all been about my father. I think I am trying to reinvent the man.

When I was thinking about what to write for the topic of "splitting," I remembered the time my father cut down a rotting tree for my grandmother. My sisters and I watched him pull his hand saw and swing his ax, splitting the wood for my grandmother's stove. By evening all that was left was a short decaying stump. Late that night my parents woke us and carried us outside to see the stump all aglow with its own cold bioluminescent light.

As I worked on that story, however, another memory intruded. I kept seeing my father reach into the coal furnace to save my art projects. I thought about how my feelings toward him were often split between fear and love. I considered how my emotions were often split between enjoying the basement and being terrified to go down there. I finally wrote about the basement and my scream that split the dusty air as my father reached into the fire of the coal furnace to save my projects. (Note: See the following story, "Into the Flames.")

At the Word Works meeting when the "splitting" assignment was due, Tom read his story about a man caught in a humdrum marriage who had won the lottery. The windfall made splitting from his wife a possibility. Alan's story was about two young boys who engaged in a fistfight in a cemetery that left one with a split lip. Bobby wrote a research piece about splitting the atom.

My first draft is usually linear—I just want to get the story down. In the second draft I ask myself questions suggested by Eve Shelnutt years before at The Experience of Writing. "Whose story is it? What is at stake?" Answers to those questions help me revise the point of view. I decided that "Into the Flames" was the child's story. I needed to let the reader see the basement and the father through the child's eyes. In subsequent revisions I asked myself which parts of what I had written were vital to the story. I also looked at word choice. If a child were telling the story, for example, would she use the word *bewildered* to describe her father's face? Would a child use the word *retrieve?* I search for a child's voice and expressions.

Word Works is the most important thing I do for myself. Years ago at The Experience of Writing, Chris Merrill reminded us to make appointments with ourselves to write. He said that discipline showed respect and that a writer, respecting herself, should use discipline to keep the appointment.

Ron Carlson commented that a writer has to ask, "Does this matter to me?" I can answer a giant YES to every piece I've shared with my Word Works group. Ron also said, "The single most important thing in writing a story, the only thing worth talking about at all is *finishing*. You must finish your work. That is the difference between writers and nonwriters." Belonging to Word Works forces me to finish a piece for the monthly deadline.

Reflecting

Attending The Experience of Writing was an important moment in my journey as a teacher of writing. I discovered the importance of revision. I experienced the fear of risking to write something important to me and the fear of sharing it with others. I learned that my students needed the kind of specific feedback on their writing that I wanted on mine. I also grew to understand the absolute joy that comes with completing a piece of writing that I cared about.

The Experience of Writing was the turning point in my journey as a writer. For the first time in my life I took time to write. Learning how to find a topic and how to revise it gave me confidence in my own writing. Knowing what I wanted to hear from my audience helped me understand what other writers needed to hear from me. In the classroom, however, I remained the guide for my students with the map and the destination.

All of us in Word Works are travelers and none of us has the map or the destination for anyone else. Cheryl, for example, writes poetry. Tim is working on "Buick Tales," a collection of memories of trips he took with his grandfather. Alan is in the middle of a novel about nuclear destruction. Barb is writing her memoirs. I continue to work on a series of stories that explores the light side and the dark side of my father. We sustain each other on our separate writing journeys with our reactions and our responses. We drift in and out of various roles; sometimes we are the presenter and sometimes we are the audience. Always we support each other and fill the cup with encouragement to keep on writing.

For some people, becoming a teacher of writing is the golden sunset of the trail; for me it was the beginning. My quest to help students understand how to write fed my own desire to write better. Learning how to write better improved my writing instruction. Perhaps the journey I've described has not been such as meandering affair after all, but a circle, one development as a writer or as a teacher of writing linked inextricably to the one before and the one after. The glue that held it all together was the community of other writers.

References

Atwell, Nancie. 1987. *In the Middle: Writing, Reading, and Learning with Adolescents.* Portsmouth, NH: Heinemann.

Calkins, Lucy. 1986. *The Art of Teaching Writing.* Portsmouth, NH: Heinemann.

———. 1991. *Living between the Lines.* Portsmouth, NH: Heinemann.

Fox, Mem. 1993. *Radical Reflections.* Portsmouth, NH: Heinemann

Graves, Donald. 1983. *Writing: Teachers and Children at Work.* Portsmouth, NH: Heinemann.

Murray, Donald M. 1968. *A Writer Teaches Writing: A Practical Method of Teaching Composition.* Boston, MA: Houghton Mifflin.

———. 1987. *Write to Learn.* New York, NY: Holt, Rinehart & Winston.

———. 1989. *Expecting the Unexpected.* Portsmouth, NH: Heinemann.

———. 1990. *Shoptalk.* Portsmouth, NH: Heinemann.

Routman, Regie. 1988. *Transitions: From Literature to Literacy.* Portsmouth, NH: Heinemann; Rigby.

———. 1991. *Invitations: Changing as Teachers and Learners.* Portsmouth, NH: Heinemann.

Into the Flames
Janice Gallagher

The basement of our bungalow at 934 Wilbur Avenue is filled with monsters. I know they are there. I feel their breath on my shoulders and their bony fingers grab at my ankles when I go up the steps. They want to keep me down in the dark basement with them. If they catch me, I will never see the sun again. The monsters hate the sunlight. They only come out at moon time. I am not afraid of the monsters in the basement during sun time. I will happily run the steps for quarts of tomatoes from the fruit cellar for my mother during daylight, but oh, if she asks me to go at night, I am so afraid.

"Janice," my mother says, "Take this hammer down to your father's workbench. While you're down there get a jar of grape jelly."

I see the night pressed against the window. "Oh," I moan in a voice so small I can hardly hear it myself.

"Surely, you are not afraid," my mother says. "Not a big girl like you. What's to be afraid of? You play down there all day. It's no different at night."

She does not know about the monsters that come in at night through the door that leads to our backyard. I have to walk past that door to get to the door that leads into the basement. There is only dim, left-over light from the top of the steps that lead from our tiny back porch to the basement—not nearly enough to scare the monsters.

"Shirley," I plead to my younger sister, "Will you go with me?"

Sometimes Shirley makes the dark trip to the basement with me. On the times that Shirley goes, no monsters come. No monsters reach for my ankles and the stairs don't even creak when Shirley's with me. She walks behind me on the way back up, and I don't feel the terrible need to race up the steps so fast that I forget to breathe.

Shirley is the one I play with in the basement during the sun time. We pretend school on rainy days. Sometimes, on sunny days when we get tired of our mud pies, we come into the cool basement to play. We wind musty old curtains around our bodies and over our shoulders to play the Count of Monte Cristo. Other times we pretend we are fancy ladies. We rummage through a box of old perfume bottles and powder boxes that Aunt Maggy gave us. When we don't feel like playing school or dressing up we jump on the bed.

My father walled off part of the basement as a kind of "guest room." It is only big enough for a double bed and a small dresser. We have no guests, but sometimes my father sleeps in the bed when he is fighting with my mother. Sometimes, he sleeps there when he is too filled with beer to make it up the steps.

An old piano guards the door to the guest room. My father got it from the Helen Thesing Post of the American Legion. They bought a new one. My dad and his cronies helped move the new one into the social hall of the Legion and then they moved the old one to our house. They celebrated their hard work with lots of cold beer.

My parents said that all of us girls would learn to play the piano, but I am the only one who takes lessons. My mother gives me $1.50 to go to Mrs. Palano's house once a week. Margaret Ann Welshans goes with me. Her mother drives us because my mother doesn't have a car. I practice the piano in the basement when the sun comes through the window in cloudy pillars.

On top of the piano Shirley and I keep all our things for playing school. There's stacks of old paper with one side, a box of broken crayons and pencils, and a pile of crumbly, faded colored paper. My father is a teacher. He pulled the paper from the trash can outside the art room at his school. Also on top of the piano are the projects I have saved from Daily Vacation Bible School.

The coal furnace is the center of the basement. Round ducts reach out from the sturdy base like branches on a tree. My father is the one who shovels coal into the furnace in the mornings before we are awake. Next to the furnace is a small dark room that is filled with coal. We call it the coal bin. When the pile gets low, the coal truck comes. I like watching the coal lumps tumble into the silver chute and fall down through the window like a black waterfall into our little coal bin.

"It is time to clean up that basement," my father announces. Without a single word of protest we all get to our feet. We know better than to cross my father. My older sister Lynda follows my mother to the corner of the basement where piles of cast-off clothing drape the army trunks. They start a load of wash in the ringer washer and then they talk about which pieces to tear into rags and which ones to keep for "around the house" clothes.

For a while Shirley and I help my father sort screws and nails. When he begins to sweep the floor with his wide push broom, we sit back watching the puffs of dust he stirs with each push. We jump when he asks for the dust pan, and one of us holds it as he sweeps the dirt into the pan. I watch a spider crawl on very skinny legs across the cement. I wonder if it will make it across before my father's broom pushes by. I don't see my father stop sweeping as his gaze falls upon the top of the piano. I don't realize that he's scooped up my pile of Bible School projects in his big hand. He is already opening the furnace door before I recognize the precious things I've saved. I leave my spider watching and I run to him yelling, "Dad! Wait! Dad!"

By the time I get to him, he has the door to the furnace open. Bright orange flames flare even brighter with the fresh air.

"Those are my projects!" I cry. "That's my stitching!"

I see the flames swallow my cotton sampler with the black embroidery that says "The Lord is My Shepherd." I see the gray sheep with the French knots that Mrs. Reese had helped me do. All on its own a scream spins inside of me. It is a scream like the ones I feel when the basement monsters chase me up the steps. It bursts out my mouth splitting the dusty air of the basement.

I see my father's puzzled face as he looks from the mouth of the furnace at me and then back at the furnace. In a flash of speed, my father reaches into those awful flames. I see his whole arm inside the fire; I smell the hair burning on his arms.

My hands fly to my face. I sob for my lost projects. I sob for my father. My tears collect in my palms and then slip out and drip from my chin.

I feel my father's fingers on my shoulder; they are firm pressing into the muscles on my back. I hear him say, "I tried to save them, but I couldn't. The fire was too hot."

At once my sadness for the projects and the papers melts. I drop my hands and I throw my arms around my father's legs rubbing my wet cheeks against his faded work pants. I am his daughter and for me, he reached into the flames.

Green Digits and Colons: Find Time to Write

Barry Peters

The only constant in my life is time. The bad part is that time is constantly leaving me, slipping away second by minute by hour. Time is my obsession. Time makes me panic. Listen to this: At any time during the day or night, I know the time within four minutes and twenty-eight seconds. At least, that's the farthest I've ever been from the United States Naval Observatory accuracy. Sometimes I wake myself up in the middle of the night to see if I know what time it is, and I'm right. I stopped setting my alarm six years ago and have never been late for work. I've run local road races where the object is not to be the fastest but to predict your finishing time; I'm always the champion. Clocks, watches, bells, and timers rule my life. I see green digits and colons in my sleep. 9:27. 6:15. 11:42. The place I'd most like to visit is Greenwich, England.

How is this sickness relevant to writing? To put it simply, I have no time to write. Time in my world, as in yours, is like a world-class sprinter—here today, gone today. The only way I can write, or the only way I can write well, is to stop time. Frank Conroy used the expression as the title of a book: Stop-time. Only stop-time isn't going to happen very often in my world—or yours, either. Family, job, social commitments, reading, eating, sleeping, O. J. (or the latest national crisis that requires my full attention on CNN). My time, like yours, is chewed up by work and play, debate and resolution, love and hate, vacuuming and mowing, shaving and showering, shopping and shitting. I know because I time it all. I know how much time it takes to do everything.

Time is everywhere in the fiction that I do find time to write. I don't write about time intentionally, but it's always there. Sometimes it has a starring role; other times it is reduced to a cameo. Digits and colons keep reappearing in my stories like little numerical men from Mars. 1:11. 7:02. 8:54.

I did stop-time once at a writers' workshop in Yellow Springs, Ohio, one summer. To stop time, I had to abandon my wife and child and job for a week. But at that writers' workshop, for once, I had time. And here's the amazing thing—it took me only one year and forty-three minutes to write my first published story. For about a year I had been thinking about a short story in which a compulsive high school student cheats on tests. That's all I did for one year—think about writing that story. Of course, it never got written. I had no time. There were always research papers to grade, gutters to clean, ballgames to watch. Then I went to the writers' workshop, where Ron Carlson gave our group a simple writing exercise. Presto—in forty-three minutes of stop-time in a small, steamy dormitory room, I wrote the story of the student who cheats. That story was published in a textbook for fiction writers, and I was on my way . . . until time started again.

Time has manipulated my entire writing life. Maybe it began when I came of age, that moment of epiphany that is contrived for fiction but happened to me in fact. Four of us were determined to make the high school basketball team—Brian Royce, Paul Kowalski, John Lentine, and me. We spent the entire summer of our sophomore year playing basketball, lifting weights, running sprints. We continued conditioning in the fall, working even harder as the season approached, a rare commitment for a quartet of sixteen-year-olds. Then one night about a week before basketball tryouts we went for a long run that took us past the high school. We noticed the gym lights were on, so we jogged over to take a look. Inside was the head basketball coach watching the school's ten best players in a full-court scrimmage. Obviously, one week before tryouts began, the coach had already chosen his team. Our dream had been voided months before and we didn't even know it. Six months of blind dedication to making the basketball team had been a waste of time. We walked home in silence, the four of us having come of age to the real world of rules violations. But this story had a Hollywood ending. When the coach cut me the next week at tryouts, he said that the local newspaper needed a stringer to cover prep sports. My English teacher had told the coach that I could write (a little bit), and bingo! I was a sportswriter.

That's when time really started eating me up. Deadline time. I would cover a high school basketball game on Friday night, party with my friends until two o'clock in the morning, then go home and write the game story on a manual typewriter, sitting on my bed so that the tapping of the keys wouldn't wake up my parents. I'd finish the story at four o'clock, my head still buzzing, and sleep for two hours. At six I would drive downtown to the newspaper building where the sports editor, Bart Fisher, would laugh at my hangover-swollen face as I wobbled into his office, my head full of bass drums banging. As a cub reporter I never missed a deadline or a party. Thank God it was an afternoon paper.

Time was my enemy every day for eight years as a journalist. I once threw a thirty-pound unabridged dictionary across the sports department of a major metropolitan newspaper on deadline. It was a record toss, twenty-two feet, seven inches, and it toppled a ceiling-to-floor bookcase of major league baseball media guides. I made that deadline.

Time killed me more slowly in the case of Charles Barkley, or the Round Mound of Rebound as he was known in his younger days. I covered Barkley's first professional basketball game in the National Basketball Association. At the time he was about six-foot-six, two hundred eighty pounds—too small and too fat to make it by NBA standards. At least that was the story that I wrote after Barkley's first game, his Philadelphia 76ers vs. the Boston Celtics. Barkley scored only one point. He couldn't jump for rebounds. He waddled up the court, a garbage truck among greyhounds. After the game, I approached Barkley with acute trepidation—sitting in the locker room he looked as if he had just been poked in the eye with a sharp stick for forty-eight straight minutes. This was a big, angry, sweaty man. But I needed a quote. So I sat down next to Barkley, glanced at his huge hands, arms, shoulders, and head, and I asked him, with typical journalistic aplomb, "How's come you stunk up the joint?" Barkley responded by shouting a series of invectives aimed at his own pitiful play, but it sure sounded as if I was included. The other players and reporters in the locker room froze as Barkley's voice echoed off the walls, his bazooka-sized index finger pointed at my face, his shaved head glistening. He ranted for about a minute but it seemed like forever, the clock in my head malfunctioning under the pressure. Barkley promised that he was never going to play that poorly again and that he would not answer any more questions. Then he stood up and stepped on my foot. I'd swear he did it on purpose. He just stood up and planted that battleship of a basketball shoe on my flimsy docksider. And then he headed for the showers.

So, on deadline, I wrote a column predicting that Charles Barkley would be a failure in basketball. Of course, time did tell that I was a fool. Charles Barkley is now one of the greatest basketball players in the world. Come to think of it, maybe that's when I started writing fiction.

Now that I'm a teacher and a writer, I can look back at my career as a sportswriter and see that I am just a victim of time. I was raised on deadline-writing, and now I am unable to write anything unless someone has a deadline pointed at my head. In fact, time is threatening me as I write these very words. Three months ago, Terry Hermsen asked me to write this essay. I said sure, and then I didn't write it. Yesterday my wife informed me that Terry called and wanted to know where my essay was. Now, Terry is a very nice man. Primarily he is a poet, which left me wondering if he would write me a nasty sonnet because I missed deadline (I get very cruel under the pressure of time). I called him and told him that I missed deadline because I didn't have time to write the essay. He said, "Find the time in the next two days." So much for the poet in him. And here I am, finding the time.

Sometimes I set my own deadlines—one story before our next writers' group meeting; two stories this month; fifteen stories this year; one story before I die. But it's not the same when you impose them on yourself. In reality, I do not have adequate time to spend with all the loves of my life—family, friends, job, reading, running, writing. I could spend twenty-four hours a day with each. It's the burden of loving life. Time could find no easier prey.

The best advice I heard at the writers' workshop in Yellow Springs came from Ron Carlson. It seems that one day Carlson was home alone—stop-time, plenty of time to write—and he decided to wash the phone. He really did. He just unplugged the phone, filled the sink with hot water and soap, and washed the phone. About that time a neighbor came by and caught Carlson in this absurd act of writing-avoidance. Carlson stood there thinking to himself, I'm washing the phone. During stop-time. And I'm supposed to be a writer?

The moral of the story is to find stop-time, not waste it. And so even I manage to find a little stop-time once in a while. I manage to crank out a short story in which time itself, inevitably, plays a part, as in the story that follows. Should you choose not to read it, I understand. You need to make judicious use of your time. Believe me, I know the feeling.

Julie
Barry Peters

Race day: Julie is awake before the radio alarm, as usual, staring at the shadows on the ceiling, thinking about everything. It's close to dawn, the first light turning the window panes silver. The rest of the bedroom is one shade lighter than black. Julie rolls onto her side and looks at the outline of Troy Aikman on the wall, the circle of his silver Dallas Cowboys helmet and the straight lines of his shoulders and legs. She can't make out the stars on his uniform yet, nor can she see the blue of his eyes, but she knows those eyes are staring into hers. The point of the football, cocked high over Troy Aikman's shoulder, is aimed directly at Julie. She raises her arms as if to catch the pass.

It's 5:53 when Julie switches on the lamp and pulls a folded newspaper from beneath her bed. She stares at the photo of Samantha Grimes, an image that is etched into her mind. In the photo Samantha is crossing the finish line in the mile run at last week's regional track meet. Samantha's lips are rolled back from her teeth, her fingers balled into fists, her arms pumped, the muscles of her biceps clearly defined. Julie studies Samantha's bowl-cut black hair, the broadness of Samantha's shoulders, the sheer size and strength that produces Samantha's speed. Then, at the right edge of the picture, in a shadow just behind Samantha, Julie finds her own tiny hand. The caption under the photo reads, *Hillsdale's Samantha Grimes wins the mile showdown between the two fastest high school runners in the state at last week's regional track and field meet. Grimes and Elmwood's Julie Pleasant (not in picture) will meet again Friday for the state title.*

Race day: Julie pulls on a Cowboys sweatshirt, a pair of checkered shorts, and her running shoes. She touches Troy Aikman on the way out of her room. In the hallway she hears the shower running way back in her parents' bedroom. Downstairs it's silent. Julie finds Prince yawning on the living room couch. She hooks a leash to the shepherd's collar; Prince's toenails click across the hardwood floor in the foyer. Julie turns off the security system and they're out the door.

It's a foggy spring dawn, the swampy air colored like burnt charcoal. Julie waits until the house is out of sight before she begins to jog. Prince is at arm's length on the strip of soft grass between the sidewalk and curb. The leash jerks and Prince does his business at the Davenports' mailbox. From there Julie knows she'll have an uninterrupted run through the twisting boulevards and cul-de-sacs of the development. Julie thinks again about the picture in the newspaper and last week's meet, when she lost to Samantha Grimes for the third time this spring, and she thinks about tonight's race for the state championship. She desperately wants to win. At least, she's been told that she desperately wants to win. Her mind drifts to school and a test she will have in algebra this morning. As she and Prince run silently, automatically, Julie also thinks about Jeremy Wallace, the best athlete in the school, who teases her at lunch, maybe even flirts with her, but she can't say anything back; she thinks about her parents, neither one a help or even a comfort to her anymore; she considers the irony of her job at Frick's Grocery; and she thinks about Samantha Grimes and wonders if Samantha has these same problems, if Samantha runs with the same pressure, if she carries the same weight on her back, if their lives are the same. Before she knows it, Julie is running faster. She strides on the balls of her feet, her arms swinging in perfect rhythm, slicing through the wet morning fog that shrouds the huge Colonial homes in her neighborhood.

Julie feels a pull on the leash and tugs at Prince. "Come on, Samantha," Julie says aloud, and she snaps Prince's head forward. They're into the third mile now and picking up speed, both of them in the middle of the street, sweating, mouths slightly open, breathing audibly in the morning silence. They race this way for about three blocks, and as the road curves they cut inside, running hard through the fog, almost sprinting. Julie's mind is focused on tonight's race. She is visualizing, the positive-thinking strategy her coach taught her. She blocks out everything else and pictures the final stretch with Samantha Grimes on her right shoulder. Their legs churn in unison, and Julie sees the thin white strip of tape stretched across the track twenty, fifteen, ten yards ahead, a yellow reflection of the setting sun at the finish line, the victory belonging to Julie finally, when suddenly something cuts across the track in front of her —a race official? another runner?—no, a car! pulling out of a driveway!— no, a boy on a bicycle with a newspaper sack slung over his shoulder! —and Julie stumbles into Prince as they stop, the boy swerving and swearing as he flies over a curb and sprawls harmlessly on a front lawn, the back wheel of his bike whirling and the newspapers scattered, his ball cap askew, cursing the girl and the dog who run away in the fog, everyone breathing heavily.

Prince's head hangs low when they walk up the driveway to Julie's house. They go into the garage and Julie finds a towel that she's hidden behind some paint cans. She wipes the sweat off her neck and forehead, then stashes the towel back in its hiding place. At the top of the driveway, on the far side of her cherry red Camaro, Julie lies down. She does fifty crunches, the last ritual of her clandestine daily workout, as Prince's big head hangs over her face, his tongue dripping. Another three-mile morning, three secret miles that she isn't supposed to run because of overtraining, injury, and/or burnout, according to her coach and her father. Julie agrees to their faces, but she runs those miles anyway every school morning of the week before most people are even out of bed. Julie thinks that if she is going to beat Samantha Grimes, she has to run more miles, and run them harder and faster. "And miles to go," Julie thinks to herself, remembering English class, "and miles to go before I sleep."

In the kitchen, Prince laps at his water while Julie stretches for a glass from the cupboard. She feels her heart lightly tapping the inside of her chest, and she breathes deeply, silently, trying to slow it down as her father walks into the room. Mr. Pleasant is tall and tan, his black hair gelled straight back in even ridges. He is dressed impeccably in a beige pinstriped business suit. Julie heard him get home at midnight from his four-day business trip in Frankfort, cut short so he can be at tonight's big race. Julie wonders, for an instant, about her father. Who he really is.

Why he is in this home. What this man is doing in this kitchen with her. Then Julie remembers that she promised herself not to care, to block it all out.

"The big day," her father says, touching the back of her neck. "Are you sweating, Julie? Must be hot out there already. Look at Prince—all lathered up from his morning walk."

Julie turns her back and opens the refrigerator. She places the inside of her wrist on a pitcher of orange juice, feeling the cold for only a few seconds, as long as she dares. She can't let her father suspect that she has been running, not walking.

The dog falls on the floor at Julie's feet.

"Prince is getting old," says her father, scratching the shepherd's neck. "He can't take the heat anymore. Maybe you guys shouldn't go so far on these warm mornings."

Julie only responds to questions, not statements. And sometimes, not even to questions. The less said, the better. She begins to fill her glass with orange juice, then reconsiders. She pours the juice in the sink and twists the top off a bottle of spring water.

"Banana?" Her father stands there, holding it like a phone.

Julie shakes her head.

"That's right. Race day," says her father. "No breakfast. A little nervous?"

Julie unfolds her arms and takes another sip of water.

"You'll get her tonight," her father says, peeling the banana for himself. "Samantha Grimes is ready to be had. Julie, this is when it counts, you know. This is your Super Bowl. This is what separates the men from the boys and the women from the girls. Or in this case, the woman from the boy."

Her father smiles and bites the end of the banana. It's his joke about Samantha, whom her dad says looks like a boy, runs like a boy, and, he laughs, might even drug-test as a boy, if they had drug testing for high school athletes.

Julie never smiles.

"It's your race to win, Julie," he says, holding the half-eaten banana in her face. "Just run her down, Julie. She's strong, but she doesn't have the natural speed that you do."

Julie hears her father's voice rising, giving more empty advice, as she leaves the kitchen and heads upstairs.

The shower is blazing hot and the radio is playing hit songs at high volume when Julie undresses and looks at herself in the full-length mirror on the back of the bathroom door. She takes a deep breath and lets her body sag. Then she stands upright, shoulders square, perfectly straight. Her brown hair, hanging halfway down her back, is the same color as her arms and legs, which have been tanned from long hours of track practice. The rest of Julie's body—her chest and stomach, her upper thighs and her ankles and feet—is yellow-white. Julie sucks in her stomach and slides her fingers slowly up her stomach, starting in the cavity between her hips. She counts her ribs as she goes, the bones feeling fragile beneath her skin. Her hands stop briefly on the tiny softness of her breasts, and for the first time she looks up from her body and into her own eyes, or rather the mirrored reflection of her eyes. She sees how deep they are in the sockets, and she wonders if Jeremy Wallace thinks they are mysterious, or even cute. A new song plays; circles of steam from the hot shower drift across the bathroom. Julie fans her fingers across the ridges of her collarbone, slowly. She thinks of Samantha Grimes, and suddenly Julie raises her fists above her head, elbows bent, and assumes a musclegirl pose, admiring herself in the cloudy silver glass. Julie tightens her biceps, but there is no rise, no mound of muscle. Posing, Julie thinks of Atlas, the god who, she remembered from English class, once held the world above his head. She can't imagine.

The music and the shower cascade. Julie puts her arms down and turns to the side, looking at her naked self in profile. She sticks out her tongue and thinks of the joke about the girl who looked like a zipper. Julie relaxes her stomach slightly, but the sight is unbearable, and she sucks it back in. Her eyes move down the reflection of her body, down her arms, waist, hips, and bottom, until they reach her legs. Julie flicks her hand against the upper part of her thigh and watches the skin vibrate. It's a slight movement, barely discernible, but it makes Julie sick. What I'd give for a runner's body, Julie thinks. Then I wouldn't be the second-best runner in the state. I'd be the first. Sensing the nausea in her stomach, she slowly steps on the bathroom scale. She opens her eyes and looks at the red digital numbers. Another new song plays. Julie is still staring at the scale when she evaporates in the steamy fog. She's going to be sick.

Mr. Stricker is in Julie's face shouting, "Kills his father! Marries his mother! Pokes his eyes out!" Julie lowers her head, embarrassed. Stricker likes to do this to her in front of the class. She sits front row center and she really doesn't mind.

"Kills his father! Marries his mother! Gouges his eyes out! Who wouldn't love this story? It's a tragedy!" This is Stricker's way of keeping the students' interest, his salesman's pitch, his strategy to get the students to read. Julie knows this but she doesn't need the motivation; she read

Oedipus during the dark hours of the night earlier in the week. In fact, she read it twice.

"Test on Monday! Test on Monday! Read this play!" Stricker is shouting when the bell rings. Julie silently stands up and begins to walk out of the classroom, half hoping that Stricker will say something to her.

"Hey, Julie," Stricker calls out. "Good luck tonight."

She wants to respond with more than a smile. She would like to say something, but she can't. She does the usual: she grins and lowers her head.

The other juniors file out behind her, and Julie wants to go with them. For now Julie remembers what she wrote in her last journal entry—the response to the Housman poem. Julie could kill herself for writing what was almost a confession. Did Stricker know? She had written about running all year in her journal—cross country in the fall, indoor track in the winter, the mile races against Samantha Grimes this spring—and she somehow related them to English class, to whatever they were studying at the time. Stricker always put these stupid smiley faces at the end of the entries, two dots and an arc, right-side-up or upside-down depending on what Julie had written. Mr. Stricker had told Julie about how he jogged with his wife and their Irish setter Thomas every night, and how they were going to train for a marathon this summer—he and his wife, not Thomas the dog, Stricker had joked.

Then Stricker assigned the Housman poem, almost as if it was intended for Julie. She couldn't believe it. And she was careless about what she wrote. She still can't get the line out of her mind: "Silence sounds no worse than cheers."

"Julie," Stricker says, "Is everything okay?"

"Yeah, I guess," she says, trying to make herself smaller, her shoulders hunched.

Stricker plays with his tie, which is a print of Sylvester the cat leaping at Tweety Bird, whose cage hangs from the knot. Stricker's crazy ties are gifts from students; Julie almost got him one once, a skeleton tie that she found in a Grateful Dead-type store in the mall. But she didn't.

"My wife and I are driving over to watch you race tonight," he says, and Julie wishes he would stop right there.

"Thanks," says Julie, and she wishes she could evaporate before he mentions the journal.

"So you like the Housman poem," Stricker says. Julie's bookbag is heavy on her shoulder. There's an uncomfortable pause. "From what you write in your journal, sometimes I can't tell whether you really like to run or not, Julie."

Julie knows it was a question but she doesn't want to answer.

"I liked the poem," she says.

"'Smart lad, to slip betimes away from fields where glory does not stay,'" Stricker says.

Julie can tell he is wondering. She tries for a laugh: "I thought the last line was about underwear."

It works. Stricker laughs, and he sits on his desk. She's gonna be outta here!

"Not too smart for an honors student," Julie says, her exit line, and she moves toward the door.

But then Stricker reaches into a pile of paper and pulls out a copy of the poem. "Well, let's look at it," he says, seriously, and Julie is stuck.

"'And find unwithered on its curls the garland briefer than a girl's.' What do you think that means, Julie?"

"I don't know," she lies.

"But you know it's not about underwear."

She doesn't say anything.

"Everything's okay?"

The nausea begins to rise.

"Julie?"

Her head begins to ache. There's pressure behind her eyes. She sees water.

"Julie?"

She nods, says thanks, smiles and walks away. He knows, Julie thinks. After all, she is an "A" student.

"Read it again," she hears him call. "Before tonight!"

At lunch Jeremy Wallace comes up with a plan.

"Here's what we're going to do, Julie," Jeremy announces to the members of the Elmwood track team. They're having lunch together, getting psyched for the state meet, which begins tonight with the mile championship for girls. "Julie, we're going to cut that beautiful long hair of yours."

From out of a paper bag, which Julie had assumed held an apple or yogurt, Jeremy pulls a large pair of scissors. Everybody laughs.

"But we're not just going to cut it," Jeremy says, looking around the table, playing to the other kids. "No, that's not good enough."

Jeremy sticks his hand back into the bag and takes out a small black razor. He flips a switch and the blade starts buzzing.

"We're going to shave your head, Julie Pleasant," he says, and the other kids are silent because the captain of the track team and school record holder in the shotput, discus, and javelin seems awfully serious.

Jeremy has done some crazy things in the past, things that Julie has found despicable and admirable.

Julie feels her face flush. She drinks from her bottle of water.

Jeremy is opening and closing the scissors in his left hand and moving the razor up and down in his right. He starts to hum the *Jaws* theme: Duh-duh duh-duh duh-duh.

Julie manages this: "Why would you do that?"

"To psyche out Grimes," Jeremy says. "I'll bet she never raced against a bald girl, and I'll bet she couldn't beat one, either."

The tension breaks, and everybody's laughing.

"I don't think so," Julie says.

"It could improve your time," Jeremy says innocently. "Less wind resistance. You'll be aerodynamic."

More laughter.

"Or maybe," Jeremy says, "I could give you a crewcut and shave a panther into the back of your head."

Then Jeremy dramatically slams his elbow onto the center of the table and slowly rolls up the sleeve on his T-shirt. "Like this one."

"Oh my God!" somebody screams. "He's got a tattoo!"

The kids crowd around Jeremy, who tells them not to touch. Carved into his left shoulder is a black panther, the mascot of Elmwood High School. Only Jeremy's panther has a mean-eyed look, with a drop of red blood falling from two bared teeth.

Jeremy moves the arm next to Julie, tightens his muscles, and puts his face six inches from hers.

"I got it done last night," he says. "Downtown. What do you think, Julie?"

Her stomach is twisting now, sick as it was this morning and will be again before she races tonight. "Gross," Julie says, which isn't what she wants to say at all. She wants to ask Jeremy all about last night. She wants to know who went with him to get the tattoo, if it hurt, what his parents said, or what they will say when they find out. Instead, Julie tries to ignore the volcano in her stomach and she says, so she doesn't seem too smart, "Gross."

Jeremy yanks the sleeve back down, almost angrily, covering the panther. Without taking his eyes from Julie's, he reaches into the brown sack again. He hesitates. Julie hates not being able to respond, being powerless. Her teammates are quiet, watching them. Then Jeremy pulls a Tiger's Milk nutritional bar from the bag.

"You eat anything yet, Julie," he says, almost kindly. "Try this. Complex carbos. It'll give you that extra energy. Just what you'll need to bring home the gold. Come on, Julie."

Julie thinks about the picture of Samantha Grimes and takes another drink of water.

As they enter the third lap Julie considers her options: stop; throw herself on the ground face-first in one of the outside lanes; run straight out of the stadium, across the parking lot, and keep on going forever. Process of elimination makes her stay right behind Samantha Grimes. The two fastest milers in the state already have separated themselves from the rest of the field. As in their previous race, Samantha has the lead and Julie is right behind her. Over Samantha's shoulder Julie sees the sun dropping behind the rim of the university stadium, the large crowd in dark shadows, cheering them on.

On the bus ride to the meet, Michelle Davis, Julie's coach, talked to Julie about strategy. They sat in the front seat away from her teammates.

"The same thing has happened each time she's beaten you," Michelle said quietly. "Samantha gets out in front and just wears you down. You're faster than she is, Julie, but she's stronger. She's a bull. An ox. Remember, that's not your style. You're a beautiful *runner*. You've got speed. Lightning speed. You've got to use that at the end of the race. You can't run the same way she does."

Julie nodded but didn't turn her face.

"You can't chase her," Michelle was saying. "Let her go early. Save your speed for the final three hundred yards. It'll be okay if she's got a big lead because she won't be able to hold it. You'll start sprinting and the crowd will begin to roar. You'll be closing the gap and Samantha won't know what's going on behind her. She'll turn her head and see that you're gaining on her. She'll try to accelerate but she'll feel like she's running in wet sand. Her legs will be dead and *yours* will be fresh. You'll pass her in the final fifty yards. The crowd will be going nuts."

Julie pictured that scenario again, just as she pictured it all week during her secret morning runs with Prince.

"Visualize," Michelle whispered hypnotically in Julie's ear. "See it happen and it will."

Then Julie visualized the photograph from the newspaper that was still lying on the floor under her bed.

"And don't forget your caffeine pills," Michelle said, grinning. "Hey, you eat anything yet?"

By the time Julie replays that conversation she and Samantha are running down the home stretch again, finishing the third lap of the four-lap race. Julie thinks about how she ignored Michelle's advice in this race, about how she had no choice but to run all the way with Samantha. She tried to let Samantha take the lead, tried to let her go, but she couldn't. She had gotten scared. What if she couldn't catch up? What if she had no speed on the last lap? She had to stay with Samantha all the way. And now she's right behind Samantha, so close that she can feel Samantha's elbow graze the fingers of her left hand after every stride.

One lap left. Julie's eyes move to the infield and she sees Jeremy Wallace standing there holding a javelin, the tip pointed at her. The field events have stopped as everyone in the stadium has turned to watch what might be the biggest race of the meet. Julie thinks about this, about her mother and father and brothers, about Mr. Stricker and Michelle, all watching her from different vantage points. Her view is still of Samantha's back.

Three hundred yards remaining. This is when Julie is supposed to begin her kick, according to the plan devised by Michelle. That's out the window, though, because Julie has no kick left. Instead she is running Samantha's race, just trying to hold on. Julie's stomach boils. To take her mind off it, Julie imagines that she and Samantha are running as one, a rope tied around both their waists. She imagines that Samantha is pulling her along, the rope taut between them. In the last fifty yards, Julie thinks, maybe she will tug on the rope and slingshot past Samantha to victory. Or maybe she will jump in the air and fly over Samantha's head like a kite. Or maybe the rope will slide up her frail torso and get stuck just underneath her chin.

And that's when the final option occurs to Julie, an option nobody else has considered except Housman. She had read the poem again, as Mr. Stricker had suggested. She had read it secretly, hidden in the stacks of the school library just after school, and now it is making sense. Perfect sense. And so when she and Samantha run the last curve, their strides synchronized as fast as any two girls had ever run a mile in state track history, one runner a tiny shadow of the other, the race entirely up for grabs, Julie puts her plan into action. Right there in the last pool of sunlight, just before the final one hundred yards down the home stretch in front of the mad crowd in the grandstand, Julie loses. The race.

IV Full Circle: Essays from Experience of Writing Faculty

As the introduction to this book makes clear, the faculty invited to conduct the workshops at the first Experience of Writing had little idea of what they signed up for. We arrived that first Saturday morning with our satchels of possible books to use—and little else. As we sat there that morning, we brainstormed. What was the institute to be? What was our role? Were we gurus? Surely not. Should we be teaching how to teach writing? The consensus was, "No." What then? The idea arose that perhaps this could be a time for teachers to experience what writers do when they tackle an inkling or follow a hunch, when a character they have invented begins to speak on his or her own, when an itch to explore a particular memory becomes so overwhelming that the words are in our heads as we drive to the supermarket.

The writers included in this last section represent only a few of the many fine faculty who have gathered for those weeks in Yellow Springs and later, Fairborn. But their answers to the knotty problems of writing mesh together with remarkable coherence. From Ron Carlson's insistence that we "turn the desk" when teaching writing, to become a student again, to Scott Russell Sanders's historical view of the advantages of using first person in an essay, to Christopher Merrill's concept of keeping all the possibilities open when one sits down to attempt a piece of writing—of even training oneself as a writer to experience all genres—they urge us to not get locked into what we thought writing was, but to let our writing guide our thinking. Their words are abrasive, humorous, reflective, discursive. Like the children's poems and stories, or the essays of the teachers, they return us to the sources of where we always begin.

With writers who teach, such as Scott, Ron, and Chris, Eve Shelnutt, Toi Derricotte, Pamela Painter, and others, collaborating on the teaching of writing with K–12 teachers, the work begun years ago in poets in the schools programs has come full circle. No longer need those who *teach* be separated from those who *write*. Contemporary writers can play an important role in exploring what it means to be educated. And if to be educated means to be fully engaged with exploring the world, contemporary writers can help students find a way. I'm reminded of a student I met at a summer workshop for high school students, whom I overheard saying to another, "Oh, I love the work of Ron Carlson," going on to explain the plot of his short story "Bigfoot Stole My Wife." She never would have known of the story's existence if her teacher, Carl Krauskopf, had not attended The Experience of Writing and participated in Ron's workshops. Clearly, Ron's witty satire spoke to this student and her teacher in a way that Twain might not, or in a way that could promote the reading of earlier writers.

Because these are writers of *our* time—because Chris is not only a poet but a journalist who has made five trips to war-torn Bosnia, trips which resulted in two important books of essays; because Scott Russell Sanders's multifaceted exploration of rebuilding community in our lives is reflected in all that he writes—we are invited to rediscover how writing can be, indeed *needs* to be, engaged with the deepest issues we face as a society. Teachers working with these writers inevitably pick up methods and inspiration for re-energizing their own lives as well. And by nature, when they do that, they find ways to help their students do the same.

Postscript

Teaching at The Experience of Writing always felt like a *homecoming* to me. Much of what happened was influenced by the environments we found ourselves in—one in which we could meet other participants and faculty by chance while walking downtown or jogging along a trail in the park. Such opportunities for exploration and discovery influenced the writing/teaching atmosphere as well. After all, how can we *experience writing* unless we have experience to write about? To draw all our inspiration from memory or invention is not enough. We need to find ways to let writing guide us into the places where we live.

Ron Carlson and Toi Derricotte found such a place one Wednesday night in the middle of the third institute. Walking home from a late conversation at the Olde Trail Tavern, I glanced to my right across the Mills Lawn Elementary School yard to see two people standing on top of a large stump. Squinting in the lamplight, I gradually realized it was Ron and Toi in the midst of a rather animated conversation, facing each other like two debaters. I was sure that the scene had come about (though I could never quite prove this) during a conversation about writer's block. I pictured Ron saying to Toi, "Hey, have you ever been really stumped?" and proceeding to invite her to act out this pun on their current perch outside the elementary school.

Similar random and wonderful connections happened frequently and became an important part of the magic we experienced together. In my "normal" life, I drive forty-five miles one way to reach the campus where I teach, but in a place where walking predominated over driving, and nooks and crannies of the campus and the town became sites of conversation, such events as Ron and Toi's "stump talk" were natural and inspiring.

—Terry Hermsen

Turning the Desk

Ron Carlson

What I want to do is turn the desk. My goal as a teacher of creative writing is to turn the desk on my students. In The Experience of Writing, this became paramount, because all of my students were teachers. They'd come from a variety of schools throughout the state and from different grade levels, but what they all had somewhere in Xenia or Dayton or Yellow Springs was a desk in the classroom, their desk full of their stuff, and this was the desk I wanted to turn. See diagram.

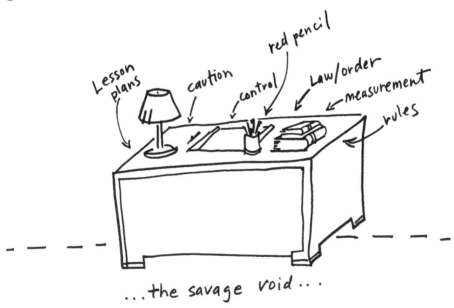

...the savage void...

Now a desk is unique among furniture because it is one of the few items that is not an accessory for the television. (All other furniture exists to serve the needs of our televisions and the soft sad universal malaise that they purvey, but this is a topic for another time.) But the classroom desk has a purpose of its own, a purpose we all know about. A teacher's desk is the law. More than a judge's bench or a lawyer's table

---

or a lectern in a law school, the desk at the head of the classroom, whether it is steel or wood or the same new space-age material they've used to construct the rest of the school, is the law. It is laden with devices for measurement, caution, and order. I don't need to go on here and talk about the confiscated toys serving time in the top drawer, the lined rollbook brimming with grades in another, the ruler, the calendar, the class schedule, the lesson plans, the syllabi, outlines, and the blue folder of school rules. The teacher's desk demarks, like an outpost at the edge of the wilderness, the needs and requirements, the ordinances and demands of *civilization*. It stands like an imposing city on the margin of the untamed void. And behind it somewhere, in a zone which can only be thought of as protected as the center of a fortress, stands the teacher on both feet—her hand full of chalk, her mouth full of yet another orderly explanation of Comma Rule 12-B.

Out beyond the desk is the unknown, and its terrifying waters lap against the walls of order. Out there the taste of chaos rides the unruly waves and there is no outline or lesson plan to cling to, no principles of grammar to shield one from harm, no regulation to, well, regulate the void. It's strange and ambiguous and pulsing with opportunity.

And my mission is to turn the desk. I want these teachers/writers out front far from their desk blotters and daytimers, a place where for the duration of writing a story they can not invoke the rules of the editor, the critic, the teacher, the judge. It is a huge and radical mission, this turning, and the surprising thing about it is (surprising to me those many blessed summers in Ohio) that when I made my intentions clear, that working with this writing was going to be different than dealing with the other writing they'd been doing and they'd been teaching, my students, these teachers helped me turn the desk and stepped willingly into places they'd never been before.

Without going into chapter and verse of the week's lessons, we started by talking about the difference between reading (a reactionary activity) and writing (a creative activity), how they involved totally different instruments. You could be in the middle of reading a book, but you were always *at the edge* of writing one. We started our writing with kernels from our real experience, choosing these for their value to us. A small moment with a charge. And then we talked a lot about the unknown. How much of a story should you know before you start? How "true" do you need to be to event? What's the difference between writing things down and making things up? How does event serve character? How can you write your way beyond the desk, into the unknown?

Of course, our credo, a fiction aesthetic was: **Did that happen? No. Is it true? Yes.** People wrote about their lives starting with moments, people, places they felt strongly about, and then the work we focused on was: how to leave "reality" behind. How to find the true path that fiction requires so that each story, each foray, each exploration into the unknown could find its way. How do people with desks, people who are well organized, masters of control, learn to let go, to tolerate not knowing, tolerate ambiguity long enough to let their story breathe a life of its own? The answer is longer than this, but not much: by staying in the room. As my students began to parrot me: **the writer is the person who stays in the room.**

Through the week we talked about all the elements of craft, of course, but these are second-draft considerations mainly. The single challenge is to write deeply enough that something is discovered to aid the writer in surviving the story. You go into the story without a compass (that's back there on the desk!) and you invent a new one; you find a new true north by writing closely. You can't outline, you can't think the story done, you must write onward into the dark.

Well, we always did. Every summer was astounding. That's not the right word. Every summer was *significant*. We all entered our endeavors with good feeling and high energy and every year it turned into something finer, something more substantial than that. We met as teachers, then together we turned the desk so that we were exposed: we were writers. It's a longer story than this, but simply put teaching public school naturally evolves—in many activities—into control; teaching and working with writers is about fostering the willingness to trust what you don't know; what the process of writing will teach you. Every year in one of those classrooms, people wept. The truth is, I wept too. I remember one teacher, a woman so skeptical of fiction writing on Monday that she could have been used in a case study. She wrote a story about a confrontation with her mother—using that strong moment as the kernel—and when she read the story on Friday, all of us in the class sat silent for a full minute afterward, our teeth in our lips, biting back the urge to cry. Other times we laughed our heads off too; you do once you've turned the desk and are out there in the naked and uncivilized process of writing.

I taught at The Experience of Writing four summers. One summer I remember as the summer of tornadoes. We had multiple tornado warnings. The conference faculty were staying at a lovely old bed and breakfast in Yellow Springs, and in the night the ponderous storm fronts would load themselves over the town and from time to time we'd hear the warning sirens. It was a summer when people exchanged tornado stories, and every time we went out to dinner, someone would point out the doorway and say, "You stand in that." It was hard to imagine: standing in a doorway while a restaurant lifted off. Restaurants, the ones we favored, were substantial buildings.

Early one humid morning the woman who ran our inn came up to my room and woke me, saying, "The police are here to see you." She hadn't had many writers staying in her house and she seemed a bit unnerved. As was I. Downstairs, I met a nice highway patrolman and behind him one of my students, Ed, a bachelor who lived and taught forty minutes away. "He wanted to stop by and let you know he won't be in class today," the officer said. Ed stepped up, "My house has been blown away; I've got to go over and pick up some of the pieces." I knew Ed pretty well; he'd been one of the people who'd told me where to stand if the sirens went off; we'd kidded at length about the storms. Now, his was bad news, but it was clear that no one had been hurt. Standing there in my pajamas, I said, "If you're going to let a little wind scare you away from writing fiction, then go ahead." I'll never forget the look on the patrolman's face. His eyes opened a little to the power of writing fiction. It is a smart alec's remark, and I'm glad I was there to make it. But there's a bit of truth in it too. This writing is real; this writing has its own power. It's not typing up your research paper on Dreiser. Ed, whom I knew well and still keep in touch with, knew what I was talking about. Writing fiction is often a personal exploration, a risk, a wrestling match, and it is an endeavor that can leave us out in the open, expose us in all kinds of ways.

Ed got his revenge with interest when he showed up in class the next day. In the group, I said something to him like this was one of the finest compliments I'd ever received as a teacher: that even with all his troubles he'd chosen to come to class. Think again, he told me, where else am I going to go?

He'd taken a roll of photographs and he passed them around: nothing was left of his apartment but one small corner. His stuff was strewn half a mile. Someone around the table waved one of the photos and said the true thing: this was going to make it harder for Ed to stay in the room. But his personal desk, wherever it was, had certainly been turned.

The net effects of the week-long Experience of Writing were obvious *even as the week closed down.* We saw a renewed commitment to each person's own writing; we'd been awakened to the rich and powerful possibilities of writing fiction. And then there was that other thing, and everybody made a point of telling me about it: they were going to approach their own teaching of creative writing differently. Assigning a short story was a profoundly different assignment than a paper on *Romeo and Juliet*. We all understood the risk better; we all knew again the tremendous rushing empathy for all the fiction writers wandering in the dangerous, sweet wilderness here far, far on the other side of the desk.

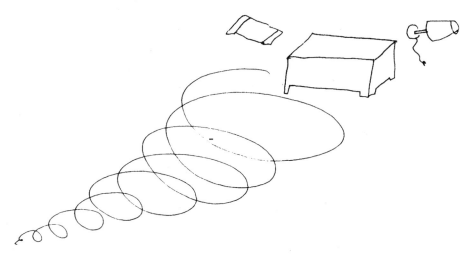

The Singular First Person

Scott Russell Sanders

The first soapbox orator I ever saw was haranguing a crowd beside the Greyhound Station in Providence, Rhode Island, about the evils of fluoridated water. What the man stood on was actually an up-turned milk crate, all the genuine soapboxes presumably having been snapped up by antique dealers. He wore an orange plaid sports coat and matching bow tie and held aloft a bottle filled with mossy green liquid. I don't remember the details of his spiel, except his warning that fluoride was an invention of the Communists designed to weaken our bones and thereby make us pushovers for a Red invasion. What amazed me, as a tongue-tied kid of seventeen newly arrived in the city from the boondocks, was not his message but his courage in delivering it to a mob of strangers. I figured it would have been easier for me to jump straight over the Greyhound Station than to stand there on that milk crate and utter my thoughts.

To this day, when I read or when I compose one of those curious monologues we call the personal essay, I often think of that soapbox orator. Nobody had asked him for his two cents' worth, but there he was declaring it with all the eloquence he could muster. The essay, although enacted in private, is no less arrogant a performance. Unlike novelists and playwrights, who lurk behind the scenes while distracting our attention with the puppet show of imaginary characters, unlike scholars and journalists, who quote the opinions of others and shelter behind the hedges of neutrality, the essayist has nowhere to hide. While the poet can lean back on a several-thousand-year-old legacy of ecstatic speech, the essayist inherits a much briefer and skimpier tradition. The poet is al-lowed to quit after a few lines, but the essayist must hold our attention over pages and pages. It is a brash and foolhardy form, this one-man or one-woman circus, which relies on the tricks of anecdote, conjecture, memory, and wit to enthrall us.

Why are so many writers taking up this risky form, and why are so many readers—to judge by the statistics of book and magazine publication—seeking it out? In this era of prepackaged thought, the essay is the closest thing we have, on paper, to a record of the individual mind at work and play. It is an amateur's raid in a world of specialists. Feeling overwhelmed by data, random information, the flotsam and jetsam of mass culture, we relish the spectacle of a single consciousness making sense of a portion of the chaos. We are grateful to Lewis Thomas for shining his light into the dark corners of biology, to John McPhee for laying bare the geology beneath our landscape, to Annie Dillard for showing us the universal fire blazing in the branches of a cedar, to Peter Matthiessen for chasing after snow leopards and mystical insights in the Himalayas. No matter if they are sketchy, these maps of meaning are still welcome. As Joan Didion observes in her own collection of essays, *The White Album,* "We live entirely, especially if we are writers, by the imposition of a narrative line upon disparate images, by the 'ideas' with which we have learned to freeze the shifting phantasmagoria which is our actual experience." Dizzy from a dance that seems to accelerate hour by hour, we cling to the narrative line, even though it may be as pure an invention as the shapes drawn by Greeks to identify the constellations.

The essay is a haven for the private, idiosyncratic voice in an era of anonymous babble. Like the blandburgers served in their millions along our highways, most language served up in public these days is textureless, tasteless mush. On television, over the phone, in the newspaper, wherever humans bandy words about, we encounter more and more abstractions, more empty formulas. Think of the pabulum ladled out by politicians. Think of the fluffy white bread of advertising. Think, lord help us, of committee reports. By contrast, the essay remains stubbornly concrete and particular: it confronts you with an oil-smeared toilet at the Sunoco station, a red vinyl purse shaped like a valentine heart, a bow-legged dentist hunting deer with an elephant gun. As Orwell forcefully argued, and as dictators seem to agree, such a bypassing of abstractions, such an insistence on the concrete, is a politically subversive act. Clinging to this door, that child, this grief, following the zigzag motions of an inquisitive mind, the essay renews language and clears trash from the springs of thought. A century and a half ago, in the rousing manifesto entitled *Nature,* Emerson called on a new generation of writers to cast off the hand-me-down rhetoric of the day, to "pierce this rotten diction and fasten words again to visible things." The essayist aspires to do just that.

As if all these virtues were not enough to account for a renaissance of this protean genre, the essay has also taken over some of the territory abdicated by contemporary fiction. Whittled down to the bare bones of plot, camouflaged with irony, muttering in brief sentences and grade-school vocabulary, peopled with characters who stumble like sleepwalkers through numb lives, today's fashionable fiction avoids disclosing where the author stands on anything.

In the essay, you had better speak from a region pretty close to the heart or the reader will detect the wind of phoniness whistling through your hollow phrases. In the essay you may be caught with your pants down, your ignorance and sentimentality showing, while you trot recklessly about on one of your hobbyhorses.

To our list of the essay's contemporary attractions we should add the perennial ones of verbal play, mental adventure, and sheer anarchic high spirits. To see how the capricious mind can be led astray, consider the foregoing paragraph, which drags in metaphors from the realms of toys, clothing, weather, and biology, among others. That is bad enough; but it could have been worse. For example, I began to draft a sentence in that paragraph with the following words: "More than once, in sitting down to beaver away at a narrative, felling trees of memory and hauling brush to build a dam that might slow down the waters of time. . . ." I had set out to make some innocent remark, and here I was gnawing down trees and building dams, all because I had let that *beaver* slip in. On this occasion I had the good sense to throw out the unruly word. I don't always, as no doubt you will have noticed. Whatever its more visible subject, an essay is also about the way a mind moves, the links and leaps and jigs of thought. I might as well drag in another metaphor—and another unfolding animal—by saying that each doggy sentence, as it noses forward into the underbrush of thought, scatters a bunch of rabbits that go bounding off in all directions. The essayist can afford to chase more of those rabbits than the fiction writer can, but fewer than the poet. If you refuse to chase any of them, and keep plodding along in a straight line, you and your reader will have a dull outing. If you chase too many, you will soon wind up lost in a thicket of confusion with your tongue hanging out.

The pursuit of mental rabbits was strictly forbidden by the teachers who instructed me in English composition. For that matter, nearly all the qualities of the personal essay, as I have been sketching them, violate the rules that many of us were taught in school. You recall we were supposed to begin with an outline and stick by it faithfully, like a train riding its rails, avoiding sidetracks. Each paragraph was to have a topic sentence pasted near the front, and these orderly paragraphs were to be coupled end-to-end like so many boxcars. Every item in those boxcars was to bear the stamp of some external authority, preferably a footnote referring to a thick book, although appeals to magazines and newspapers would do in a pinch. Our diction was to be formal, dignified, shunning the vernacular. Polysyllabic words derived from Latin were preferable to the blunt lingo of the streets. Metaphors were to be used only in emergencies, and no two of them were to be mixed. And even in emergencies we could not speak in the first person singular.

Already as a schoolboy, I chafed against those rules. Now I break them shamelessly, in particular the taboo against using the lonely capital *I*. Just look at what I'm doing right now. My speculations about the state of the essay arise, needless to say, from my own practice as reader and writer, and they reflect my own tastes, no matter how I may pretend to gaze dispassionately down on the question from a hot-air balloon. As Thoreau declares in his cocky manner on the opening page of *Walden*: "In most books the *I*, or first person, is omitted; in this it will be retained; that, in respect to egotism, is the main difference. We commonly do not remember that it is, after all, always the first person that is speaking. I should not talk so much about myself if there were anybody else whom I knew as well." True for the personal essay, it is doubly true for an essay about the essay: one speaks always and inescapably in the first person singular.

We could sort out essays along a spectrum according to the degree to which the writer's ego is on display—with John McPhee, perhaps, at the extreme of self-effacement, and Norman Mailer at the opposite extreme of self-dramatization. Brassy or shy, center stage or hanging back in the wings, the author's persona commands our attention. For the length of an essay, or a book of essays, we respond to that persona as we would to a friend caught up in a rapturous monologue. When the monologue is finished, we may not be able to say precisely what it was about, any more than we can draw conclusions from a piece of music. "Essays don't usually boil down to a summary, as articles do," notes Edward Hoagland, one of the least summarizable of companions, "and the style of the writer has a 'nap' to it, a combination of personality and originality and energetic loose ends that stand up like the nap of a piece of wool and can't be brushed flat" ("What I Think, What I Am"). We make assumptions about that speaking voice, assumptions we cannot validly make about the narrators in fiction. Only a sophomore is permitted to ask if Huckleberry Finn ever had any children; but even literary sophisticates wonder in print about Thoreau's love life, Montaigne's domestic arrangements, De Quincey's opium habit, Virginia Woolf's depression.

Montaigne, who not only invented the form but nearly perfected it as well, announced from the start that his true subject was himself. In his note "To The Reader" at the beginning of the *Essays*, he slyly proclaimed:

> I want to be seen here in my simple, natural, ordinary fashion, without straining or artifice; for it is myself that I portray. My defects will here be read to the life, and also my natural form, as far as respect for the public has allowed. Had I been placed among those nations which are said to live still in the sweet freedom of nature's first laws, I assure you I should very gladly have portrayed myself here entire and wholly naked.

A few pages after this disarming introduction, we are told of the Emperor Maximilian, who was so prudish about exposing his private parts that he would not let a servant dress him or see him in the bath. The Emperor went so far as to give orders that he be buried in his underdrawers. Having let us in on this intimacy about Maximilian, Montaigne then confessed that he himself, although "bold-mouthed," was equally prudish, and that "except under great stress of necessity or voluptuousness," he never allowed anyone to see him naked. Such modesty, he feared, was unbecoming in a soldier. But such honesty is quite becoming in an essayist. The very confession of his prudery is a far more revealing gesture than any doffing of clothes.

A curious reader will soon find out that the word *essay*, as adapted by Montaigne, means a trial or attempt. The Latin root carries the more vivid sense of a weighing out. In the days when that root was alive and green, merchants discovered the value of goods and alchemists discovered the composition of unknown metals by the use of scales. Just so the essay, as Montaigne was the first to show, is a weighing out, an inquiry into the value, meaning, and true nature of experience; it is a private experiment carried out in public. Whatever Montaigne wrote about— and he wrote about everything under the sun: fears, smells, growing old, the pleasures of scratching—he weighed on the scales of his own character.

It is the *singularity* of the first person—its warts and crotchets and turn of voice—that lures many of us into reading essays, and that lingers with us after we finish. Consider the lonely, melancholy persona of Loren Eiseley, forever wandering, forever brooding on our dim and bestial past, his lips frosty with the chill of the Ice Age. Consider the volatile, Dionysian persona of D. H. Lawrence, with his incandescent gaze, his habit of turning peasants into gods and trees into flames, his quick hatred and quicker love. Consider that philosophical farmer, Wendell Berry, who speaks with a countryman's knowledge and a deacon's severity. Consider E. B. White, with his cheery affection for brown eggs and dachshunds, his unflappable way of herding geese while the radio warns of an approaching hurricane.

E. B. White, that engaging master of the genre, a champion of idiosyncrasy, introduced his own volume of *Essays* by admitting the danger of narcissism:

> I think some people find the essay the last resort of the egoist, a much too self-conscious and self-serving form for their taste; they feel that it is presumptuous of a writer to assume that his little excursions or his small observations will interest the reader. There is some justice in their complaint. I have always been aware that I am by nature self-absorbed and egotistical; to write of myself to the extent I have done indicates a too great attention to my own life, not enough to the lives of others.

Yet the self-absorbed Mr. White was in fact a delighted observer of the world, and shared that delight with us. Thus, after describing memorably how a circus girl practiced her bareback riding in the leisure moments between shows ("The Ring of Time"), he confessed: "As a writing man, or secretary, I have always felt charged with the safekeeping of all unexpected items of worldly or unworldly enchantment, as though I might be held personally responsible if even a small one were to be lost." That may still be presumptuous, but it is a presumption turned outward on the creation.

This looking outward helps distinguish the essay from pure autobiography, which dwells more complacently on the self. Mass murderers, movie stars, sports heroes, Wall Street crooks, and defrocked politicians may blather on about whatever high jinks or low jinks made them temporarily famous, may chronicle their exploits, their diets, their hobbies, in perfect confidence that the public is eager to gobble up every least gossipy scrap. And the public, according to sales figures, generally is. On the other hand, I assume the public does not give a hoot about my private life. If I write of hiking up a mountain with my one-year-old boy riding like a papoose on my back, and of what he babbled to me while we gazed down from the summit onto the scudding clouds, it is not because I am deluded into believing that my baby, like the offspring of Prince Charles, matters to the great world. It is because I know the great world produces babies of its own and watches them change cloudfast before doting eyes. To make that climb up the mountain vividly present for readers is harder work than the climb itself. I choose to write about my experience not because it is mine, but because it seems to me a door through which others might pass.

For the essayist, in other words, the problem of authority is inescapable. In searching for your own soapbox, a sturdy platform from which to deliver your opinionated monologues, it helps if you have already distinguished yourself at some other, less fishy form. When Yeats describes his longing for Maud Gonne or muses on Ireland's misty lore, everything he says is charged with the prior strength of his poetry. When Virginia Woolf, in *A Room of One's Own*, reflects on the status of women and the conditions necessary for making art, she speaks as the author of *Mrs. Dalloway* and *To the Lighthouse*. The essayist may also lay claim to our attention by having lived through events or traveled through terrains that already bear a richness of meaning. When James Baldwin writes his *Notes of a Native Son*, he does not have to convince us that racism is a troubling reality. When Barry Lopez takes us on a meditative tour of the far north in *Arctic Dreams*, he can rely on our curiosity about that fabled and forbidding place. When Paul Theroux climbs aboard a train and invites us on a journey to some exotic destination, he can count on the romance of railroads and the allure of remote cities to bear us along.

Most essayists, however, cannot draw on any source of authority from beyond the page to lend force to the page itself. They can only use language to put themselves on display and to gesture at the world. When Annie Dillard tells us in the opening lines of *Pilgrim at Tinker Creek* about the tomcat with bloody paws who jumps through the window onto her chest, why should we listen? Well, because of the voice that goes on to say: "And some mornings I'd wake in daylight to find my body covered with paw prints in blood; I looked as though I'd been painted with roses." Listen to her explaining a few pages later what she is up to in this book, this broody, zestful record of her stay in the Roanoke Valley: "I propose to keep here what Thoreau called 'a meteorological journal of the mind,' telling some tales and describing some of the sights of this rather tamed valley, and exploring, in fear and trembling, some of the unmapped dim reaches and unholy fastnesses to which those tales and sights so dizzyingly lead." The sentence not only describes the method of her literary search, but also exhibits the breathless, often giddy, always eloquent and spiritually hungry soul who will do the searching. If you enjoy her company, you will relish Annie Dillard's essays; if you don't, you won't.

Listen to another voice which readers tend to find either captivating or insufferable:

> That summer I began to see, however dimly, that one of my ambitions, perhaps my governing ambition, was to belong fully to this place, to belong as the thrushes and the herons and the muskrats belonged, to be altogether at home here. That is still my ambition. But now I have come to see that it proposes an enormous labor. It is a spiritual ambition, like goodness. The wild creatures belong to the place by nature, but as a man I can belong to it only by understanding and by virtue. It is an ambition I cannot hope to succeed in wholly, but I have come to believe that it is the most worthy of all.

That is Wendell Berry in "The Long-Legged House" writing about his patch of Kentucky. Once you have heard that stately, moralizing, cherishing voice, laced through with references to the land, you will not mistake it for anyone else's. Berry's themes are profound and arresting ones. But it is his voice, more than anything he speaks about, that either seizes us or drives us away.

Even so distinct a persona as Wendell Berry's or Annie Dillard's is still only a literary fabrication, of course. The first person singular is too narrow a gate for the whole writer to squeeze through. What we meet on the page is not the flesh-and-blood author, but a simulacrum, a character who wears the label *I*. Introducing the lectures that became *A Room of One's Own*, Virginia Woolf reminded her listeners that "'I' is only a convenient term for somebody who has no real being. Lies will flow from my lips, but there may perhaps be some truth mixed up with them; it is for you to seek out this truth and to decide whether any part is worth keeping." Here is a part I consider worth keeping: "Women have served all these centuries as looking-glasses possessing the magic and delicious power of reflecting the figure of man at twice its natural size." It is from such elegant, revelatory sentences that we build up our notion of the "I" who speaks to us under the name of Virginia Woolf.

What the essay tells us may not be true in any sense that would satisfy a court of law. As an example, think of Orwell's brief narrative, "A Hanging," which describes an execution in Burma. Anyone who has read it remembers how the condemned man as he walked to the gallows stepped aside to avoid a puddle. That is the sort of haunting detail only an eyewitness should be able to report. Alas, biographers, those zealous debunkers, have recently claimed that Orwell never saw such a hanging, that he reconstructed it from hearsay. What then do we make of his essay? Or has it become the sort of barefaced lie we prefer to call a story?

Frankly, I don't much care what label we put on "A Hanging"— fiction or nonfiction, it is a powerful statement either way—but Orwell might have cared a great deal. I say this because not long ago I was bemused and then vexed to find one of my own essays treated in a scholarly article as a work of fiction. Here was my earnest report about growing up on a military base, my heartfelt rendering of indelible memories, being confused with the airy figments of novelists! To be sure, in writing the piece I had used dialogue, scenes, settings, character descriptions, the whole fictional bag of tricks; sure, I picked and chose among a thousand beckoning details; sure, I downplayed some facts and highlighted others; but I was writing about the actual, not the invented. I shaped the matter, but I did not make it up.

To explain my vexation, I must break another taboo, which is to speak of the author's intent. My teachers warned me strenuously to avoid the intentional fallacy. They told me to regard poems and plays and stories as objects washed up on the page from some unknown and unknowable shores. Now that I am on the other side of the page, so to speak, I think quite recklessly of intention all the time. I believe that if we allow the question of intent in the case of murder, we should allow it in literature. The essay is distinguished from the short story, not by the presence or absence of literary devices, not by tone or theme or subject, but by the writer's stance toward the material. In composing an essay about what it was like to grow up on that military base, I *meant* something quite different from what I mean when concocting a story. I meant to preserve and record and help give voice to a reality that existed independently of me. I meant to pay my respects to a minor passage of history in an out-of-the-way place. I felt responsible to the truth as known by other people. I wanted to speak directly out of my own life into the lives of others.

You can see I am teetering on the brink of metaphysics. One step farther and I will plunge into the void, wondering as I fall how to prove there is any external truth for the essayist to pay homage to. I draw back from the brink and simply declare that I believe one writes, in essays, with a regard for the actual world, with a respect for the shared substance of history, the autonomy of other lives, the being of nature, the mystery and majesty of a creation we have not made.

When it comes to speculating about the creation, I feel more at ease with physics than with metaphysics. According to certain bold and lyrical cosmologists, there is at the center of black holes a geometrical point, the tiniest conceivable speck, where all the matter of a collapsed star has been concentrated, and where everyday notions of time, space, and force break down. That point is called a singularity. The boldest and most poetic theories suggest that anything sucked into a singularity might be flung back out again, utterly changed, somewhere else in the universe. The lonely first person, the essayist's microcosmic "I," may be thought of as a verbal singularity at the center of the mind's black hole. The raw matter of experience, torn away from the axes of time and space, falls in constantly from all sides, undergoes the mind's inscrutable alchemy, and reemerges in the quirky, unprecedented shape of an essay.

Now it is time for me to step down, before another metaphor seizes hold of me, before you notice that I am standing, not on a soapbox, but on the purest air.

Reveling in the World: An Interview with Christopher Merrill on the Power of Language and Teaching

Terry Hermsen

One evening in 1995, during The Experience of Writing, Chris and I sat down for dinner near the Wright State University campus, where this interview was recorded.

—T.H.

TERRY: Since you write in a wide variety of genres (poetry, journalism, translation, art criticism, social/historical analysis) and since you seem to believe in writers exploring these various genres—as opposed to being tracked into just one—is there anything that variety tells you which would help teachers when they approach their classrooms?

CHRIS: I think that on the grandest level we are talking about the creative process, and therefore a writer in the largest sense of the word is a generalist. And by generalist I mean somebody who writes in a variety of forms, a variety of genres about a variety of subjects. The writer is someone who looks at the world in a spirit of wonder or awe and wants to try to discover meaning and pattern in what he or she sees.

It's a given that the world, various as it is, will demand of its writers a variety of forms of expression. Poetry, fiction, nonfiction. It seems to me that we can't answer all of the questions that we have about our experience in a limited number of forms, and insofar as we can work against the prevailing tendency in our culture to specialize—a tendency which also exists in creative writing programs—it seems useful to me to think

---

about writing as a way to break down those categories, break down those compartments and find ways to address everything. Because, after all, we never know what we're going to be best in as a writer. We may start out as a poet and end up as a journalist, we may start out as a novelist and end up writing plays, we may find at some point in our lives that personal essays are what we are most interested in writing. For us the best examples among writers may be those who have tried their hands at everything so that when the muse truly decides to speak we're ready, we have all the tools with which to express whatever it is we most desperately need to say.

TERRY: So, when you think about the average high school students' experience, as far as we are able to picture it, how might they make use of this need to write in a variety of forms? Many are still taught to develop one style only, that being the expository mode. Analyze that poem, analyze that topic, find the thesis, etc. Where is the limitation in that?

CHRIS: That encourages learning by method, learning by rote; creative writers are people who are interested in learning by means of discovery. We hope that through the act of writing we will discover something about the world that we did not know before. That works against the notion of systematic attempts at knowledge, systematic attempts at learning. Writers are people who do not work in a linear fashion, in the way that perhaps the elementary levels of mathematics can be taught. Writers work in a more circular method. We cast our net out as far as we can and we hope to gather in a lot of different fishes, some of which we'll want to keep and some of which we'll throw back, but it is the act of casting which is most interesting to a writer. It's very much an experimental sort of operation and that goes against the memorizing of the periodic table, which is necessary for learning chemistry, or learning the laws of evolution in biology. The laws of art, which is what we're talking about, work on more intuitive levels, in a more creative fashion. And even if our students do not go on to become writers, hopefully we are teaching them how to solve problems in a creative fashion. How to adapt to circumstances in their lives in a flexible manner. What any long-standing long-term immersion in the arts can teach us is a more open approach to life itself, which in a changing and adaptable economy like ours is necessary.

TERRY: So suppose you're a teacher in seventh grade in a middle school where the dominant force in the school is based on fitting into one mode. You've just been hired. In the light of what you've just been talking about, how do you change the approach? How would you structure the year?

CHRIS: First of all, every writer that we know can look back to one teacher in grammar school or high school or college, who makes all the difference to his or her career. So it's important to remember that one teacher can make a change in a student's life. Secondly, I think of the poet and writer Brewster Ghiselin, who in the mid-forties teaching at the University of Utah put together this wonderful symposium on the creative process. I've often thought: what a straight-laced institution he was teaching in at the time, just after the Second World War, when all of the emphasis in education was toward rote memorization. Brewster Ghiselin decided that he would try to assemble a number of writings on the creative process, to try to understand the way in which breakthroughs are made in the sciences, in mathematics, and in the arts.

Now if a Brewster Ghiselin could do that in the mid-forties in Utah, then in the 1990s, in Ohio, a seventh-grade teacher can make similar kinds of strides by trying to teach students that the way to creative breakthroughs in our work is to go against the circle; it is to think about the habitual way, the familiar manner in which we look at the world, and try to break that up. That's what the arts are doing, they are trying to teach us ways to look at the world with new eyes, and see the world freshly. The only way to do that is to try to break those old familiar patterns of association, the old familiar ways of looking at the world.

So if I were a seventh-grade teacher, the first thing to do would be exercises designed to spring the students' imaginations free. For example, take five words and say to the class, you have to put all five of these words into a fifteen-line poem or a one-page story. And make sure one of the words is a word as strange, for example, as Tanzania. A place that the students, we can assume, have never been. If it belongs to the unknown and to the imaginary, then the students are automatically in that realm of the imagination, and they can begin to learn the ways that the imagination can be—is, in fact—a fluid place. That fluidity is what I hope to find, to teach in young writers. So a seventh-grade teacher begins with an exercise like that and builds up from there, accustoming the students to the strangeness, miracle and mystery of their own imagination. And then you can build up to more formal exercises after having given them the chance to make the plunge into the unknown.

TERRY: What would you say to people who would claim that poetry, or exercises like that are okay for Friday afternoon when everyone is too tired for anything else, or the spring when we've finished the curriculum guidelines, and they think of it as frivolous time, fooling around time, cherry-blossom time or whatever they call it. What would you say to people who react with, "That sure won't get my students into college"?

CHRIS: Well, it's quite likely that this sort of educational approach may not prepare them for certain university courses, but what I'm talking about is the longer-term preparation for life. It is important that at least every week you make some time for that sabbath, as it were, a kind of sacred space where even if it's the most playful activity we're going to engage in, we are going to engage in it, and it will be that activity that we call art.

I know that our culture is moving and is insisting dramatically that students do things that are appropriate only for college and for getting a job; however, if our culture is to remain healthy and vibrant and alive and creative, it will in and of itself find ways to keep that spirit alive, so whether it becomes a formal part of your curriculum, or you have to find a way to make it seem like something extra, you've got to find a place for it each week, in the same way that once upon a time people found time each week to go to church. There has to be that space, preferably every day, even if it comes down to making sure that each day you read a poem to the kids, or read a story to them, or insisting that every week they memorize a poem. Somehow or other, that type of learning, which goes against the grain of a lot of learning in this day and age, has got to find its place.

TERRY: Could we talk for a few minutes about teacher as writer, since that's the focus of this particular conference? When teachers approach writing freshly from their own need to write, how does that change how they teach? Is it important that people who teach writing take some time for writing themselves? Because in many cases, they don't. Not that they couldn't, but often the time isn't there. How essential is it that they go through the same process their kids will be going through?

CHRIS: On one level, I think it's probably not essential. However, teachers who do write and who do take their chances and who do make themselves vulnerable and risk making fools of themselves by failing on the page, understand much more deeply the consequences of any creative act, and therefore approach the teaching of the art with the same passion that real writers do. If you're a writer or if you're trying to be a writer, you can come into the classroom with a full head of steam. When you have spent the morning, or the early morning, or the late night trying to make a poem work, or bring a scene to life in a story, or get something right in a memoir—when you come in to teach the next day, you have some of that same energy informing what you do. Whatever you read, for example, becomes a way to learn something that might be useful for teaching your students. Don't go through life automatically. The act of writing demands that you pay attention to the world itself. And if you're doing that then you can come into the classroom and ask your students to pay the same kind of attention to the world around them and that's where writing comes from.

TERRY: So teachers don't necessarily have to write. . . .

CHRIS: No. But they have to understand the process of making yourself vulnerable on the page. They also have to do that enough to understand the playful nature of writing. The fact of the matter is that a lot of writing comes out of the simplest question, "What if? What if I try this. . . . What a crazy idea, but maybe I'll go with that a little ways." Now that's how many breakthroughs come, in all areas of human experience. Somebody says, "Now this seems like a real tangent to me, but maybe I'll give it a try." The arts are the place in school where we can give sanction to that idea.

It is very much as John Elder has remarked in that wonderful book called *Imagining the Earth*, that poetry is akin to wandering into a wilderness area. This is a place where all the rules of civilization no longer apply. So you go in there and find it's a place where you can go wild. This is the place where you can walk off the trail. Where everything you've been taught by society and the culture at large doesn't necessarily hold. Because right now we're going to play around, we're going to mess around and see what happens. Because something interesting might happen that might bring about new ways of looking at the world, which is of course what the human condition has always been about. Throughout history writers hook into new ways of looking.

TERRY: One of the problems or concerns for teachers in this process is that the teacher needs to maintain control. If the teacher loses control of the classroom, big problems can result. You're saying writers take risks, they go off in many directions. I think one of the problems teachers have with giving students the kind of range and free rein that you're talking about, is what happens then? We're certainly asking a lot of the teacher. When a poet comes into a classroom, who has had perhaps that morning you were talking about, and can say, "Hey, listen to this . . . ." it's a different kind of energy. But Poetry in the Schools has been around for thirty years now. We've seen in The Experience of Writing these last few years some teachers taking that same kind of enthusiasm with them. How can teachers do that even more? And how can they maintain control while also giving their students new freedom to write?

CHRIS: I think of a man I once saw teaching teachers how to teach poetry. One of the student teachers had an African mask as his prop, and in the middle of getting ready to ask the students to write poems, his mask fell on the ground and he froze. And there was a moment when he didn't quite know what to do. Even though this was just a class of student teachers you could feel him losing control. But the man in charge of the class was really quite brilliant. He ran up and said, "No, no, you did that wrong." He grabbed his ruler, and he put the African mask back up on the lectern and he let it fall over, and then he took the ruler, looked at the mask, and just swatted it, saying, "Take that. . . ." Of course everybody laughed.

The key to teaching poetry and to teaching writing in the schools is to be quick on your feet, to be willing to improvise, and to recognize that you're going to lose control in all kinds of ways. Instead of being frightened by that loss, turn it into an occasion for play. Lose control, lose the prop, write something badly yourself, make yourself as vulnerable as your students. You will make a more congenial kind of atmosphere.

It's a matter of recognizing that even if you lose control, you can always turn that around a bit. For example, think of the blues. How did the blues turn into such a wonderfully improvisatory experience but by a musician hitting a "wrong" note and then just bending it far enough so that it came back in tune; when you hear that little slide from dissonance into consonance you think, wow, that's exciting, that sounds nice. Teachers can do the same thing. Because, after all, that's what writers are doing. They try something on the page, which seems completely crazy or completely wrong, and suddenly they realize that if they add this word to that, then it might just be interesting.

TERRY: Let's address the question of quality. Say a teacher gets his or her class writing, and things are going fine. One thing they want to do is be encouraging, to show the students where the writing is strong. But where do you introduce the question of cutting, revising, or being able to say, "That *doesn't* work"? A lot of teachers struggle with how do they bring up the question of what makes a strong poem or story without squelching the bubbling up of energy in their students' writing.

CHRIS: We know that in every piece of writing in its first draft there are clichés or awkward phrases, places that are simply uninteresting. I look at those places as being opportunities for the writer to open up the poem or story again, and say, this is a place where I was asleep in the first draft, a place where I've stumbled on some emotional or aesthetic material for which I don't yet have the language.

If as teachers we don't approach that as a "mistake" or something that needs to be corrected, but as an opportunity, a chance to delve into the material a little further, we have the chance to write something more meaningful. I have a private hunch that the more awful a first draft is, the better chance I have of writing something interesting. Because there are two things I'm thinking. One is: "My God, I've lost all my talent," so I have to work harder to make it come to light, and secondly, "Well, this may be badly written now because I've found something pretty vital for which I have yet to find the language." And if I'm patient, if I'm willing to take some chances and if I can engage as much of my imagination as possible, it may be that I will find my way to something altogether new, something I will find aesthetically and emotionally satisfying.

TERRY: To follow up on that, teachers are used to marking, correcting. I've met a number of them who say, "With poems I just don't say much of anything at all, because I don't know what to say. So I just write something like 'Good' and put a smiley face on the page." And there are others who say, "Well, that's cheating, it's not really giving them very much," and who can sometimes go the other way and act like they're critics for the *New York Times* and start ripping the poem apart.

CHRIS: The middle ground is to take all those places that are clichéd, boring, or awkward, and just put a question mark by them. The student poet can then look at that and say, "Well, it hasn't quite worked here for the teacher yet, and maybe if I look at it again, I'll realize that it hasn't yet come to life for me. Maybe I can dig deeper there."

TERRY: So this is a very technical device we're talking about here. Along with underlining good lines, or putting an asterisk beside strong sections, we can add the use of a question mark to indicate where things are unclear or not yet fully developed.

CHRIS: If you could combine the positive comments with the questions, then students can begin to see, "Ah, that's language that's interesting, and that's language that just isn't there yet." And the student can quickly deduce what the difference is.

Similarly, we could talk about grading—how do you grade assignments like this? Obviously, the students have to have some kind of grades. I'd be less interested in grading someone on what they have produced than on the chances that they take, their willingness to rewrite awkward sections and make them into new poems and their efforts to engage their imaginations. The more creative the solution, the more interested I would be in giving them a better grade.

TERRY: Yes, that's a question teachers face all the time. If I make this a key part of my curriculum, how do I judge the end product?

CHRIS: It's interesting when we think about the example of the Polish poet Czeslaw Milosz—maybe the best poet of this last half-century—who took no creative writing classes in college. He had a creative writing club. So it may be that this is an activity that we find a place for in the classroom, but maybe it *isn't* graded. You've got various things you have to cover in the curriculum, and you can always cover them a little bit faster if you knew you were going to save some time to work in the arts, for which there may not be a need to grade, subversive as that may sound.

TERRY: And you're saying, Milosz didn't have classes. . . .

CHRIS: He had no classes. He had a club that got together and they showed each other work. Of course, they were all geniuses. . . . (laughter)

TERRY: Milan Kundera in *The Book of Laughter and Forgetting* says that when we have too many writers the world will become deaf. This leads us to a rather weird question, because we're on the other side of what Milosz experienced. We have a lot of writing classes, a lot of seminars proposing to strengthen our poetry, and workshops like this one where teachers come to write. In addition, we have the writing process movement in the schools. I'm wondering if it might be possible that we have too much. Are there any dangers in overtalking the writing process?

CHRIS: I look at it this way. At this particular point in history, and particularly in America, the media has a stranglehold on the public imagination and on our disclosure. And the media by its very nature has to work in rather simplistic terms—in sound bites, in black and white ideas. Creative writing and literature is that place where we can see our questions addressed in a serious fashion in all of their complexity. The more we have people, poets and writers, trying to address serious questions in that complexity, the better chance we have of creating a level of public discourse that will lead us to better and more fulfilling answers to the great problems of the day. So I find it interesting that even as the media grows by the hour there is a contrary effort on the part of writers and teachers around the country to create these systems in which people talk seriously about poetry, that great accelerator of consciousness, or fiction, that great place in which we can see how other people live. Because I think it is an effective—though not effective enough—balance and counter to that stranglehold of the media.

TERRY: So that's why it may be more important here than it would be in Italy, say, or elsewhere.

CHRIS: We're not talking about creating a plethora of writers. That's not what's going to happen. We're really talking about creating a culture of readers, people attuned to the sensitivities of language, to ways that poetry and fiction can shape our ideas about the world. And exact from us more discriminating answers to our deepest rooted problems.

TERRY: It's like Richard Hugo saying that a creative writing class is one place where you might be treated as an individual.

CHRIS: And where you're taken seriously. It's no accident that as television's power has grown so has the urge for creative writing programs. Of course they are outgunned by the power of the media, by perhaps a million to one, but that's always been the case when it comes to the ways that cultures change and are shaped throughout history. I like to think that poets and writers in their small ways can keep the media honest, even if the media has no clue as to what poets and writers are trying to do.

TERRY: Because you are primarily a writer and have not followed a traditional path of getting a Ph.D., etc., how does your experience as a writer affect how you approach teaching? Do you ever get tired of teaching, do you ever feel drained by it? Or does it awaken a new sense of what writing is about?

CHRIS: I really don't teach enough to be drained by it, so it's difficult to say. That's why during the weeks I spend here in Ohio I marvel at the teachers who spend week after week, period after period, day after day teaching, because I spend most of my hours as a writer, which is to say, researching, traveling, taking notes, giving readings, whatever. But nevertheless, when I go into the classroom to teach, and it's usually for short periods, where I'm giving my all, I find that the opportunity to speak about the thing I love most, which is writing, is always a rich one for me. Because as the old adage puts it, "He who teaches learns twice." And it's useful to articulate to yourself what it is you're trying to do. Because after all, when you write, you are on one level confronting yourself on the page. And if you take that energy into the classroom what you're doing is trying to figure out how to make it through your life, how to make meaning out of your life, how to understand how you've done what you've done, or how you've ended up where you are, and where you might be going. Teaching and writing can therefore feed each other.

Of course I'm speaking more from the writing point of view, but I assume it can go the other way as well. I know my teaching has been immensely rewarding, so I imagine that a writer who writes full time can go into teaching in the same way that a teacher who teaches full time can get from writing some of that same reward.

TERRY: How about formal styles versus more open-ended forms? Some teachers are torn about that question, too, in that they were raised on Frost, Browning, and Keats. How would you balance that? Is it important for kids to spend some time trying out villanelles and sestinas?

CHRIS: Early on in the writing process, I'm most interested in finding ways to spring their imaginations free, to give them the kinds of exercises I spoke of earlier. However, at a certain point, having shown them the glories of the imagination and the fun they can have with exercises that have them repeat rhetorical structures, or throw words in a poem, or imagine a crazy situation and see what might happen with it, I then want to teach them ways that form, too, can be a playful arena in which to wander; writing villanelles or sestinas for more sophisticated students should not be a straightjacket or prison but a possibility. If you play around with a form, say the sonnet, and try to get the rhymes straight, as long as you don't settle for the first rhyme that occurs to you, which is usually the trite rhyme, but find a rhyme that doesn't seem to make sense, then the sonnet, the strictest form of all, can be an occasion to take you someplace you haven't been before.

I always look at writing in form as an occasion to wander into a strange and alien territory. If it is viewed as a prison, as it has been for too long in contemporary American practice, then it will be. But if it's viewed as a possibility, then it will be a possibility. And it's always necessary for students who want to learn their craft. That's why I insist at a certain point that students memorize poems so that they have by heart the great poems of the English language, have those sounds and rhythms somewhere inside them, so that in some way they know those forms, because you never know when the muse talks to you what form he or she wants you to speak in. You should have as much available as possible. Why restrict yourself?

Think of Rilke, in that marvelous month of February 1922, when he completed in one fell swoop the Duino Elegies, which are written in free verse, and at the same time he received the great gift he talked of which comes from the muse or the gods or the angels, the fifty-six sonnets to Orpheus. On the one hand, a free and open meditative poem and on the other hand, the strictest poem of all. He could not have done that if he hadn't already in his career tried his hand at every single form of writing, and every single form of poetry. So that when the muse finally chose to speak, he was ready for both, he didn't mangle the transmission.

TERRY: Frost found the same thing, too.

CHRIS: And think of Auden, who seemed to write in every possible form. Whatever had to be said, he knew how to get it down on the page.

TERRY: I want to talk about Bosnia for a minute, in light of the effort that you've made to emotionally and analytically engage what's going on now at the end of the century. Because it seems to me that we can have a good time (I find this in my own classes) doing dream poems and language poems and situation poems, and then there's a time when I think, "What does this have to do with what's going on?" What does poetry and writing have to do with politics, with the disasters of this century? How can teachers use this exploring you're speaking of, that could be very personally engaging and enlightening and satisfying for their students, how can they also use it to deal with the drive-by shootings they see in their cities, and the rest of the news that they can't even digest?

CHRIS: One hopes that by engaging in literary work, opening oneself to the imagination, listening to what the language has to offer, what will come from that is a more open understanding of the way that the world works. It seems to me that wherever things get broken down into black and white, us versus them, we're on our way to bloodshed. That's nowhere more apparent today than in Bosnia, or in certain inner cities in this country with the drive-by shootings. It's easier to blow somebody away for whom you have no human feeling. But of course it's in literature where we imaginatively engage ourselves in other people's lives.

So it may seem like a small thing to play around in the language writing a poem or writing a story, but I think that what we're also doing is inculcating a more open understanding of the world and efforts to empathize with the other. And of course, in a country of 170 ethnic groups like our own, we have at least 170 different reasons to try to empathize with those who are different from what we are. We can read the poems of Black poets or Hispanic poets or Asian poets or White poets, men and women poets, and each poet that we read should ideally give us a sense of all of the range of human possibilities. And give us respect for those possibilities and thus break down those borders that we are all too quick to build between one another. The sense that this person is different from me and therefore they don't deserve to live: we as writers can find ways to break down that way of thinking.

I think that's what the war in Bosnia is teaching. The Bosnian Serb madness of believing that the most interesting way to live is to be only with one's fellow Serbs to me is anathema. After all, the rich tapestry of life, as a European military monitor said to me once, is what we should be reveling in. Even though it has its share of tragedy and loss and grief, we are on this planet together, we are all different, and it's much more fun to revel in those differences than to be afraid of them. In its own small way literature teaches us to take pleasure in those differences and the way we look at the world. Tonight, for instance, I was thinking about Herb Martin reading Paul [Lawrence] Dunbar's poems. Now, of course I could never write those poems, or create what Herb can so beautifully capture in his performances, but I sat there absolutely captivated by his performance, and thinking, "That's right, that's what poetry does, at least on one level, it teaches us how other people live." It makes what is utterly unfamiliar to us familiar, and then what is all too familiar to us mysterious again. It can work in both ways, and I think that's what we need to prize about it.

TERRY: How to do that? I agree with all you've just said, the need to do that on a national scale, on a metropolitan scale, on a world scale, but on a level of a teacher trying to make that happen, how do you avoid didacticism? How is it possible for the teacher to make that exercise as significant and freeing as the dream poem, for instance?

CHRIS: The short answer would be to think of Carolyn Forche's poem, "The Colonel." You and I have talked about this—we've used this poem in our classes together. Take a poem like that and try to rewrite it from the colonel's point of view. In the '80s that would have been a useful exercise. For here's a poem that those of us on the left wing could sympathize with, at least with its politics. But now let's make the larger imaginative leap and write it from his point of view. This is Jorie Graham's exercise, and I think it happens to be a terrifically imaginative one. Or think about the story that Eudora Welty wrote on the night that Medgar Evers was assassinated in her town of Jackson, Mississippi. She stayed up all night writing "Where Is the Voice Coming From," and she wrote it from the point of view of a man who might have been the white assassin of Medgar Evers. Because even though she didn't know him, she found a point of correspondence in her own self between herself and that assassin. So we need to ask ourselves to think about some of these characters that in our waking life we can't find points of correspondence with but in a poem or story we might try to. That would be the simplest way to do it.

TERRY: Yes, flip it around and do the same kind of discovery that you were talking about before.

CHRIS: Take it as a challenge. As a chance to get deeply inside someone else's skin. Octavio Paz went to Spain in the 1930s during the Spanish Civil War. He went there of course on the side of the Republicans, but at a certain point he was in Madrid, with his back against a wall, and on the other side of the wall were soldiers fighting for the Loyalists. And he heard them talking. They were talking about girls, I think, and they were talking about cigarettes, and he realized the futility of war because he saw that on the deepest level they were just men on the other side, just like the men on this side of the wall.

Every way that literature can find a point of correspondence between those on the other side of the wall and those on this side of the wall, that's a plus. It works against the efforts to build up that wall and therefore justify war. That's the lesson of Bosnia, that's the lesson of the Spanish Civil War, and that's the lesson of every war that the human race engages in. No doubt we will never eradicate war, but in their own small ways writers work against that impulse to divide things into us versus them.

TERRY: To close, let's return to something you said earlier about teachers who influenced you and made you want to teach and write strongly. I'm thinking also of the selections Scott Russell Sanders was reading today, emphasizing the teachers in his life. Who did influence you?

CHRIS: One was a novelist by the name of Tom Gavin, who taught at Middlebury College. When I was starting out as a poet, he was somebody who looked at what I was doing, crazy as it was, and said, "Keep doing it."

There was a family friend named Franny Pingcon when I was in high school and trying to write my first poems and stories. She certainly couldn't have understood what I was trying to do but she said, "This is a good thing for you to do." And of course when I got to graduate school, I met Brewster Ghiselin, who was for me the most important because what he taught me in every possible way was how to live the creative life, how to work against the circle, how to break up my habitual ways of looking at the world in order to find something original to say. That was of immeasurable importance.

Think of all the teachers we've had by the time we get to graduate school. Dozens, really. Almost none of them that I can remember left any kind of imprint on me at all and of course many left very negative imprints. But the ones that I went to, the ones I searched out, they made all the difference in the world. I suspect that if I hadn't met Brewster, and I met him at a very sad period of my life, maybe I would have stopped being a writer. But he was there, he listened to me, he looked at my first efforts at writing and he said, "You're on your way, who knows where it will go." That's the right attitude to take with the young, and that is why even though he's ninety-one years old today he is vital, curious about the world, full of wonder, still trying to write. Three years ago he published a book called *Flame*, and that's what I hope for all of us, to keep open to the world and its possibilities.

TERRY: I was drawing a couple key things for teachers out of what you just said. One is encouragement, the urge to keep trying. The other is to break the habits. . . .

CHRIS: Particularly in grammar school, in high school and college, no one knows who's going to become a writer; all that we know is that some at that age start showing talent and signs and seem desperately to want to do it. Encourage them. Why discourage somebody who's showing artistic inclinations? You never know where it will lead. I remember hearing about Stephen Koch telling his class that his job was to water and fertilize all the flowers in front of him because he had no idea who was going to blossom. That's how teachers need to be. If someone shows signs of going off in their own directions as a writer, let him go. It might be the right thing. Maybe that person will find his or her own way, and the best thing we can do as teachers is to honor that effort.

Experience of Writing Faculty

Richard Bullock	1995, 1996
Ron Carlson	1991–94
Toi Derricotte	1993–94
Frank Dobson	1995, 1998
Nikky Finney	1997–98
Terry Hermsen	1991–94
Nancy Mack	1995–97
Nancy Mairs	1998
Herbert Woodward Martin	1995
Irene McKinney	1995–96
Christopher Merrill	1991–98
Pamela Painter	1991–95
Constance Pierce	1997–98
Scott Russell Sanders	1995
Lori Segal	1993
Eve Shelnutt	1991–92, 1994
Mark Shelton	1991–92, 1994
James Thomas	1997

Robert Fox and James Thomas, Co-Directors
C. J. Baker, Administrative Assistant

Editors

Photo by Doug Martin

Terry Hermsen taught in the Ohio Arts Council's Arts in Education program for fourteen years and for four years in The Experience of Writing. He has two chapbooks of poetry, *36 Spokes: The Bicycle Poems* and *Child Aloft in Ohio Theatre,* both from Bottom Dog Press, for whom he has also edited *O Listen,* and *Food Poems* (with David Garrison) in the Pocket Poems series directed toward high school students. He lives in Westerville, Ohio, and teaches at the Ohio State University in Marion.

Photo by Doug Martin

Robert Fox is Literature Program Coordinator for the Ohio Arts Council. He has taught at Ohio University and Rider College, and as a writer in the schools. His poems, stories, and essays have appeared in such magazines as *The North America Review, The Massachusetts Review,* and *Witness.* In 1992, he won a Nelson Algren Short Fiction Award from the *Chicago Tribune.* Two collections of his fiction were published by December Press: *Destiny News* (stories) and *The Last American Revolution/Confessions of a Dead Politician* (two short novels in one volume). He co-directs The Experience of Writing.

Contributors

Ron Carlson teaches at Arizona State University. He is the author of five books of fiction, most recently the story collection *The Hotel Eden*. His fiction has appeared in *The New Yorker, Harper's, Playboy, GQ, Ploughshares*, and many other magazines.

Debra Conner was born in Cambridge, Ohio, raised in Marietta, and now lives across the Ohio River in Parkersburg, West Virginia. She has an MFA in Poetry from Warren Wilson College and has taught English and Creative Writing at Parkersburg Community College, at special workshops for ESL families, and since 1992, in the Ohio Arts Council's Arts in Education program.

Janice M. Gallagher has taught English at Cloverleaf High School in Medina County and currently serves as Director of Special Programs for Euclid City Schools. She attended the first Experience of Writing in 1991.

David Hassler is the author of *Sabishi: Poems from Japan*. He is co-editor of the anthology *Learning by Heart: Contemporary American Poetry about School* to be published in March 1999. He holds a BA from Cornell University and an MFA from Bowling Green State University. He conducts school residencies in the Ohio Arts Council's Arts in Education Program and is an Associate Artist for the Shaker Heights High School Theater Program in Cleveland, Ohio.

Carl H. Krauskopf III, 1995–96 Excellence in Education Award Winner, lives in Dayton, Ohio, and teaches at Northmont High School. He attended The Experience of Writing from 1991 to 1993.

Michael London lives in Dayton, Ohio, where he writes plays, teaches English at Wright State University, and serves as an arts consultant to school systems and arts organizations. His plays include *Beyond Freedom* (about the fall of the Berlin Wall) and *Chaplin: The One-Man Band*.

Christopher Merrill is a poet, editor, journalist, and critic. In 1994 White Pine Press collected his three books of poems into a single volume entitled *Watch Fire*. His prose includes *The Old Bridge*, an extended essay on refugees from the Balkans, and *Grass of Another Country*, a portrait of the 1990 World Cup in Italy. He has edited *Outcroppings: John McPhee in the West* and *The Forgotten Language: Contemporary Poets and Nature* among other books. Currently he holds the Jenks Chair in Contemporary Letters at Holy Cross University in Worcester, Massachusetts, and is at work on a book of essays about the war in Bosnia.

Nick Muska is the author of *Elm: The Warehouse Poems* and *Living My Night Life Out Under the Sun*, both from the Toledo Poetry Center. Originally from Lorain, Ohio, he has degrees from Antioch College and the University of California, Santa Barbara. With Joel Lipman and Sybil James, he has presented several programs of translytics. Every October 21 he may be found directing his theatrical presentation, "Back to Jack" in Toledo on the anniversary of Jack Kerouac's death.

Mary L. Noble lives and teaches in Dayton, Ohio. She was a participant in The Experience of Writing in 1993 and 1994.

Barry Peters has worked as a journalist and currently lives and teaches in Centerville, Ohio. One of his stories appears in *Sudden Fiction (Continued)*, and he has stories forthcoming in *Riverwind* and *Oxford Magazine*. He was an Experience of Writing participant in 1992 and 1993.

Lynn Powell has been awarded Individual Artist Fellowships from both the Ohio Arts Council and the New Jersey State Council on the Arts. Her book *Old and New Testaments* won the Brittingham Prize for Poetry from the University of Wisconsin Press. She has worked extensively as an artist in the schools in grades K–12 and has taught at Cornell University as a Visiting Writer. She lives in Oberlin, Ohio.

Scott Russell Sanders was born in Tennessee, raised in Ohio, and currently teaches at Indiana University. His books of essays include *The Paradise of Bombs, Secrets of the Universe: Scenes from the Journey Home, Staying Put: Making a Home in a Restless World*, and most recently, *Writing from the Center*.

MaryAnn Titus attended The Experience of Writing from 1992 to 1995 and in 1997. She teaches at Wilder Elementary School in Westerville, Ohio. Her poems have appeared recently in *Vol. No., Chiron Review*, and *Pudding Magazine*.

This book was typeset in Avant Garde and Baskerville by
Electronic Imaging.
The typefaces used on the cover were Bauer Bodoni and Charlemagne.
The book was printed on 60-lb. Finch Opaque by Edwards Brothers, Inc.